The Ebony Success Library

The Ebony Success Library

Volume II
Famous Blacks
Give Secrets of Success

By the Editors of Ebony

Johnson Publishing Company Inc.
Chicago 1973

Copyright © 1973 by Johnson Publishing Company, Inc.
Chicago, Illinois

Printed in the United States of America

Library of Congress Cataloguing in Publication Data

Main entry under title:
Famous Blacks give secrets of success.

  (The Ebony success library, v. 2)
    1. Negroes—Biography.   *I. Ebony*   *II. Series.*
E185.96.F23   1973   920'.0092'96073   73-5724
ISBN 0-87485-061-4

R.R.D. 1-73

Publisher
John H. Johnson

Editor
Charles L. Sanders

Designer
Cecil L. Ferguson

Production Coordinator
Brenda M. Biram

Production Assistants
Editorial: Brenda J. Butler
Photographs: Basil O. Phillips

Introduction

In this volume are seventy-two articles about black persons who have achieved success in fields as diverse as publishing, chemistry, entertainment and structural engineering. There are stories of men who have made fortunes as comedians, and stories of men who are owners of their own businesses and management executives of national firms. There is a profile of the Reverend Jesse L. Jackson, national president of Operation PUSH, and one of Miss Barbara Watson, an administrator at the U.S. Department of State. As was stated in Volume I, almost all the persons selected for inclusion in this volume began their lives in circumstances quite similar to those of black youths of today. Thus it is hoped that they will serve as inspirational examples for young blacks, especially those who are growing up in deprived circumstances and who may have begun losing hope of ever bettering the quality of their lives.

The major contributors to this volume are Peter A. Bailey, William Earl Berry, Hamilton J. Bims, Philip E. Brown, Warren Brown, Robert A. DeLeon, Robert E. Johnson, B. J. Mason, Hans J. Massaquoi, Herbert Nipson, Carole A. Parks, Alex Poinsett, Osborne Roberts, Fredrick Salsman and Caryl V. Terrell. We thank each contributor and the subject of each article for the cooperation that made the volume possible.

The Editors of Ebony

Contents

Famous Blacks
Give Secrets of Success

Milton B. Allen

State's Attorney, Baltimore City

At luncheon, State's Attorney Milton B. Allen (seated, 3rd from l.) is joined by George H. Beall, U.S. Attorney for the District of Maryland (at Mr. Allen's left) and Baltimore Police Commissioner Donald D. Pomerleau (seated, extreme r.). Others include Maryland Attorney General F.B. Burch (standing, c.).

He Saw What Was Wrong with the System, Moved Inside to Change It

"A person with the proper outlook . . . can move the entire system, but he must be inside with policy-making power."

When Milton Burk Allen was a successful defense lawyer in Baltimore, Maryland, he knew just about every way there was to take advantage of all the things that were wrong with the system of justice in his town. For twenty-five years, he either won acquittals or wangled light sentences for scores of defendants by exploiting what he calls "the gross ineptitude of law enforcement generally and prosecutors in particular." During that quarter-century, what concerned him was not reform of the system but how to use what was wrong as "an arena in which I made a living—in which I 'did my thing.' " He was, he says, "very busy making money, enjoying the adulation that comes to a successful lawyer and planning how to acquire a bigger and better law practice." He was delighted to meet young, stumbling prosecutors, or the policeman who had done a poor investigative job. " 'Fair trial' to me meant getting the defendant out by any acceptable strategy or device. The more inept the system, the fatter I grew," he says.

2

Milton Burk Allen, state's attorney in Baltimore, Md.; born Dec. 10, 1917 in Baltimore; graduate of Coppin State Teachers College (1938), University of Maryland (LL.B., 1948; J.D., 1971). Wife: Martha Allen. Children: David, Peter and Milton Jr. Address: 204 Court House, Baltimore, MD 21202 (See full biographical sketch in Volume I.)

In his office at Baltimore Court House, Mr. Allen confers with his deputy for operations, Benjamin L. Brown. The state's attorney is responsible for prosecution of all crimes—approximately 50,000 a year—that occur in City of Baltimore. His 140-member staff includes 90 assistant state's attorneys.

But Mr. Allen got tired of taking advantage of the system's faults. In 1966, he was asked to chair the Baltimore Criminal Court Committee and a few years later was named a member of a federally funded advisory group that studied the city's criminal court system. In both cases Mr. Allen found grave deficiencies in the whole justice system. And that's when he decided that a good way to help correct what he had found wrong would be to seek public office, to work from the inside.

". . . the system is not fair, but battling it from outside is impossible. A person with the proper outlook, the determination to be fair, the determination to cover the whole spectrum of crime, the determination to use his vast powers to shut off unjust prosecution or unjust failure to prosecute can move the entire system, but he must be inside with policy-making power," Mr. Allen contends. With this contention, he campaigned and was elected state's attorney by the people of Baltimore—the only black elected chief prosecutor of a major city in the United States.

In this position, Mr. Allen is responsible for the prosecution of all crimes that occur in Baltimore. He sets the overall policy of his office and supervises 140 employes (90 assistant state's attorneys included). His office prosecutes approximately 50,000 criminal offenders each year.

3

Milton Burk Allen's beginnings were like those of many blacks in America. Born December 10, 1917 in Baltimore, the son of poor parents, he attended one of the two public high schools for the education of black youths in that city. From there, he went on to Coppin State Teacher's College on a scholarship. Unable to find a job in the segregated school system upon graduating in 1939, young Allen went to work for a governmental agency in Washington, D.C. until he was drafted into the United States Army in 1943.

Serving approximately two and a half years in the military as a naval training officer, he was assigned to instruct general education courses for United States Navy recruits. He was later assigned to establish an on-base functional educational program for remedial-through-college courses in Hawaii. The program was used as a model for in-service educational systems in the Pacific area. For this innovation, he received a U.S. Navy honors award.

Two months after being honorably discharged (December, 1945), Mr. Allen embarked upon his legal training at the University of Maryland Law School under the GI Bill. He was admitted to the practice of law in 1948, a full year before receiving the bachelor of law degree. In 1970, he was awarded a doctorate in law from the same university.

With two other young black lawyers, he opened a law office in Baltimore, intending, he said, to "... aspire to elevate, to truly professional status, the [black] lawyer who was all too often bypassed by black clients because they felt that black lawyers could exert so little influence in the courtroom. And he wanted the office, he said, "to make a substantial contribution to the community it served." It was this philosophy that later earned Mr. Allen the title, "Dean of the New Breed of lawyers," and he has been rated in the *Martin Dale and Hubble Law Directory* as one of the "A"-rated legal personnel in the country.

Dubbed "a flamboyant courtroom lawyer" by the press, Mr. Allen had an extensive legal practice before becoming state's attorney. He tried more than seven thousand cases—from simple misdemeanors to death penalty cases—at all jurisdictional levels in all parts of the country, and he argued more than one hundred appeals before state and federal courts, many resulting in landmark decisions in criminal law, voting rights and civil rights.

One of Mr. Allen's most significant civil liberties cases was initiated in 1952 when numerous citizens, suspected of "communist sympathies," were victimized by "loyalty" investigations. A black female federal employee was fired because of "unfounded suspicion of disloyalty, accusing her of 'guilt by association.'" Mr. Allen took the case to federal court, and finally won it in 1957 in federal appeals court.

4

State's Attorney Allen visits chambers of Judge Albert L. Sklar.

The historic decision resulted in the reforming of the Civil Service merit system; in new grievance procedures for federal employees; made possible new avenues of entry to federal service for many people, particularly blacks, and created better promotional advantages for those who, regardless of their qualifications previously had been relegated to the most demeaning positions without the hope of ever advancing to better jobs.

With this impressive legal background, in mid-1970 Mr. Allen launched his campaign for the state's attorney position—which paid only $27,000 a year, less than a third of what he earned in private practice. His main campaign assertion was: "The office of the State's Attorney must serve all the people." The voters believed him; he won with a margin of 25,000 votes.

"Whatever success I have achieved," Mr. Allen says, "is in getting a black person into a position of authority in one segment of the justice system that must survive if America is to survive. Black lawyers have customarily shied away from working in the prosecution or law enforcement agencies, feeling they can be more effective elsewhere. I think this is a position that is 180 degrees inaccurate. The backbone of our society is its justice system, and a large part of our problems dealing with racism and all its attendant evils grow out of a malfunctioning justice system in which the black man plays a very tiny role."

The Milton B. Allen who now presides as the dedicated state's attorney of Baltimore City is a far cry from Milton B. Allen, defense lawyer, who once took advantage of every loophole that he could find in the justice system.

Mr. Allen takes a break from his duties to visit his uncle, Major Allen, 92.

Harry Belafonte

Entertainer

Above, earlier in his career, Harry Belafonte leads a Calypso scene in the musical *Almanac* at the Imperial Theater in New York City.

Harry Belafonte, singer, actor and film director; born March 1, 1927 in New York, N.Y.; attended high school; served with U.S. Naval Reserve (1943–46); became hit folk-ballad singer at the Village Vanguard in New York City, 1950; set many concert attendance records world-wide; his RCA record albums are among world's leading sellers; starred or co-starred in eight films, produced or directed four others; his TV special, Tonight with Belafonte, won him the Emmy award. Wife: Julie Robinson Belafonte. Children: David and Gina. Address: c/o The Mike Merrick Co., 9000 Sunset Blvd., Los Angeles, CA 90069 (See full biographical sketch in Volume I.)

He Combines Show Business Success With Social Awareness, Commitment

"No matter how much we stick now to finding our own uniqueness, we'll find that we're just part of the human race and that this is a phase in the history of it all."

Harry Belafonte was one of the first black entertainers to attain the status of superstar. Acclaimed widely for his highly individualistic rendition of folk-type songs, his extraordinary good looks and his acting ability, he has firmly established himself among the most durable personalities in the entertainment world. He is also one of the first entertainers—black or white—to combine his preeminence in show business with social awareness and commitment, a commitment that has led him to give consistently of his time and energy to the cause of black liberation.

Of West Indian extraction, Mr. Belafonte was born March 1, 1927,

Top photo (l. to r.): Lena Horne, Harry Belafonte, George Barrie, Cary Grant, Mrs. Harry Belafonte and Mrs. George Barrie talk during a party. Above, at rehearsal for TV show "A Time to Laugh," Mr. Belafonte shares a moment with (l. to r.) Godfrey Cambridge, Diana Sands, director Arthur Storch and "Moms" Mabley.

in New York City. While he was still quite young, his family moved to Jamaica, where they lived for five years, then returned to New York where Harry attended George Washington High School. There was a war on at the time and, rather than sticking it out in school until graduation, he dropped out in 1944 and joined the U.S. Navy for a two-year hitch. When he returned to civilian life, he considered himself too old at nineteen to go back to school. He found a job as a maintenance man instead. It was during this period that he received two tickets to an American Negro Theatre production. The play stimulated his interest in theater and he became a member of ANT, along with his close friend, Sidney Poitier. It was not until one of Mr. Belafonte's roles required him to sing that he discovered his special talent as a singer. Some time later, he signed a two-week contract to sing at the Royal Roost, a New York night club. Because of his almost instantaneous popularity with the club's patrons, the two weeks stretched to twenty. Before long, he had established himself as a moderately successful pop singer, an achievement that left him artistically unfulfilled and frustrated. Quite unhappy about his failure to find his "groove," he quit show business and, with what little money he had been able to save, joined two friends in buying a small restaurant in New York's Greenwich Village. Occasionally, he would join his guests in an impromptu song to the accompaniment of someone's guitar. These informal singing sessions prompted him to have another try at show business, but this time as a singer of ethnic folk tunes, ballads and calypso songs. By the end of 1950, following the building of a sizable repertoire of old and modern folk ballads, he appeared at the Village Vanguard nightclub and immediately "caught on." A subsequent recording contract with RCA Records was followed by his first starring roles in two motion pictures, *Bright Road* and *Carmen Jones*.

In 1955, already fully established as a recording artist, Mr. Belafonte became a full-fledged Broadway star in the Paul Gregory production, *Three for Tonight*, following his Broadway debut in a minor role in *John Murray Anderson's Almanac*. A year later, he began what became a Belafonte trademark—the breaking of attendance records— by breaking the thirty-nine-year record at New York's Lewisohn Stadium.

Perhaps Mr. Belafonte's greatest exposure to the public has been through his many television appearances, especially his top-rated specials, including Revlon's "Tonight With Belafonte" in 1959, which won him an "Emmy award" for top musical performer. He scored again a year later with his second television special, " Belafonte: New York 19." Moving farther up the ladder of success, he became executive producer and creator of the 1966 CBS-TV special, "The Strollin' Twenties," a musical flashback to Harlem during the colorful decade

Mr. Belafonte meets with the Reverend Jesse L. Jackson, president of Operation PUSH, before performing at a 1972 dinner in Chicago to raise funds for PUSH. A strong supporter of black rights, Mr. Belafonte has been closely associated with civil rights activists.

following World War I. Later, another special, "A Time for Laughter," a look at black humor, which he produced for ABC-TV, further enhanced his reputation.

Since the establishment of his own motion picture production firm, HarBel, Mr. Belafonte has produced three films: *The World, the Flesh and the Devil, Odds Against Tomorrow* and *The Angel Levine.* He had a starring role in each. He also starred opposite Joan Fontaine in *Island in the Sun*, a 1957 20th Century Fox film that caused much controversy because of its theme of interracial romance. His first western, *Buck and the Preacher*, a 1972 release in which he co-starred with Sidney Poitier, was a joint effort of the two actors' respective production companies.

Commenting on black awareness, as far as black film-makers are concerned, Mr. Belafonte says: "I think that after we have gone through a period of our blackness, which I consider therapeutic because it brings out all of our frustrations and our angers, we have to face the universe. No matter how much we stick now to finding our uniqueness, we'll find that we're just part of the human race and that this is a phase in the history of it all."

Mr. Belafonte became the first entertainer to be named a cultural advisor to the Peace Corps by the late President John F. Kennedy and, in recognition of his active involvement in a wide range of causes, he has been honored many times by such groups as the National Association for the Advancement of Colored People, the American Jewish Congress, the City of Hope, Fight for Sight, and Bonds for Israel. Because of his close friendship with Dr. Martin Luther King Jr. during the latter's civil rights campaigns, he was named one of the executors of the slain leader's estate and a member of the board of directors of the Southern Christian Leadership Conference.

Early during his rise to fame, Harry Belafonte was introduced to the work of the Wiltwyck School for Boys in upper New York state by the late Mrs. Eleanor Roosevelt. Since then, he has consistently supported the school to assure its survival, an effort the school recognized by naming the performing center in its new arts building the Belafonte Theatre.

Mr. Belafonte has four children—two girls, Adrienne and Shari, by a former marriage to Marguerite Belafonte, and a son and daughter, David Michael and Gina, born to his wife Julie, a former actress. The Belafontes live in New York City in a large, comfortable apartment filled with many paintings, trophies and records. An avid water skier, Belafonte also enjoys spending his leisure time at his farm in upstate New York.

8

Above, Mr. Belafonte and the late Dr. Martin Luther King Jr. during a planning session in Atlanta, Ga. for the Southern Christian Leadership Conference. At right he escorts the Reverend and Mrs. M. L. King Sr. at an affair (top) and performs for inmates of Rikers Island prison in New York City.

Mr. Belafonte and actor Sidney Poitier run into each other at airport in Nassau, Bahamas as they arrive for premiere of their film *Buck and the Preacher.*

Lerone Bennett Jr.

Journalist and Historian

The Truths of Black History Are Revealed in His Articles and Books

Lerone Bennett Jr., senior editor of Ebony magazine; born Oct. 17, 1928 in Clarksdale, Miss.; Morehouse College (A.B., 1949; hon. Litt.D., 1965). Wife: Gloria Sylvester Bennett. Children: Joy, Constance, Courtney and Lerone III. Address: 820 S. Michigan Ave., Chicago, IL 60605 (See full biographical sketch in Volume I)

"I found history exciting and fascinating, but it was usually written so dryly. I knew people would become interested if it were presented in a popular, dramatic way."

In its July, 1961 issue, *Ebony* magazine published the first in a series of articles on black history that quickly made their author, associate editor Lerone Bennett Jr., a familiar and respected name in thousands of black American homes.

"A series of revolutionary discoveries by archeologists and historical anthropologists is forcing the world to change its mind about the strong bronzed men and regal black women from whose loins sprang one out of every ten Americans. This reappraisal has already yielded a new perspective on African history. Africa, long considered the Dark Continent, is now regarded as the cradle of humanity. Ancient Africans, long considered primitive and ignorant, are now regarded as creative contributors to Egyptian civilization and ingenious builders of powerful states in the Nile Valley and the Western Sudan."

Those were the introductory words to the articles that popularized black history among millions of Americans in a way that no historian had been able to do before. The articles eventually were compiled into a book, *Before the Mayflower*, which has, since it was published in 1962, sold more than 50,000 hardcover copies. By 1973 it was in its fourth revised edition.

On opposite page, Lerone Bennett Jr. delivers one of his frequent speeches. Above, at a conference, he is greeted by historians Dr. John Hope Franklin (l.) and Prof. Sterling Stuckey. At right, he speaks at dedication of "Wall of Respect" in Chicago, Ill. ghetto.

Born October 17, 1928 in Clarksdale, Mississippi, Lerone Bennett Jr. knew intimately many of the racial paradoxes he would explore with authority in later years. In Jackson, Mississippi, he attended segregated schools and was barred from the public library, yet learned that one did not have to be literate to understand the difference between signs reading "White Only" and "Colored."

Fortunately, he inherited a strong sense of tradition from, and had a healthy respect for, his parents, Lerone Bennett Sr. and Alma Reed Bennett. Mrs. V. M. Manning, a high school history teacher, taught him to see the continuity between the past and the present. "That influenced me a great deal," he says. "It seemed a logical progression to apply that to journalism, too, by interpreting events against their historical background." His high school coach, Ben Allen Blackburn, also impressed him: "He carried himself as a man. And it was very difficult for a black man to be a man in Mississippi and other Southern states at that particular time."

11

In addition to social studies and history, young Bennett showed a talent for writing, and local black newspapermen encouraged him by printing some of his articles. He also played alto saxophone well enough to earn the nickname "Duke" at age thirteen. With his own band and with other bands, he often performed as a featured soloist in nightclubs in his home state and in Atlanta, Georgia. When the five foot, eight inch, 120-pound high schooler expressed interest in football, too, he recalls that the athletic staff "laughed me off the field." They finally let him play, however, and he quarterbacked his team to an almost unblemished record. An academic scholarship enabled him to attend Atlanta's Morehouse College, though he had to moonlight as a musician and newspaper writer. He graduated from Morehouse in 1949 (he had been editor of the college newspaper) with an A.B. degree in political science and economics.

After his graduation, Mr. Bennett was hired by the *Atlanta Daily World* as a reporter; he was promoted to city editor in 1953. In the same year, he left for Chicago to begin his long and distinguished association with Johnson Publishing Company, first on the *Jet* magazine staff, then on *Ebony*. In 1958, he was promoted to senior editor of *Ebony*, the position he holds today. "It was my desire to work in the black media," he says of his exclusive work in that area. "I was fortunate that breaks in black journalism made it unnecessary to go to the white press."

The decision that Lerone Bennett would provide *Ebony*'s frequent articles on black history opened up fruitful possibilities for him. He already possessed "the material and the passion" for the project. "I found history exciting and fascinating, but it was usually written so dryly. I knew people would become interested if it were presented in a

Students at LeMoyne-Owen College in Memphis, Tenn. surround Mr. Bennett and ask for his autograph after his speech there during a celebration of Negro History Week.

At a meeting of the Black Academy of Arts and Letters, Mr. Bennett and his wife, Gloria, talk with writer-educator John Henrik Clarke.

Mr. Bennett visits a Chicago black history exhibition with writer Margaret Goss Burroughs and photographer-film director Gordon Parks.

popular, dramatic way." In the preface to *Before the Mayflower*, Mr. Bennett explained: "The book, like the series, deals with the trials and triumphs of Americans whose roots in the American soil are deeper than those of Puritans who arrived on the celebrated *Mayflower* a year after a Dutch man-of-war deposited twenty Negroes at Jamestown." The same kind of dramatic, revealing presentation of fact characterizes the six other books that he had written for Johnson Publishing Company by 1973: *The Negro Mood* (1964), *What Manner of Man: A Biography of Martin Luther King, Jr.* (1964); *Confrontation: Black and White* (1965); *Black Power U.S.A.: The Human Side of Reconstruction, 1867–1877* (1967); *Pioneers in Protest* (1968), and a collection of essays and speeches, *The Challenge of Blackness* (1972). He also was editor of the three-volume *Ebony Pictorial History of Black America* (1972).

In his article, "Lerone Bennett: Social Historian" (*Freedomways*,

13

After speaking at 75th Commencement at Florida A & M University, Mr. Bennett signs a program for one of his young fans.

Fall, 1965), historian John Henrik Clarke assessed Mr. Bennett's role as a scholar. He noted that both Mr. Bennett and his Morehouse classmate, Dr. Martin Luther King Jr., belonged to "the generation of new black thinkers who, before and after the Montgomery bus boycott, started insisting and demanding their full manhood rights in the United States. This generation literally grew up and matured within the eye of the civil rights storm . . . As an editor, [Bennett] is an active participator in the civil rights movement as well as an astute interpreter of it."

In the opinion of George E. Kent, Professor of English at the University of Chicago, *Before the Mayflower* "reveals the qualities which have caused [Bennett] to be quoted in schools, on quiz programs, and by blacks whose struggles for bread leave time for only the most essential reading: solid documentation complimented by the perception of one who has known the fire and not forgotten the intensity of the flame."

Lerone Bennett's writing has not eclipsed other important activities in which he has been engaged. He has taught at Northwestern University, given countless speeches, contributed to many periodicals, served as Senior Fellow at Atlanta's Institute of the Black World, travelled in Europe and Africa, and been a member of several boards of directors. His poetry has appeared in such volumes as *New Negro Poets: U.S.A.*, edited by Langston Hughes, and his *Negro Digest* short story, "The Convert," has been anthologized numerous times in a half-dozen languages. He still blows his saxophone occasionally, though he devotes most of his time away from work to his family—his wife, the former Gloria Sylvester, and children: Lerone III, Joy, and twins Constance and Courtney.

Mr. Bennett is the first to acknowledge that he has benefited from the groundwork of brilliant black scholars of earlier years. Few of them, however, touched so many lives directly or received so many plaudits in their own lifetime. Morehouse College presented him an honorary doctor of letters degree in 1965. In 1972, hundreds of people assembled to see him receive a Black Liberation Award from Chicago's Kuumba Workshop.

To the program booklet printed for the Kuumba occasion, Chicago writer Eugene Perkins contributed his poem, "Tree of Knowledge (For Lerone Bennett)," which sums up the general assessment of the man and his work:

At first glance
he appears like a fragile tree
. . . . Yet beneath his ebony trunk
lies a fierce

14

determination. . . .
His roots are planted in wisdom
blossoming relevant knowledge
to clarify the aberrations
of our painful history.
Not just a scholar
but an Evergreen man;
a consistent exemplifier
of Black excellency.

In his books, articles, speeches, classes and creative writing, Mr. Bennett has taken on some of the most tenacious myths and fantasies of the twentieth century. Above all, he has, for the layman, "demystified" the past—that haunting past black people have not wanted to remember and the Western world has tried so terribly hard to forget.

A collector of books by Mr. Bennett and other black historians is entertainer Sammy Davis Jr., shown during a visit to Mr. Bennett's office at Johnson Publishing Co.

At an autographing party at Chicago's Independence Bank, Mr. Bennett and his publisher, John H. Johnson (r.), talk with bank's president, Alvin Boutte (l.) and A. M. Schweich of Chicago Metropolitan Mutual Assurance Co.

Edward W. Brooke III

United States Senator

Edward William Brooke III, U.S. senator (Republican, Massachusetts); born Oct. 26, 1919 in Washington, D.C.; Howard University (B.S., 1941), Boston University Law School (LL.B., 1948 and LL.M., 1950). Wife: Remigia Ferrari-Scacco Brooke. Children: Remi and Edwina. Address: 421 Old Senate Office Bldg., Washington, DC 20510 (See full biographical sketch in Volume I.)

Sen. Brooke stands in front of the U.S. Capitol shortly after he is sworn-in on Jan. 10, 1967 as a member of the Senate by Vice President Hubert H. Humphrey (top photo).

The First Black Senator in Modern Times

"I can't just serve the Negro cause. I've got to serve all the people of Massachusetts."

By any measure, Massachusetts Senator Edward W. Brooke is a remarkable man. He was the first black since 1881 to win membership in one of the world's most exclusive clubs, the United States Senate, and he did it in 1966, when racial animosity throughout the United States was at its peak. Despite the fact that he is an Episcopalian and a Republican in heavily Catholic and Democratic Boston, he has proven himself the top vote-getter in his state's history. He may be the only public official who can boast of endorsements from top black leaders as well as Harvard liberals, staid Yankee conservatives and right- and left-wing extremists. He probably is also the only black in American politics who could have caused the Republican party tremor that occurred after the 1972 Republican presidential landslide, when he announced that he was "considering" running for the presidency in 1976.

Edward William Brooke was born on October 26, 1919, in Washington, D.C., the only son and the youngest child of Edward W. and Helen Brooke. His father was a lawyer with the Veterans Administration. Edward grew up in an atmosphere of well-being, mostly in middle class neighborhoods. For a time, the family—and a few other "select" black families—lived in a "white" neighborhood so "restricted" that other blacks were not permitted to pass through without a note from a white person. He spent summers on his mother's family plantation in Virginia

Sen. Brooke listens intently during a Senate hearing.

Sen. Brooke joins three other Republican freshmen senators shortly after arrival in Washington in January 1967. From left are: Sen. Clifford P. Hansen (Wyo.), Sen. Charles H. Percy (Ill.), Sen. Brooke and Sen. Howard H. Baker (Tenn.).

where his grandparents told him he was a descendant of Thomas Jefferson and British Admiral Sir Philip Bowes Broke, and that he was related to the poet Rupert Brooke. "I was a happy child," Senator Brooke has recalled. "I was conscious of being a Negro, yes. But I was not conscious of being underprivileged because of that."

After completing public school in Washington, he went to Howard University, where he received his bachelor's degree in 1940. When the United States entered World War II, Mr. Brooke, who had been in the ROTC at Howard, was inducted as a second lieutenant. He served five years with the all-black 366th infantry, was awarded the Bronze Star and Infantryman's Badge, and attained the rank of captain.

Several months after the end of the war, Mr. Brooke entered Boston University Law School. He received the bachelor of laws degree in 1948 and the master of laws degree in 1949. In 1950, when it was still legal to cross-file in primary elections, he declared as both a Republican and a Democratic candidate for the Massachusetts state legislature. He won the Republican nomination and has been a Republican ever since. In his next two attempts at public office, he lost. In 1960, he was the first black ever to be nominated for a statewide office in Massachusetts. He lost to his Democratic opponent by less than 12,000 votes, and in doing so ran up the startling total of 1,095,054. He attained public prominence in 1961 when he was appointed chairman of the Boston Finance Commission, a watchdog agency. Several well-publicized exposures of civic corruption propelled him into the state attorney general's office in 1962. In seeking reelection in 1964, he received 1,543,900 votes and a plurality of 797,510 votes, the largest plurality of any Republican in the United States that year, and the largest of any

Sen. Brooke receives an honorary LL.D. degree at Emerson College in Boston, Mass. (above) and (right) with his daughter, Remi, accepts cheers of crowd on "Senator Edward W. Brooke Day" in Oak Bluffs, Mass. in August 1967.

Sen. Brooke joins others to greet the Rev. Leon H. Sullivan upon his return from a tour of Africa. From left are: Virgil Day of General Electric, Sen. Brooke, Sen. Hugh Scott, Rev. Sullivan, Sen. Richard Schweiker, Ambassador Ebenezer Debrah of Ghana, Dr. Samuel Adams and Valor Jordan.

Republican in the history of Massachusetts. As attorney general, Senator Brooke was criticized when he warned a predominantly white village that reading of the Bible in schools was unconstitutional, and ruled that a school boycott by blacks was illegal.

Mr. Brooke's 1966 Senate victory was largely attributed to his easy, affable style of campaigning, eloquent speech and long hours of criss-crossing the state. Another asset was his wife Remigia, whose husky Italian voice and delightful way with the English language made a favorable impression on voters.

What sets Senator Brooke apart is not that "he thinks he is white" as some of his critics have charged, but that he has had the tenacity to

During his 1960 campaign for election as secretary of state in Massachusetts, Mr. Brooke rejected any Communist support and sent a "warning letter" to U.S.S.R. Premier Nikita Khrushchev. At right, during a 1962 campaign for election as attorney general of Massachussetts, he explains his program to workers.

20

Sen. Brooke and his wife, Remigia, spend a moment together in their home.

resist pressure to become a civil rights leader. "I can't serve just the Negro cause. I've got to serve all the people of Massachusetts." (At the time of his Senate election, the state was only 2 percent black.)

Senator Brooke's determination to hold a middle-of-the-road course does not mean that he has not tried to change the road's direction. In the Senate, he has voted to reform and broaden welfare legislation, to make the cities more livable, to clean up rivers and streams and to provide better schools for ghetto areas. He serves on several important Senate committees, including the Committee on Appropriations, the Committee on Banking, Housing and Urban Affairs, the Select Committee on Equal Educational Opportunity and the Special Committee on Aging. His subcommittee assignments include Foreign Operations, Labor, Military Construction, Small Business and Securities. Not incidentally, he wants to reform the Republican party. In 1966, his book, *Challenge of Change: Crisis in Our Two-Party System*, proposed that the Grand Old Party cease being grandfatherly and cold. He not only castigated the party and its 1964 presidential candidate, Arizona Senator Barry Goldwater, but criticized Republicans for being blind to America's needs. "We often have no solutions at all," he wrote. "We give the appearance of being afraid of social progress."

Senator Brooke has served as board chairman of the Boston Opera Company, and enjoys tennis and swimming as well as the opera. He is a trustee of Boston University and Northeastern University. He is the recipient of numerous awards and more than twenty honorary degrees. The senator's wife is the former Remigia Ferrari-Scacco of Genoa, Italy. They met when he was an intelligence officer during World War II and were married in 1947. They have two daughters, Remi Cynthia and Edwina Helene.

21

Gwendolyn Brooks
Poet

She Cannot Remember When She Did Not Want to Be a Poet

Gwendolyn Brooks, poet; born June 17, 1917 in Topeka, Kan.; graduated from Wilson Junior College, Chicago, Ill. (1936); first black winner of Pulitzer Prize (1950); named Illinois poet laureate (1969); recipient of several honorary degrees and numerous citations and prizes; author of several books of poetry. Husband: Henry L. Blakely; children: Henry L. and Nora. Address: 7428 S. Evans Ave., Chicago, IL 60619 (See full biographical sketch in Volume I.)

"In my writing I am proud to feature people and their concerns, their troubles as well as their joys. It is my privilege to present Negroes not as curios but as people."

It may not be true that Gwendolyn Brooks was born to be a poet—but then again it just might. Today the soft-spoken black woman from Chicago who weaves words as adroitly as a Ghanaian artisan patterns kente cloth cannot remember when she didn't want to be a poet.

She remembers that when she was growing up she was writing all the time—sometimes actually putting it down on paper and sometimes writing it in her mind as she lay on her back on the grass in Chicago's Jackson Park on a summer day and watched the clouds fill and thin against a bold blue sky.

Gwendolyn's mother, Keziah Corinne Wims Brooks of Topeka, Kansas, says that Gwendolyn started writing in rhyme when she was just seven years old. Mrs. Brooks was a schoolteacher and church worker who early taught Gwendolyn to recite poems and pieces at programs at Carter Temple Church on Chicago's South Side when Gwen (as she has always been known to her friends) was only four or five years old.

Miss Brooks knows that she was writing very carefully rhymed verse when she was eleven. She knows it because she still has notebooks from that period. In her autobiography, *A Report From Part One,* Broadside Press, 1972, she talks of the "careful rhymes, lofty meditations" in her pre-teen poem, "Forgive And Forget."

If others neglect you,
Forget; do not sigh,
For, after all, they'll select you
In times by and by.
If their taunts cut and hurt you,
They are sure to regret.
And, if in time, they desert you,
Forgive and forget.

Poems like that let Gwendolyn's family know that she was serious about becoming a poet and her family encouraged her in every way. Her father, David Anderson Brooks, worked most of his life as a janitor but, like many blacks who took menial jobs to support their families, he had the mind and feeling for far greater things. Born in Atchison, Kansas, David Brooks moved with his family to Oklahoma City, Oklahoma when he was nine. The death of his father when David was a teenager left him the head of a family of young brothers and younger and older sisters. He still managed to finish high school and to study for a year at Fisk University, planning to become a doctor, although poverty kept him from completing school. He married Keziah Wims on July 16, 1916, and their daughter Gwendolyn was born June 17, 1917. Five weeks later they moved to Chicago where Mr. Brooks soon found himself working as a janitor but with a great love and respect for education.

Gwendolyn's mother and father and her younger brother, Raymond, all respected her desire to become a poet and helped her in every way they could. Gwen found that she was never overloaded with chores and that her desire for privacy when she wrote—even as a child—was respected. Her father secured a desk at which she could work—a desk that even had a place for books, particularly for her "Emily" books, a series by L. M. Montgomery about a young Canadian girl who wrote and kept notebooks just as Gwendolyn did, and her favorite volume, *The Complete Paul Laurence Dunbar*.

Even today, Miss Brooks laughs about how her mother early announced that Gwen was going to be "the *lady* Paul Lawrence Dunbar." It was prophetic that Mrs. Brooks said that the budding poet would be a "Paul Lawrence Dunbar" and not a "Phillis Wheatley"—America's first famous black woman poet who, in the mid-1700s, wrote in the classical style. Like Dunbar, Gwendolyn was destined to write about the real people she knew and the real world around her.

Timid, dark, not much of a dancer, and poor, Gwendolyn was anything but a social butterfly during her teen-age years. You had to be light, bright, or rich and a little fast to be popular in those days. She was somewhat of a loner, spending almost all her spare time in her room

Miss Brooks acknowledges praise for her work at the Illinois Institute of Technology's 75th Anniversary ceremony in Chicago. She has been the recipient of numerous honors and awards.

Miss Brooks sits among recipients of honorary degrees at 1968 ceremony at Illinois Institute of Technology.

reading and writing. She admits that she often daydreamed of "some little boy or other" but seldom went out on dates. Even then, she thought of herself as a poet. She wrote at least one poem every day and knew that it was only a matter of time before the whole world would know her genius.

Gwendolyn was right. In 1950, Gwendolyn Brooks became the first black Pulitzer Prize winner when she was awarded the Pulitzer Prize for Poetry for *Annie Allen*, her second volume of poetry, published in 1949. Her first published volume, *A Street in Bronzeville*, had also been an award winner. Published in 1945, the thin volume of poetic pictures of Chicago's black South Side and South Siders won for its author the Merit Award as outstanding woman of the year from *Mademoiselle* magazine.

The years from her early teens to the Pulitzer Prize were not empty. At fourteen, she had her first poem published in *American Childhood* magazine, though most of the manuscripts she submitted to magazines during her "growing years" were returned. She kept writing and she began to hang out with other young blacks on the South Side who were interested in writing or painting or photography. The late 1930s marked the beginning of a renaissance in the arts among blacks in Chicago and Miss Brooks was right in the center of it. The federally sponsored Works Progress Administration provided work for writers like Richard Wright and artists such as Charles White and Archibald Motley. The mature artists took the youngsters under their wings. Word of the promise among young blacks reached Chicago's North Side and it had a profound effect upon Inez Cunningham Stark, a wealthy and talented patron of Midwest poets. Somewhat to the dismay of her friends, Miss

A favorite poet of black youth, Miss Brooks accepts 1970 award from Lew Jackson (l.), president of the Black Students Association at Western Illinois University, and Don Poindexter, vice president of the BSA.

Stark started a poetry workshop at the South Side Community Art Center in 1941. For several years she provided books, free subscriptions to *Poetry* magazine and professional guidance to young black poets. Among her students were Margaret Goss Burroughs, Margaret Danner Cunningham and, of course, Gwendolyn Brooks. Miss Stark taught them to teach one another, encouraging them to write and then to read their work to the class. In lively discussions, they learned how their poems affected other people and they learned how to listen to what others were saying. It was a happy time for Gwendolyn and when it was over she had made giant strides.

In class with Miss Brooks was Henry Blakely, also an aspiring writer who, shortly before the workshop was started, had married Gwendolyn. Friends had introduced them two years earlier, feeling that two people so interested in writing should know each other.

Gwendolyn and Henry were married for thirty years but separated in 1969. They have two children, Henry, born October 10, 1940, and Nora, born September 8, 1951.

In 1943, Miss Brooks won the Midwestern Writers' Conference poetry award and was asked to submit poems for a book to the publisher, Alfred Knopf. She sent the firm forty poems on a variety of subjects and got them back with a notation that "the Negro poems" had been liked the best and that when there were enough of them she should try again. Miss Brooks rushed together a group of poems about black South Siders and sent them, not to Knopf but to Harper Brothers. Harper's editor, Elizabeth Lawrence, sent back an acceptance, telling Miss Brooks to take her time in completing a sufficient number of poems for a book. In 1945, Harper published *A Street in Bronzeville* and Gwendolyn Brooks was on her way to greatness.

The Pulitzer Prize in 1950 opened all doors, and magazines that had turned down her submitted poetry now begged her to write for them. In 1953, her novel *Maud Martha* was published, followed in 1956 with a volume of verse, *Bronzeville Boys and Girls*, and in 1960, the book of poems *The Bean Eaters*.

In 1969, one of her strongest books of poems, *In The Mecca*, firmly established Gwendolyn Brooks as one of the most powerful poetic voices in the world. Commenting on urban living, she had once said, "The city is the place to observe man *en masse* in his infinite variety. In my writing I am proud to feature people and their concerns, their troubles as well as their joys. It is my privilege to present Negroes not as curios but as people."

The title poem, "In The Mecca," was a strong piece of life lifted from experiences in a once luxurious development that had become one of the worst slums on Chicago's South Side. The new volume showed new strain—stronger and more militant—and there was good reason. Just a year before, Miss Brooks had gone to speak at a workshop for black writers at Fisk University. There, listening to the young and learning from dedicated writers such as Lerone Bennett Jr., Hoyt W. Fuller, Don L. Lee, John O. Killens and Imamu Amiri Baraka, Gwendolyn Brooks rediscovered her blackness.

Her earlier success, including her being named poet laureate of the state of Illinois in 1968, had been, to a large extent, in the white world. Now she was hearing black. And she began to live black, helping other black writers, visiting children in all-black schools, giving money to black cultural groups. She conquered her fear of flying and travelled to Kenya and Tanzania to experience living for a brief time in black nations.

Miss Brooks is presented flowers at a 1971 autographing party for *To Gwen With Love* (Johnson Publishing Co., 1971), an anthology dedicated to her. She has inspired numerous young writers and poets.

Miss Brooks, at 1972 dedication of the new Johnson Publishing Co. Building in Chicago, reads a poem she composed for the occasion. Her work has appeared in *Ebony* and in numerous other periodicals.

Gwendolyn Brooks' conversion was so complete that when her autobiography, *Report From Part One*, was published in 1972, the publisher was not Harper and Row, but a smaller, black company, Dudley Randall's Broadside Press in Detroit.

Miss Brooks has been a book reviewer, editor, teacher and lecturer. She has taught at Columbia College in Chicago, the University of Chicago, Elmhurst (Ill.) College, Northeastern Illinois State College, the University of Wisconsin and the City University of New York.

One of the most honored of poets, Miss Brooks, a graduate of Wright Junior College, has honorary degrees from twelve colleges and universities. She has also been named in *Esquire* magazine's One Hundred Most Important People in the World, *Ebony* magazine's One Hundred Most Influential Black Americans, the *Ladies Home Journal*'s Seventy-Five Most Important Women in America, *Mademoiselle* magazine's Ten Women Of The Year, *Town and Country* magazine's Who's Who In Chicago, *Panorama* magazine's Sixty-Two Best People In Chicago and *McCall's* magazine's Seventy-One People Who Made A Difference in 1971.

Although she was born in Topeka, Kansas, Miss Brooks has lived most of her life in Chicago. She was only a month old when her family brought her to Chicago and she knows no other home. She says she wouldn't have it any other way.

James Brown

Entertainer

James Brown, one of the world's most successful show business personalities, has entertained fans around the world. In photos above, he goes through his strenuous routine.

James Brown, entertainer and businessman; born May 3, 1933 in Augusta, Ga; worked in fields, did odd jobs, shined shoes, etc. before beginning to entertain U. S. Army soldiers at Fort Gordon, Ga. to earn money to help support his family; by 1971 his single records had sold more than 39 million copies; though criticized by some for his support of the re-election of President Nixon in 1972, he gained widespread respect for anti-narcotics songs and crusades; is owner of several radio stations and other businesses, and plans a $21 million shopping center and an office building in Georgia. Wife: the former Deidre Yvonne Jenkins. Children: Terry, Daryl, Teddy, Venisha, Deanna and Yamma. Address: Man's World Enterprises, 1122 Greene St., Augusta, GA 30902 (See full biographical sketch in Volume I.)

He Now Owns the Place Where He Once Shined Shoes

". . . I knew I had to make it. I had the determination to go on, and my determination was to be somebody."

As a boy growing up in segregated Augusta, Georgia during the late 1930s, James Brown picked cotton, did odd jobs, and shined shoes for three cents a pair on the steps of radio station WRDW in order to help his family pay the $7-a-month rent on their tarpaper-roofed shack. Today, James Brown, millionaire entertainer and businessman, owns radio station WRDW—plus a string of other enterprises.

"I had to do all those things in order to survive as a little black boy growing up in the South—pick cotton, work wherever I could, shine shoes . . . ," Mr. Brown recalls. "I started shining shoes at three cents, then I went up to five cents, then six cents. I never did get up to a dime. I was nine years old before I got a pair of underwear from a real store; all my clothes were made from sacks and things like that. But I knew I

28

In the White House, Mr. Brown has a talk with President Richard M. Nixon prior to endorsing him for re-election.

Mr. Brown has lent support to various civil rights groups and has been a crusader against the use of drugs. Above, after becoming a life member of the NAACP, he is awarded a plaque by NAACP Executive Director Roy Wilkins. Below, Los Angeles Mayor Sam Yorty presents him a certificate during "Anti-Drug Week."

had to make it. I had the determination to go on, and my determination was to *be somebody* . . ."

By the time he was twelve years old, poverty had pushed James out of the seventh grade. In his "dropout" status he was better able to help support his family by picking up nickels and dimes as a singer and dancer for World War II soldiers stationed at Fort Gordon, near Augusta. "I had a very, very big family," he recalls. "Not brothers and sisters, but a lot of close relatives, and I had to help feed them. My family was so poor you wouldn't even believe it. My father [Joseph] greased and washed cars in a filling station. Sometimes I worked with him. Other times I picked cotton, worked on a farm, worked in a coal yard . . . In the afternoon, I had to walk home along the railroad tracks and pick up pieces of coke left over from the trains. I'd take that home and we'd use it to keep warm."

At sixteen, James was convicted of stealing an automobile. He was paroled after three years in a reform school. He began singing gospel songs in Baptist churches. Later, he married and became a father. Still determined to "make it," he followed the traditional entertainer's route of performing for years wherever he could get a "gig." In 1956, he recorded his first hit song and was on his way to becoming "Mr. Dynamite" in the rhythm 'n' blues field, then "Soul Brother No. 1" in the world of music called "Soul."

"I'm 75 percent businessman and 25 percent talent," is the way he describes himself now. In a typical successful year, the business-talent combination enables him to: perform 335 days; give away 5,000 autographed photos and 1,000 pairs of James Brown cuff links each month; wear his choice of 120 shirts, more than 80 pairs of shoes and 150 stage costumes, and perform some of the 960 (or more) songs that he has either composed or arranged.

In 1968, the year in which he wrote "Say It Loud, I'm Black and I'm Proud," a "black anthem for black youths," Mr. Brown employed eighty-five people (his annual payroll was $1.1 million) to help him run James Brown Productions, James Brown Enterprises, Man's World, three

On stage in the Apollo Theater, Mr. Brown is presented with a crown and gold record after being dubbed "The King of Soul."

record companies, two real estate interests, and two radio stations—the one in Augusta, and WEBB (We Enjoy Being Black) in Baltimore, Maryland. By 1971, he had added a third radio station, WJBE (With James Brown Enterprises) in Knoxville, Tennessee. And by 1973, he had bought stations in Mobile, Ala., and Oklahoma City, Okla.

Spending money to make money, he used promotions and an extensive advertising schedule in *Jet* newsmagazine to boost gross from personal appearances from $450,000 in 1963 to $2.5 million in 1968. Recordings, publishing and investments increased his 1968 gross income to $4.5 million. He donated 10 percent of his earnings to black charities, youth groups and scholarship projects.

In 1971, at age thirty-seven (fifteen years after he made his first record, "Please, Please, Please,") Mr. Brown's black fans crowned him "King of Soul" at Harlem's Apollo Theatre. He was by then not only king of "soul" gold record sellers (he sold over thirty-nine million singles for King and Polydor record companies), but he was king of the one-nighters, travelling 100,000 miles a year in his five-passenger, $713,000 Lear jet airplane to entertain more than three million fans—including a growing number of young whites. At New York's Yankee Stadium, with only his name on the marquee, Mr. Brown drew an estimated 43,000 persons—more than the New York Yankees baseball team had drawn in any game in that year. About 95 percent of the audience were black.

In November 1970, Mr. Brown married the former Deidre Yvonne Jenkins. Today they live on a four-acre estate in Augusta. Their sprawling ranch-style house was built at a cost of $115,000, and at their disposal are three automobiles—a Rolls-Royce, an Excalibur and a Lincoln Mark IV—and a new Jet Commander plane.

In recounting his rags to riches saga, Mr. Brown considers three events in his career with special pride. First, he was inspired by the favorable nationwide response he received in the spring of 1968 following his appeal to blacks to end the racial strife which had been triggered by the assassination of Dr. Martin Luther King Jr. Second, in 1969 he was presented the Humanitarian Award by the Music and Performing Arts Lodge of B'nai B'rith in New York City. In addition to the award, Congressman William L. Clay of Missouri gave him a portfolio of letters of commendation. In making the presentation, the congressman said: "Men of good conscience, men of good will are proud to stand up and be counted. You kept your color and by doing so you made color less of an obstacle." Third, although he was frequently seen in different countries and cities in the company of presidents, kings, governors, mayors and army generals, his acceptance in Africa,

where he was received with extraordinary warmth, left him almost speechless. In 1970, President Kenneth Kaunda of Zambia introduced him at a State House reception with these remarks: "I have often been privileged to introduce to you several heads of state, and tonight I am privileged to introduce to you a different head of state, a head of music, Soul Brother James Brown." In Lagos, Nigeria, Mr. Brown was named a "freeman of the city" by Oba Adeyinka Oyekan and was presented with a "chain of office" and a scroll detailing the story of the soul singer and his contribution to making black men everywhere black and proud.

In top photo, Mr. Brown visits a Los Angeles school to warn children against drugs. In center photo, he entertains American troops in South Vietnam. Above, he visits with Oba Orkan II of Lagos, Nigeria during a 1970 visit to the African capital. At right, he and his wife, Deidre, share a moment together.

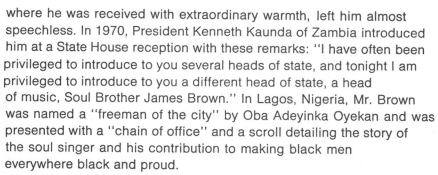

Yvonne Brathwaite Burke

United States Congresswoman

Yvonne Watson Brathwaite Burke, congresswoman, was elected in November 1972 to the U.S. House of Representatives from the 37th Congressional District in Los Angeles, Cal.; born Oct. 5, 1932 in Los Angeles; graduate of UCLA (B. A., political science, 1953) and the University of Southern California School of Law (J.D., 1956); in private practice of law in Los Angeles (1956-66); member of California Assembly (1966-72); member of numerous professional and civic groups. Husband: William A. Burke, a Los Angeles businessman. Address: House of Representatives, Washington, D.C. 20515 (See full biographical sketch in Volume I.)

She Is 'Too Pretty
Not to Be in Show Business'

"My approach has always been to be nice until I'm pinned to the wall. Then I blow up—this when all else fails."

Yvonne Brathwaite Burke, who in November, 1972 became the first black woman from California to be elected to the United States House of Representatives, has been described by admiring newswriters as "too pretty not to be in show business." While her unquestioned good looks may have helped her in winning votes, she is well qualified for her position, having entered the House race with impressive credentials as a lawyer, politician and legislator. Prior to her election to Congress, Mrs. Burke served for six years with distinction in the California General

In the California General Assembly, where she served from 1966 until her election to Congress in 1972, Mrs. Burke discusses legislation with Assemblymen Leon Ralph (c.) and Bill Green.

At right, Mrs. Burke is sworn-in as a member of Congress by Speaker of the House Carl Albert of Oklahoma. Below, during a break in her duties as vice chairman of the 1972 Democratic National Convention, she stops to talk with Mrs. Mervyn Dymally, wife of the California state senator.

Assembly, to which she was elected in 1966. As an assemblywoman, she supported such issues as increased federal aid to education, child care for the poor, court reform, prison reform and equal job opportunities for women.

Mrs. Burke was born October 5, 1932 in southeast Los Angeles, the only child of Mr. and Mrs. James Watson. At the time, her father was a janitor at Metro-Goldwyn-Mayer movie studios. Little Pearl Yvonne (she later dropped the "Pearl" because she didn't like it) impressed her public school teachers with her keen intelligence, causing the principal to urge her parents to have her transferred to a more challenging school environment. Consequently, she was enrolled at a model school affiliated with the University of Southern California. Mrs. Burke, who says that she was the only black pupil in that school, remembers that she was usually treated harshly by her classmates. This did not deter her, however, from making her mark as an excellent student. Having won state and local honors as an orator, and after having been elected vice president of the student body at Manual Arts High School, she decided that the profession of law

33

After her election as the first black congresswoman from California, Mrs. Burke strides from the California General Assembly (top) and is congratulated (above) by a friend.

would provide an excellent outlet for her special talents. On the basis of her high scholastic standing, her father's union awarded her a scholarship to the University of California at Berkeley in 1949. When she reached her junior year, she transferred to the University of California at Los Angeles, where she graduated with a bachelor's degree in political science in 1953. She then entered the University of Southern California Law School, becoming the school's first black woman student in thirty years. Discovering that a women's law society on the campus refused to admit blacks and Jews, she and two Jewish girls started a chapter of a rival law sorority. Her "take-charge" ability has remained a trademark throughout her political career.

Mrs. Burke was graduated from law school in the top third of her class in 1956. After passing her bar examination, she began private practice in probate, civil and real estate law. She also became known in Los Angeles as an aggressive civil rights attorney and as a member of the executive board of the Los Angeles Branch of the NAACP. Eventually, she served as an attorney for the McCone Commission, which conducted an investigation into the causes of the rebellion in Watts, the same area that today makes up part of her 37th Congressional District.

In 1957, she married Louis Brathwaite, a mathematician. After seven years, the marriage, which was childless, ended in divorce. Shortly after winning the 1972 California Primary, she married Los Angeles businessman William Burke.

A highlight in Mrs. Burke's political career—one which brought her to national attention—was her officiating as vice chairman of the 1972 Democratic National Convention in Miami, Florida. She impressed delegates as well as millions of television viewers with her thorough knowledge of parliamentary procedure, resolute handling of the gavel—and her beauty.

Mrs. Burke's election to Congress—simultaneous with that of Miss Barbara Jordan, a Texas state legislator—brings the number of black women serving in the U.S. House of Representatives to three. The first black woman to make the historic breakthrough was Representative Shirley Chisholm from Brooklyn, New York. Following her election, Mrs. Burke expressed relief over the fact that she did not have to carry the burden Mrs. Chisholm had carried as the only black woman in Congress. "There is no longer any need for anyone to speak for all black women. I expect Shirley Chisholm is feeling relieved. As for me, I'm going to try to work out something as pleasant as possible, and, most of all, keep my sanity."

Discussing the strategy she intends to employ as a congresswoman, Mrs. Burke says: "My approach has always been to be nice until I'm pinned to the wall. Then I blow up—this when all else fails. My reaction will just have to come issue by issue."

Mrs. Burke's father, James T.
Watson, gives her a "victory hug"
after election returns show that
she has won election to Congress.

LeRoy Callender
Structural Engineer

LeRoy Callender, professional engineer (licensed in 13 states ranging from New York to Mississippi, Texas and Ohio), proprietor of the firm, LeRoy Callender, Consulting Engineer, in New York, N.Y.; born Feb. 29, 1932 in New York City; City College of New York (B.C.E., 1958). Divorced. Son: Eric. Address: 401 E. 37th St., New York, N.Y. 10016 (See full biographical sketch in Volume I.)

LeRoy Callender (in foreground) and some members of his staff in the firm's drafting room.

36

He Wasn't Satisfied Until He Proved He Could Compete on His Own

"Wherever I go and whatever I do I will never forget where I come from, or my commitment to help make things easier for younger blacks and for future generations."

In 1969, LeRoy Callender, Consulting Engineer, was a one-man firm with only a drafting table, a telephone and a file drawer crammed into thirty square feet of space in a friend's office in New York City. By 1972, Mr. Callender had a full-time staff of twenty-one and had completed, or had in progress, projects worth more than $300 million.

Mr. Callender was born in New York City on February 29, 1932 and spent almost all his life in Harlem. He attended Brooklyn Technical High School, one of several New York City public schools noted for academic excellence, and graduated in 1950, first in his class in architectural design. He was awarded a scholarship by the *Amsterdam News*, Harlem's black newspaper, to attend the Columbia University School of Architecture, but chose instead to study civil engineering at City College of New York.

"As far back as I can remember," he says, "I had a strong interest in architecture and related fields, but I can't recall anything special that caused me to feel that way." He worked as a draftsman for a major structural engineering firm while attending CCNY at night. Two years later, in 1952, he was drafted into the United States Army where, because of his aptitude and abilities in engineering, he was assigned to a special drafting school. Upon completion of his training, he was sent to Korea, where he designed small office buildings and other facilities for the army. After being honorably discharged from the army, he returned to his studies at CCNY. During summers, he worked for the same engineering firm he had been with prior to his military service.

Graduating from college in 1958, Mr. Callender joined another engineering firm and worked on the first nuclear power plant ever built in the East—the Consolidated Edison plant at Indian Point, New York. In 1959, he rejoined the structural engineering firm he had been with through college and remained there until shortly before founding his own firm in January, 1969.

"The challenge and the opportunity were irresistible," he recalls. "I knew I could compete successfully on my own and I knew I'd never be satisfied until I proved it . . . building a successful organization is one of the most gratifying accomplishments imaginable."

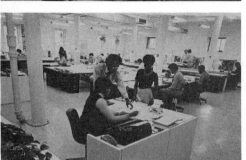

In top photo, Mr. Callender dictates to his secretary, Urmi Raval. Above, he checks appointments with receptionist Helen Nesbitt and secretary Deborah Jamison.

37

Mr. Callender gives instructions (top, left) to Everton Alkins, a draftsman; discusses plans (top right) with draftsman Ray Acevedo (c.) and designer Andrew Mireku, and (above) watches as senior designer Anis Baig explains plans for a high-rise building in one of the Callender firm's housing development projects.

Construction projects for which the Callender organization has provided consultation include the $3.2 million dormitory and student union buildings for Mary Holmes College in West Point, Mississippi; the $6.3 million Whitney M. Young Complex in Yonkers, New York; the $30 million Lindsay-Bushwick Houses in Brooklyn, New York; a $6 million housing project for the elderly (sponsored by St. Philip's Church in Harlem); the $18 million Simpson Street Housing in Bronx, New York, and the $14 million Douglas Circle project in New York City.

Members of Mr. Callender's interracial staff speak a total of fourteen different languages. He believes that the staff's racial and ethnic integration has contributed to the firm's success. "I'm sure," he says, "that this balance and openness adds spice to the organization and makes us livelier and more imaginative as a team. That's a very important factor for any professional organization where teamwork plays a big role. It also proves that people of diverse backgrounds can function productively as a unit."

One unusual aspect of the Callender organization is the absence of a strict nine-to-five routine. "No punch clocks," Mr. Callender says. Employees set their own work hours, and as long as they put in a specified amount of time and all projects in design are covered each day, no one cares when they arrive or depart. "Some people can't get their mental machinery going before ten in the morning," Mr. Callender believes. "We feel that it's better to have a thinking professional on the job at all times than to have someone who's with you in body only."

Mr. Callender has two major goals for himself. One is the continued growth of his organization. "However," he says, "right now in early 1973 we have some projects actually frozen on the drafting board because of President Nixon's eighteen-month moratorium on Section 236 subsidized housing. That's hurting black architects and

The Callender firm's chief draftsman, James Perrone, conducts a class for some of the young draftsmen being trained by Mr. Callender and his associates.

engineers all over the country. I just hope that some consideration will be given to us for all the reconstruction work that will now be going on in post-war Vietnam." His other goal is more personal than professional. "I want to continue my contribution to the advancement of the black community, both through this organization and by my personal efforts in community involvement," he says. "Wherever I go and whatever I do I will never forget where I come from, or my commitment to help make things easier for younger blacks and for future generations."

Mr. Callender is a member of the board of directors of the Central Harlem Police Athletic League track teams. In 1971, he ran a Workshop for Engineering for the National Black Science Students Organization and presented seminars for the opportunity programs at several colleges. He holds open house periodically in his offices so that black students can see for themselves how a consulting engineering concern functions.

"It's a particular desire of mine," Mr. Callender says, "to interest more young blacks in entering the engineering field. We all know that the rebuilding of our urban black communities is not just a matter of money and effort. Perhaps the most important consideration is a sharp sensitivity to the needs and desires of the community, a feeling for the things that will add to the quality of life as well as improve the physical surroundings. Blacks should provide this special creative input, and there is still a shortage of our people in this field."

Mr. Callender—with his field representative, David Flores (in hard hat), and Bill Clark, a registered architect with the Callender firm—makes a field investigation of work being done at one of his projects, a 14-story concrete building in Harlem.

39

Wilt Chamberlain

Professional Athlete

Wilton N. ("Wilt") Chamberlain, professional basketball player; born April 21, 1936 in Philadelphia, Pa.; attended Kansas University and was twice selected as All-American; played with San Francisco Warriors, Philadelphia 76ers, traded to Los Angeles Lakers in 1968; holds all-time record for points scored (more than 30,000), and holds numerous other records. Address: The Forum, 3900 W. Manchester Blvd., P.O. Box 10, Inglewood, CA 90306 (See full biographical sketch in Volume I.)

He Sets the Records That Other Players Seek to Match

"There is only one thing, one disenchantment. . . . It is impossible to get lost in a crowd."

Wilton Norman Chamberlain is one of the greatest basketball players in the history of the game. In fourteen professional seasons, he has set more records than any other player. High on his list of career achievements are the all-time leads in points scored (more than 30,000) and rebounds captured (more than 29,300); the most consecutive games played without disqualification (all of his professional games); and the most points scored in one game by an individual (100 points).

40

Career highlights: At left (below), Wilt Chamberlain ponders some of the 202 scholarship offers he received (1955) from colleges. At left, after enrolling at Kansas University, he plays against Marquette University (1957). Above, as a professional with the Los Angeles Lakers, he wins a battle against the N.Y. Knicks' Willis Reed.

Born April 21, 1936 in Philadelphia, Pennsylvania to William and Gloria Chamberlain, Wilt was one of nine children (six sons, three daughters). His father was a porter for a publishing company and his mother was a maid. Wilt grew at a normal rate until he entered Overbrook High School in Philadelphia. At the end of his sophomore year, he measured six feet and eleven inches. In addition to playing basketball at Overbrook, he participated in track and field. He has run a forty-seven-second quarter mile, put the sixteen-pound shot fifty-five feet, and high-jumped six feet and ten inches. In his three-year high school basketball career, he scored 2,252 points.

Upon graduation from high school in 1955, Wilt, now measuring just over seven feet, received offers from 77 major colleges and 125 smaller schools. He chose Kansas University at Lawrence. In two years there, he helped lead his team to a 42–8 won-lost record while averaging 30 points per game; he was twice selected All-American. By the end of his second year, opposing teams had taken to guarding him with two, three and sometimes four men at a time. Feeling that these tactics hindered his development as a player, he quit collegiate basketball and his communications studies in 1958 to join the Harlem Globetrotters for a year at a salary of $65,000.

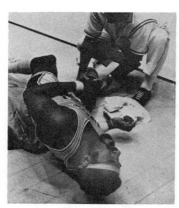

Los Angeles Lakers trainer Frank O'Neil bends over injured Wilt Chamberlain after the player's knee collapsed during a 1969 game. After treatment and rest, he continued setting record after record. At right, he gets instructions from Lakers Coach Bill Sharman during a 1972 game.

In 1959, Mr. Chamberlain signed a contract with the Philadelphia Warriors of the National Basketball Association (NBA). He set eight new records in his first year and garnered Rookie of the Year and Most Valuable Player of the Year honors. For seven successive seasons from 1959 to 1964, he led the league in total points scored per season. In three successive years, 1965 to 1968, he was named the Most Valuable Player. In March 1962, he scored 100 points in a single game against the New York Knicks and ended that season with an unprecedented scoring average of more than 50 points per game. He considers his scoring statistics and his playing all but two minutes of that season the greatest of his achievements.

In 1967, playing wih the Philadelphia 76ers, Mr. Chamberlain led his team to an NBA record sixty-eight victories (only thirteen losses) and the NBA championship. During the 1972 season, following his trade to the Los Angeles Lakers, he established fourteen new NBA records. Included on his list of new marks were the most seasons leading the NBA in rebounds, 10; the most seasons leading the league in field goal percentage, 8; the most minutes played in a career, 44,319; the most field goals made in a career, 12,255; and the most field goals attempted in a career, 22,933. In addition, he led the Lakers to sixty-nine victories (an NBA record), thirty-three of them consecutive (an all-time professional sports record), and to the team's first NBA title in twelve years. Though playing with a broken wrist in the final game of the championship, he scored 24 points, grabbed 29 rebounds and blocked 10 shots. He won unanimously in the voting for the Most Valuable Player of the playoffs. He has been voted Most Valuable Player of the year or of playoffs eight times in his career and has played on thirteen All-Star teams. On a number of occasions, he has overcome serious injuries to lead his team to the championship playoffs. He made his most memorable comeback in 1969 when he recovered in five months from what was thought to be a career-ending knee injury.

Among the many business enterprises in which Wilt Chamberlain has invested is Big Wilt's Smalls Paradise, a nightclub in New York's Harlem (top). In center photo, he attends the funeral of Dr. M. L. King Jr. Above, he plays with dogs on lawn of $1½ million home he built on a California hilltop.

Wilt's annual salary is in excess of $300,000 (one of the highest in professional sports), and he receives additional income from numerous advertising endorsements and business interests. Fond of high-style living, he lives just outside Los Angeles in a lavish $1.5 million home, which he helped design.

In 1968, following the assassination of Dr. Martin Luther King Jr., he joined presidential candidate Richard M. Nixon's campaign to help sell Mr. Nixon's "black capitalism" economic program in ghetto areas. Mr. Chamberlain said of his decision to become a Nixon aide, "I attended the funeral [Dr. King's] and saw Nixon there. He convinced me that I could be helpful to my people and to him by joining his staff. So that's how I came to be his aide on community relations."

Wilt enjoys a wide range of hobbies and pastimes, including racing cars, playing volleyball and water skiing. He likes being called the Big Dipper, a nickname he picked up at the University of Kansas, as much as he dislikes his better known nickname, "The Stilt." Of his unusual height, he says, "I tell you that as the years have gone by I have enjoyed being seven feet tall a lot more. There is only one thing, one disenchantment . . . the fact that it is impossible to get lost in a crowd. I'm the kind of guy who someimes would like to go out and do some things and not let everyone know about it. . . ."

In a 1964 photo, the famous athlete poses with his parents, William and Gloria Chamberlain. He is one of nine children.

James E. Cheek

University President

James E. Cheek, president, Howard University, Washington, D.C.; born Dec. 4, 1932 in Roanoke Rapids, N.C.; Shaw University (B.A., 1955; L.H.D., 1970), Colgate-Rochester Divinity School (B.D., 1958), Drew University (Ph.D., 1962; LL.D., 1971); wife: Celestine Williams Cheek; children: James and Janet. Address: Howard University, Washington, DC 20001 (See full biographical sketch in Volume I.)

He Envisions a University In Which All Students Are Teachers

"We shall seek to lead and not to imitate and, in all we undertake, we shall try to fashion a community of scholars where all students are teachers."

On July 1, 1969, Dr. James Edward Cheek stood before a capacity crowd to receive the symbols of office as the fifteenth president of Howard University in Washington, D.C. In an eloquent, probing address, he said " At Howard, academic freedom is to be cherished and valued; human freedom is cherished and valued more. Hence, we cannot stand aloof, morally neutral and socially passive. For us, the business of education must be conducted not in the atmosphere of the museum where men are gathered to contemplate the past, but in the atmosphere of the true university where men are gathered to create the future. . . . We shall seek to formulate new norms of excellence and more effective methods of extending the university beyond the campus to enhance the community which is our home as well as the community across the seas. We shall seek to lead and not to imitate and, in all we undertake, we shall try to fashion a community of scholars where all students are teachers."

The long road from his hometown of Roanoke Rapids, North Carolina to Howard's spacious presidential office was a rough one for Dr. Cheek. Born on December 4, 1932, he was threatened with loss of his eyesight. Doctors expected him to be totally blind at fifteen. When he was ten years old, he underwent eye surgery. After fourteen operations, his vision was saved.

The son of insurance agents, young Cheek—described as

44

Dr. Cheek is inaugurated as president of Howard University (above). On opposite page, he chats with students on campus.

"serious"—became interested in theology. In 1955, he received a bachelor of arts degree from Shaw University in Raleigh, North Carolina, and three years later, a bachelor of divinity degree from Colgate University in Rochester, New York. He earned his doctor of philosophy degree from Drew University in Madison, New Jersey, in 1962. While at Shaw, he had also secured the affection of Celestine Williams, whom he married in a June wedding in 1958. Dr. and Mrs. Cheek have two children, James Edward Jr. and Janet Elizabeth.

Dr. Cheek, a chain-smoking, intense and energetic man, never intended to become a minister, even though he was deeply interested in theology. Instead he aspired to a career in teaching and writing. At Virginia Union University in Richmond, Virginia, Dr. Cheek was executing his life's plan when Shaw University was casting about for a dynamic leader who could stimulate its growth. University officials at Shaw, Dr. Cheek's alma mater, thought that he was such a man. Thus, eight years after his graduation from Shaw, Dr. James Cheek returned to become its youngest president.

Within a year, Dr. Cheek wrested Shaw University from the brink of destruction. He devised the Shaw Plan of Education and asserted himself as an imaginative innovator, designing programs to meet the special needs of black people. With skill and dignity, the young president persuaded foundations and corporations such as Gulf Oil to assist in building "a stronger Shaw." By 1969, the annual operating budget of the once-foundering university rocketed from $700,000 to an unprecedented $5.9 million.

There was an irony, however, about the slim young man who, as its president, saved Shaw University. That same man had, as a student in the 1950s, taken part in boycotts of classes to protest "poor quality of teaching and absurd student regulations."

Dr. Cheek was called to save another institution from possible destruction. Howard University was in the aftermath of two violent student uprisings, which had left many scars on the campus and on the out-going president of nine years, Dr. James Nabrit, and which threatened the college's survival. When Dr. Cheek ascended to Howard's presidency in 1969, the label "rebel" came along with him.

Like many a student protester, the new president of Howard strongly favored more activism from the nation's colleges. Dr. Cheek asserted that the wall that divided the college from the community had to fall. A university could not exist in a void, he realized, and he designed new programs to accelerate Howard's participation in change. He listened to the angry voices of the young and to the silent fears of the old. In listening, half the battle was won and Howard began to stabilize.

Students and faculty attend inaugural ceremony of Dr. Cheek as fifteenth president of Howard University.

"Universities like Howard," President Cheek explained, "can and must broaden their concept of service. The entire community is the campus. . . . Universities can directly influence society's direction by what they choose to do. Can you imagine what would have happened in the area of race, for instance, if the whole university had on its own said, 'We are going to have an integrated society.' It would have changed the whole character of the century."

One day early in his presidency while sitting at his desk, Dr. Cheek was seized with a partial paralysis. Physicians found him to have spinal cord compression and ordered major surgery. But from his hospital bed, where he lay in a waist cast, James Cheek continued to work to quell whatever student unrest remained and to handle the myriad details of administration. His courage won the respect not only of administrators and faculty but of students as well.

When peace again settled over the sprawling Howard campus, Dr. Cheek's voice grew louder and carried even further—until it reached the White House. Appalled by the deaths of two black students shot down by state troopers at Jackson State College, Dr. Cheek wrote President Richard M. Nixon about the need for a White House meeting on the future of black colleges. The president responded promptly and scheduled the meeting for the summer of 1970. Heading the delegation of fifteen black college presidents, Dr. Cheek was the most vocal and

46

President Cheek is flanked by his two brothers, Dr. King V. Cheek (l.), president of Morgan State College, and Albert Cheek, a medical student at Howard University.

dramatic. In a much publicized face-to-face confrontation with the president of the United States, Dr. Cheek tried to drive home the urgency of the problems faced by all blacks in the nation. At the close of the meeting, the group requested the president to reassure them by saying, "We are with you," but no such reassurance was given.

Disturbed by the Administration's policy of "benign neglect" toward black people, Dr. Cheek began to speak even more loudly for the survival of black colleges and the rights of black Americans.

The man, who as a child had prepared himself for a life of blindness, has consistently stressed his vision of the dangers facing black academia: "A large number of black people claim not to understand and a large number of white people claim they clearly do not want black colleges, but we cannot afford to lose them because they represent our history, our present and our future.

"Black colleges in the North are more than one hundred years old and they did not become [controversial] . . . so long as this country was committed in philosophy and in practice to segregation. . . . And now they have become an issue . . . because of the notion that the nation is committed both philosophically and ideologically and in practice to integration."

Dr. Cheek has repeatedly stated his conviction that there is no contradiction in the existence of black colleges in an integrated society. In this light, he reflects the spirit of all the other builders of great black institutions—those who sought triumph in an earlier era of "benign neglect."

Dr. Cheek's family includes (l. to r.) his wife, Celestine, and their two children, James E. Jr. and Janet Elizabeth.

47

Shirley Chisholm

Congresswoman

America's First Black Woman Candidate for the Presidency

"By the time I was two and a half . . . I was already dominating other children around me—with my mouth!"

"Every time people look at me, I'm screaming and yelling. So they get to the point where they say, 'What's wrong with her? She's half crazy!' I'm not half crazy, man," insists the first black woman to be elected to the United States Congress. "The fact is I'm trying to do what many politicians aren't interested in: restore trust and integrity to the political profession."

The words reflected the spunkiness, charisma and determination that carried Mrs. Shirley Chisholm to the 1972 Democratic National Convention as a candidate for her party's nomination for president of the United States. Mrs. Chisholm, who was elected in 1968 to the U.S.

Shirley A. Chisholm, U. S. Representative (New York) since 1969; born Nov. 30, 1924 in Brooklyn, N.Y.; Brooklyn College (B.A.), Columbia University (M.A.). Husband: Conrad Chisholm. Address: House Office Bldg., Washington, DC 20515 (See full biographical sketch in Volume I.)

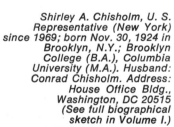

48

House of Representatives from New York's 12th Congressional District, (Brooklyn), was the first black woman to seek the presidency.

She was an underdog at the 1972 Convention in Miami Beach, Florida. However, unlike several other candidates who withdrew from the race before balloting for the party's nominee began, Mrs. Chisholm angered party leaders by remaining in the race until the very end. As expected, she lost, collecting only 101.45 of the 1,509 delegate votes

The first black woman in U.S. history to seek the presidency joins other candidates—(l. to r.) Sen. Hubert H. Humphrey, Sen. George McGovern and Sen. Henry Jackson—in victory salute at the 1972 Democratic National Convention where Sen. McGovern became the nominee. An effective speaker, Congresswoman Chisholm campaigned across the nation to provide an alternative for blacks, women and other minorities.

needed to win the nomination. But the forty-seven-year-old candidate was not disappointed, After the balloting, she said: "Since I first emerged in politics, I have tried to provide a breath of fresh air for people. I think I have succeeded at that."

It was Mrs. Chisholm's insistence on honesty, integrity and "fresh leadership" that won her a seat in the New York State Assembly in 1964. The victory, which came after nearly fourteen years of pushing her way up through political organizations such as the mostly male and white 17th Assembly District Democratic Club in Brooklyn, was her first for public office. During her four years in the assembly, she said in her autobiography *Unbought and Unbossed*, "I had a liberal education in how politics is run in our country—a sort of graduate course to follow my basic education in ward and county politicking."

Mrs. Chisholm and Gloria Steinem, editor of *Ms.* magazine, discuss women's liberation on a television talk show.

The "course" paid off. Mrs. Chisholm's first run for Congress was against black city councilman William C. Thompson, a former state senator who had been handpicked by powerful Democratic bosses to seek the 12th Congressional District House seat. She also had to run against James Farmer, a nationally prominent figure who once served as national chairman of the Congress of Racial Equality. Using the same type of people-to-people, grass-roots campaigning that was so effective in the assembly race, and running on the record she established as an assemblywoman, she swept the predominantly black and Puerto Rican Brooklyn district and defeated both opponents.

As a freshman congresswoman, Mrs. Chisholm upset Congressional protocol by refusing to accept the "left-over" committee assignments that routinely are given to first-term House members. "I found out what my subcommittee assignments were to be: rural development and forestry. Forestry! That did it!" she said. Her protests did not get her the assignment to the House Education and Labor Committee that she wanted, but it did bring about a review of the congressional seniority system (the "senility system," she called it) in which the lawmaker with the longest tenure is assigned to the top committee. She was later assigned to the House Veterans Affairs Committee. "It was an improvement," she said. "There are a lot more *people* in my district than there are *trees*."

The congresswoman, born in New York in 1924 to Charles and Ruby Seale St. Hill, immigrants from the West Indies, had always been a "pushy" person. "By the time I was two and a half, no bigger than a mite, I was already dominating other children around me—with my mouth," she says. "I lectured them and ordered them around. Even mother was afraid of me." One of three girls, Shirley St. Hill was sent to Barbados at the age of three to live with other family members until her parents in Brooklyn could earn a better living. Eight years later she returned to Brooklyn where she attended grade school and high school. Brooklyn was also where she met her husband, Conrad.

A graduate of both Brooklyn College and Columbia University, and the holder of a master's degree in elementary education, Mrs. Chisholm worked as a nursery school teacher, director of a day care center, and consultant before entering politics.

Clockwise, from top left: Mrs. Chisholm speaks to a 1972 meeting of the Conference of Black Elected Officials; from the floor of the Conference; gets a kiss from Congressman Ronald V. Dellums (D., Cal.) after announcing her candidacy for the presidency, and speaks to a group of Chicagoans during her campaign.

Algernon J. Cooper

Mayor of Prichard, Alabama

Young Lawyer Returns South, Becomes Mayor of Alabama Town

Algernon J. Cooper Jr., mayor, Prichard, Ala., born May 30, 1944 in Mobile, Ala.; University of Notre Dame (A.B., 1966), New York University School of Law (J.D., 1969), also attended Spring Hill College, Roosevelt University and the University of Southern California; wife: Madora Cooper. Address: P.O. Box 10515, Prichard, AL 36610 (See full biographical sketch in Volume I.)

"Whites don't really believe we have enough political sophistication to take over. We have the rest of this decade to prove them wrong."

Among the biggest obstacles that faced Mayor Algernon Johnson (Jay) Cooper when he assumed office in September, 1972 was to clear Prichard of its $121,000 debt. More than 60 percent of its 41,578 residents lived in substandard housing. The annual median income of the 52 percent black city was under $5,000 and about 52.5 percent of its families were on welfare. Indeed, Prichard's economic decline had been so severe since 1960, some 5,793 of its citizens had migrated to Mobile (which surrounds it on three sides) and to other communities.

Born in Mobile on May 30, 1944, the third of six children of insurance executive Algernon J. and Gladys Cooper, "Jay" attended St. Peter Claver Grade School in Mobile and Marmion Military Academy in Aurora, Illinois. He earned a bachelor's degree from the University of Notre Dame in 1966, and enrolled at New York University Law School. In 1967, he helped found the Black American Law Student Association, which soon represented 80 percent of the nation's black students. He received his law degree in 1969.

As a neophyte lawyer, Mr. Cooper was struck by the glaring contrast between legal services available to blacks and whites. Nationally, whites had one lawyer for every seven hundred persons while the ratio for blacks was one in seven thousand (one in 28,000 in

When Mr. Cooper (r.) ran for mayor, Atlanta Vice Mayor Maynard Jackson (l.) came to Alabama to offer help. Others are Mr. Cooper's campaign manager, John Dean, and Floyd King.

Mayor Cooper reads letter to town council (above) and listens intently to council discussion (above, right). Flanking the mayor are council members Shafter Summers (l.) and John Langham.

Visiting a high school (top), Mayor Cooper checks student's work. Above, with Col. Harry A. Griffith of the Army Corps of Engineers, he examines an open sewer which city wants to eliminate.

the South). In southern Alabama, a single lawyer served about three hundred thousand blacks. Nowhere else in the nation was there a greater need for young black lawyers. So when he returned to Mobile in 1970 as an NAACP Legal Defense Fund attorney, jumping into the legal battles over school desegregation, "Jay" Cooper became known among embittered whites as "that nigger lawyer." Though he distinguished himself in the courtroom, he believed the greatest challenges for young blacks were in Southern politics.

Thus Mr. Cooper announced his candidacy for mayor on the steps of Prichard's City Hall in August, 1971. In both 1964 and 1968, three blacks had run unsuccessfully for the Prichard City Council and for the post of mayor. Not one of them had received more than 1,700 votes. But Mr. Cooper was something new on the political scene. Armed with organizational expertise acquired on Robert F. Kennedy's campaign staff in 1968, the young, ambitious pragmatist set up three campaign offices staffed with about one hundred high school volunteers, plus friends who had cut their political eye teeth in Washington, New York, Ohio and in states as far away as Minnesota. Threading through the campaign was the terse theme: "Together we stick, divided we're stuck." The boundaries of that togetherness extended up North where "Jay" Cooper's friends printed sixty thousand pieces of campaign literature, then shipped the batch to Prichard. Certain handbills were earmarked for the black community while others, worded differently, went into the white neighborhoods. Campaign posters were carefully placed thirteen feet above ground to prevent them from being defaced or torn down.

In his speeches, "Jay" hammered away at Prichard's high unemployment, poor housing, unpaved streets, open drainage ditches, weak law enforcement, long food stamp lines, City Hall corruption and the public's general discontent with Mayor Vernon O. Capps, who had held office for twelve years. Mr. Cooper insisted he cared about all of Prichard's citizens, that he would help them "save" it from its decline as a viable city, bring competence to local government, expand social services, improve law enforcement, bring in federal programs and

53

On Prichard's main street (top), Mayor Cooper seeks views of teen-agers. Near his home (above), he and his wife, Mado, joke with youngsters from neighborhood.

attract private industry to boost job opportunities.

The young attorney won endorsements from the Mobile *Beacon*, a black newspaper, and the Mobile *Press-Register*, a white daily which endorsed only one other candidate in the field of seven running for mayor. It was the first time in Mobile's history that the *Press-Register* had endorsed a black man for public office. But on election day, whites boycotted the polls in droves. Only 7,646 of the 15,707 eligible voters cast ballots in the August, 1972 non-partisan election. Blacks were harassed at the polls. Either black poll watchers were not permitted to observe closely the signing in of voters, thus making challenges difficult, or illiterate black voters were denied in-the-booth assistance for "Mickey Mouse" reasons. While Mr. Cooper polled 3,587 votes to Capps' 1,762, his failure to receive a majority of the votes cast, as required by law, forced a September run-off.

Meanwhile, because Mobile County officials extended voter registration an additional twenty-five days, Mr. Cooper organized a new drive to sign up at least one thousand more black voters and thus wipe out the 55 to 45 percent edge which Prichard's whites held over blacks. The imbalance had been partially because the city had 1,900 more voting-age whites. On the very first registration day, Cooper staffers carried four hundred candidates to the registration site. But officials slowed up the 8 A.M.-to-noon process by permitting only eight persons to register at a time. Thus only three hundred candidates became voters that day.

Despite the annoying delays, about 2,000 new voters were eventually registered; more than 1,300 were taken to the registrar's office by Cooper's campaign workers. Even so, he won the run-off by only 544 votes (out of 10,648 cast) to become the first black man since Reconstruction to defeat a white incumbent in a major Alabama city. Almost immediately, three white members of the five-man City Council seized control of important municipal committees from the minority faction led by the mayor, countermanded orders he had given to department heads, then called a closed meeting to discuss his powers. Mayor Cooper insisted his powers were non-negotiable, that only *he* had day-to-day control and supervision over clerical personnel, firemen, policemen, building inspectors, street and sanitation employes, etc. He promised to obtain a court injunction if the City Council persisted in interfering with his administration.

The new mayor's confrontation with the council was only the first of a series of obstacles he had to hurdle. His forty-nine-member police force had only four blacks, all of whom were assigned exclusively to black neighborhoods. Prichard's forty-man fire department had more equipment than men to handle it, and the

54

sanitation department operated inefficiently. But the young mayor did not believe Prichard's problems could not be turned around. He was optimistic because the city is only eight minutes from the nation's seventh largest seaport, within ten minutes of two major airports and is located on two major interstate highways. Very early in his administration he persuaded the United States Department of Housing and Urban Development to list Prichard as one of eight cities requiring special attention. But Mayor Cooper has already shown that skillful political organizing can overcome voter apathy, archaic and discriminatory voter registration and even poverty. He is impressed with black political potential in the South. "Whites don't really believe we have enough political sophistication to take over," Mayor Cooper observes. "We have the rest of this decade to prove them wrong."

At a dinner reception given by a paper company in nearby Mobile, Mayor and Mrs. Cooper talk with other guests.

Sammy Davis Jr.
Entertainer

Sammy Davis Jr., entertainer; born Dec. 8, 1925 in New York, N.Y.; began his professional career in 1928, appeared in film Rufus Jones for President (1930) and in numerous other films, appeared with Will Mastin Trio (1930–48), has been a single act since. Wife: Altovise Gore. Children: Tracey, Mark and Jeff. Address: 9000 Sunset Blvd., Los Angeles, CA 90069 (See full biographical details in Volume I.)

He's Called 'The Greatest Entertainer in the World'

"If you want to be the best . . . not just the black best . . . you've got to work harder than anybody else."

Born into show business on December 11, 1926 in New York, New York, Sammy Davis Jr. has known no other life. He made his debut before the footlights when he was one year old—even before he could walk. As his parents, Sammy Davis Sr. and Elvira Davis, went through their vaudeville dance number in a theater in Columbus, Ohio, little Sammy toddled onstage to get a closer look. His surprise walk-on almost ruined his parents' number but it brought down the house. Shortly thereafter, he quickly demonstrated his talent as an entertainer. Barely out of infancy, he so impressed Bill "Bojangles" Robinson with his dancing that the late tap-dance king offered to help him develop his style. Sammy absorbed every trick that Bojangles taught him, and eventually he could "hoof it" almost like the old master.

At the age of two, Sammy became a regular trouper in his uncle's flashy family act, the Will Mastin Trio. By his fourth birthday, he was considered a full-fledged professional who could take his cues, curtain calls and plaudits just like the grownups in the cast whenever the Mastin troupe hit the Orpheum circuit. Times were hard and Sammy endured his share of poverty and suffering right along with the adults. However, he says, "If my dad or uncle had a dollar, I always got it.

During a visit to London, Mr. Davis performs in the street for photographers. Later, with comedians Tommy Steele and Jerry Lewis, he is received by the Queen Mother.

In one of his numerous movie roles, he plays a gunslinger (below) in *One More Time*.

They went hungry, but not me. Everything they ever had was mine. Now it's the other way around."

Playing the vaudeville circuit during his early childhood, Sammy learned about "law and order" before he reached his tenth birthday. Once, when the act played a burlesque house, juvenile authorities yanked him off the stage because they thought he had no business in the company of strippers and smutty jokesters. Sammy was simply billed as "a midget" and continued to perform.

In 1943, at the height of World War II, Sammy Davis Jr. was drafted into the army. He was assigned to Special Services, where he produced, directed and starred in camp shows, many of which he wrote himself. When the war ended in 1945, he returned to the Will Mastin Trio. Although the Depression had curtailed many of their engagements and had left them stranded without work, Sammy kept his hopes up and continued to polish his talents. In April, 1946, after they arrived unheralded in Los Angeles to fill the spotlight at Slapsie Maxie's, they electrified the opening-night audience and scored a surprise hit. An instant box-office draw, Sammy, his dad and his uncle were signed to return as headliners. On their return engagement, they broke every previous record at the club, and Sammy Davis Jr. was on his way to the top.

Big promoters began bidding for the threesome, whose billing as the "Will Mastin Trio, starring Sammy Davis Jr." spelled cash in the bank. Now a fast-moving act, they scored successively in major theaters and nightclubs throughout the country. From Las Vegas to New York, it was the same story: one record-breaking date after another. Between nightclub triumphs, the trio appeared on national television shows. And Sammy's hit recording of "Hey, There" soared to the top of the disc charts.

After a number of years as a team, in 1948 Will Mastin and Sammy Davis Sr. retired from show business and Sammy Davis Jr. stepped onstage as a single. Six years later, while driving from Las Vegas to Hollywood in November, 1954, he barely escaped death in an auto collision which cost him his left eye. "Recovery became a tonic to me," he recalls. "It gave me the energy, the spirit and the determination to return to show business."

In his first movie role (1930), five-year-old Sammy Davis Jr. appears with Ethel Waters in *Rufus Jones for President*. He has made numerous other films.

In one of his frequent appearances on network television, Mr. Davis squares off against Wilt Chamberlain on the popular "Laugh-In" program.

A year later, his comeback at Ciro's in Hollywood was a night to remember. Greats and near-greats showed up to pay homage to the most dazzling performer in the entertainment industry. Mr. Davis, however, nursed an ambition to become a film actor. In 1959, shortly after he converted to the Jewish faith, he co-starred with Eartha Kitt in *Anna Lucasta*. This was followed by the coveted role of Sportin' Life in Samuel Goldwyn's *Porgy and Bess* (1959) and a co-starring role with his friends, Frank Sinatra, Dean Martin and Peter Lawford, in *Oceans 11* (1960). He later starred on Broadway in *Golden Boy* and made it a long-running hit. Meanwhile, he magnetized television viewers with stellar performances in "Sammy Davis and His Friends," appearances on "Hullabaloo" and guest stints on a number of major variety shows. Another movie, *A Man Called Adam,* followed in 1966 with Sammy in the lead role—topped by his own weekly television program, "The Sammy Davis Show," both of which preceded the writing of his autobiography, *Yes I Can* (1965).

Mr. Davis married Loray White, a singer, in 1958 but they were divorced a year later. In 1960, he married Swedish actress Mai Britt, (she later changed her name to May); they were divorced in 1968 and she received custody of their daughter, Tracey, and two adopted sons, Mark and Jeff. In 1970, Mr. Davis and dancer Altovise Gore were married. Despite many television, movie and theatre obligations, he finds time for home life in Beverly Hills, California. He feels a compulsion to help others as much as he can—by doing benefits, by making contributions to charity and by talking to young black people.

58

Mr. Davis is shown (above) with Dr. M. L. King Jr. (1965) and with the NAACP's Roy Wilkins after being awarded the Spingarn Medal (1969).

Mr. Davis and his wife, Altovise, are hosted by President Nixon at the White House.

During a 1969 visit to Israel, Mr. Davis prays at the Wailing Wall (above). Below, he and his former wife, May Britt and their children, Tracey and Mark, in 1963.

His stature as a humanitarian has been acknowledged by practically every major organization in the nation. He has received citations as Entertainer of the Year by *Cue* magazine, Personality of the Year by the New York Press Association, Man of the Year by B'Nai B'Rith, the Cultural Achievement Award of the State of Israel, the NAACP Spingarn Medal, and recognition by the Police Association of America and the League of Crippled Children. In addition, he has been chairman of the NAACP Life Membership Committee since 1966.

"If you want to be the best," he says, "... not just the *black* best or the Jewish best or the female best or male best, but the best, period—you've got to work harder than anybody else. When you've suffered and sweated all your life and your turn comes up to bat, you either swing at the ball or bunt it. If you want to be the best, you swing, like me. There's nothing wrong with ambition."

Mr. and Mrs. Davis spend a moment together at poolside of their California home.

James DePreist

Symphony Conductor

James DePreist, associate conductor, National Symphony, Washington, D.C.; born Nov. 21, 1936 in Philadelphia, Pa.; University of Pennsylvania (B.S., 1958; M.A., 1961), Philadelphia Conservatory of Music (1959–61). Wife: Betty Louise Childress DePreist. Children: Tracy and Jennifer. Address: National Symphony, Washington, DC 20009 (See full biographical sketch in Volume I)

"Once I conducted, there was no question about what I wanted to do. I was hooked!"

Musician Conquers Polio to Become a Symphony Director

It must have been an unusual sight for the audience to deal with. Moving slowly onto the stage at the 1963 Dimitri Mitropoulos International Conductors Competitions was an imposing black man with crutches and various metal braces supporting his partially paralyzed body. Just a year before, James DePreist had been struck down by polio while in Thailand. Now he was on stage to compete in one of the most prestigious events in the world of classical music. He remembers thinking "My braces must make me look like an armored knight." Perhaps so, but the young Philadelphia-born conductor, who is the only child of Ethel Mae Anderson DePreist and the late James Henry DePreist, and the nephew of retired concert artist Marian Anderson, certainly did not conduct like one. Competing against the best of his peers from around the world, he reached the semi-finals of the competitions. And he did it while sitting on a specially built stool.

That performance by Mr. DePreist, a man who has been involved with music for most of his thirty-four years, was the starting point of a steady rise to the top. Since his performance elicited no offers from any major orchestra, he returned to Thailand, this time with his wife, Betty, a physical therapist whom he met when she was his nurse in the hospital. There

60

Conductor DePreist and the National Symphony accept plaudits (opposite page) of crowd after a concert.

Mr. DePreist and his famous aunt, singer Marian Anderson, are honored by Rittenhouse Square Woman's Committee in Philadelphia, Pa.

he became conductor-in-residence for three Thai orchestras. The following year he returned to the United States to compete once again in the Mitropoulos Competitions, and won the $3,500 first prize, a gold medal and an opportunity to conduct the New York Philharmonic Orchestra. Once again, however, he had to go abroad to get work. He says: "American conductors, like American-made handbags, are considered less worthy than imported ones." He and his wife eventually made plans to join many other young American conductors in Europe where opportunities were considered greater. "We wrote to all the European consulates in New York requesting information on their orchestras. Exactly one reply came and that was from Johanna Beck of Holland who offered to be my European manager. There was no firm job offer, but we decided that if we had to starve, it would be better to do it slowly in Europe." In 1967 they were off to Rotterdam. It was December of that year before an offer was made—an invitation to guest-conduct the Rotterdam Symphony Orchestra in 1969. Meanwhile the DePreists had to make it through 1968, which they contrived to do with the help of a couple of free-lance concerts. When his chance did come, Mr. DePreist was ready. The reviews were excellent. One critic exulted "Whoever is able to conduct an orchestra so well after only a short preparation and can bring it to such outstanding heights with simple gestures and from memory must be a truly great conductor." He

61

Conducting from a stool (below), Mr. DePreist leads the Philadelphia Orchestra. At left, he talks with concertgoers after a performance.

credits his ability to memorize the most difficult scores to the way he used his time in the hospital. "I studied scores, soaking up everything until it became a total commitment and a total diversion."

The Rotterdam success was followed by concert appearances with such prestigious orchestras as the Stockholm Symphony Orchestra, the Philadelphia Orchestra and the New York Philharmonic. Then Mr. DePreist received an offer to become associate conductor of the National Symphony in Washington, D.C. He accepted only after assurances from Antal Dorati, the orchestra's principal conductor, that he would have the opportunity to conduct important subscription concerts. He commutes between New York City and Washington during the concert season so he can spend time with his wife and two daughters, Tracy and Jennifer, to whom he is an affectionate and devoted father. His New York apartment is located a mere two blocks from the Lincoln Center for the Performing Arts, which gives him quick access to the New York Philharmonic, the Metropolitan Opera and other cultural institutions housed there.

Now that he has achieved success, James DePreist finds it hard to believe that it was not until 1962 that he began conducting. During his undergraduate years at the University of Pennsylvania, he played drums in a jazz quintet. After graduation, he studied composition at the Philadelphia Conservatory but still had no plans for a conducting career. That interest did not really develop until, at the urging of conductor Leonard Bernstein, he accepted an offer from the United States Department of State to teach American music in the Near and Far East. While in Thailand, he was asked to conduct a rehearsal of the Thailand Orchestra, and as he puts it: "Once I conducted, there was no longer any question about what I wanted to do. I was hooked." But the joy was short-lived. It was then that polio struck and he was flown home for treatment. It was during his recuperating period that his friends, especially Mr. Bernstein, encouraged him to continue his conducting career.

The young conductor still has one major goal: to reach the point in his career where conducting invitations are "almost automatic." That time should not be too far off.

Outside the opera house, Mr. DePreist and his wife, Betty, stand with concert pianist Giuseppe Lalicata (l.) and manager William Denton.

Robert Dunham

Businessman

Robert Dunham, president, Harlem's McDonald's in New York, N.Y.; born Sept. 12, 1932 in Kannapolis, N.C.; joined U.S. Air Force in 1951, attended its Food Service School. Wife: Jeanette. Son: Bradley. Address: 215 W. 125th St., New York, NY 10027 (See full biographical sketch in Volume I.)

Former Policeman Becomes
A Business Success in Harlem

"[My personal philosophy is] to endeavor to achieve—without any thought of public recognition—whatever goal I set for myself."

That lady who "has come a long way, baby" in the advertisements for Virginia Slims cigarettes hasn't got a thing on Robert "Lee" Dunham, who has come from a sharecropping background in the South to the position of president and major stockholder of one of the most lucrative franchises in the entire McDonald's fast-food chain. Since Mr. Dunham's store opened in March, 1972 on busy 125th Street in the Harlem section of New York City, it has grown into a hamburger haven that services some 3,500 people each day (nearly 5,000 on weekends). It grosses more than $100,000 each month, and anticipated earnings of $1½ million by the end of its first fiscal year. This makes Harlem's McDonald's, as Mr. Dunham calls his place, the third most successful of nearly 2,800 McDonald's outlets in the United States. Early in 1973, a second McDonald's franchise was awarded to Mr. Dunham and his partners.

The man behind this business success is a rugged-looking former air force cook, former policeman, former machine-operator and former woodworker (he designed the layout in his store and all the furniture in his home) who exudes a kind of infectious self-assurance, energy and determination that immediately lets one know that here is a brother who knows how to put things together; one who doesn't shuck and jive once he decides what he wants to do. Anyone who doubts this should check out a member of one of the youth gangs that thought they were going to either take over Mr. Dunham's store or drive him off 125th Street when he first opened the doors. When Mr. Dunham talks about his first three months in business, it sounds more like a chronicle of war. He can laugh now when telling of the grim encounters: "Man, right after we opened, four gangs regularly converged on the place, sometimes with pipes and knives. There were fights and other harrassments which completely drove away all our family trade." Finally, he and his two partners, Nathaniel Jones, also a former policeman, and William Richards, a social worker, decided they would meet force with force. "We let them know that, if they wanted to get it on, then we'd get it on, but we weren't going to be driven out or taken over." They began collaring troublemakers and throwing them out of the place. Once, Mr. Dunham scattered an unruly bunch by firing four pistol shots into the ceiling. And gang leaders were told in no-nonsense language that they would be held personally responsible for any damage to the store. The tactics worked. The

Robert Dunham works (below) with assistants in kitchen of his restaurant that has become one of the most successful in the McDonald's chain.

gangs realized that Harlem's McDonald's was not to be messed with. After that was settled, Mr. Dunham and Mr. Jones started talking to gang members and ended up hiring several of them. The store also began to sponsor a junior basketball team and provide food for the Black Panther party's free breakfast program. "We do have a sense of responsibility to the community," notes Mr. Dunham, who lives in the large black community of Bedford-Stuyvesant in Brooklyn, New York. "That was my first location site choice but the Harlem site was available sooner."

Though the most severe, the gang problem was only one source of trouble for the young entrepreneur. Another was the pilfering of food, supplies and money by employees. Machines were also abused by people who didn't know how to use them properly. Mr. Dunham moved decisively. He set up a training program for employees and gave them a stake in the store's survival by paying them well. Anyone caught stealing was fired immediately and the three partners made sure that their presence was felt in the store by working twelve to fourteen hours a day. "I know at all times where everything is and where it should be," Mr. Dunham says, "and I keep close tabs on what's happening. I also take a personal interest in my people and try to maintain a business-like but relaxed atmosphere." With this combination of determination, skill and sensitivity, Mr. Dunham built his store so fast that officials of McDonald's urged him to open another.

Operating a fast-food restaurant was not "Lee" Dunham's first objective when a bad back forced him to retire from the police force after fourteen years. He wanted to open up "a really plush place with art pieces and original paintings on the walls." (He has carried this idea through in his McDonald's store with original art work done especially for the store by two friends, Greg Ridley, who contributed hand-tooled copper portraits of Malcolm X, Dr. Martin Luther King Jr., Frederick Douglass and others, and Harper Phillips, who contributed several collages.) Financial help was supposed to come from the Presbyterian Economic Development Corporation, but the deal fell through when the church-related agency balked at financing a place that sold liquor. That's when Mr. Dunham decided to get in touch with McDonald's.

Mr. Dunham remembers the small town of Kannapolis, North Carolina, where he was born in 1932. "They [the white farmers for whom his family worked] wouldn't give us money. We used to get $200 a year in credit for clothes and things. We were supposed to grow our food. My family got tired of that life and we decided to sneak away one night—my mother, grandparents, two brothers and myself. That white man hunted us with dogs and caught my mother and grandmother and put them in jail for three months. The rest of us escaped to South

66

Mr. Dunham stands in the restaurant that has made him one of Harlem's fastest-rising businessmen. He was awarded a second McDonald's franchise early in 1973.

Carolina. After my mother and grandmother got out, my mother went to New York to work and sent money to my grandparents to take care of us. Finally, in 1947, we all came to New York." While a child in the South, Mr. Dunham shined shoes, picked cotton, picked and sold strawberries and blackberries, and slaughtered hogs. "I learned early that one has to work to survive," he says. He also learned to cook. "Since I came from a family of three boys and my mother worked for a white family, she used to leave the food cooking on the stove and tell us to watch it. And man, if anything burned, Momma would whip us good. When the biscuits got a certain shade, we knew it was time to take those babies out!"

In 1951, Mr. Dunham joined the United States Air Force and was sent to the Food Service School. He became such a good cook that they transferred him from the Enlisted Men's mess to the Officer's Mess. After leaving the military, he worked as a machine operator and later as a salad man at New York's Waldorf-Astoria Hotel. Eventually, he joined the New York City police force and acquired some of the skills—certainly the physical ones—which proved helpful when he opened his store.

Mr. Dunham now devotes most of his time to the store. What time is left is spent with his wife, Jeannette, and their thirteen-year old son, Bradley, with whom he skis, bowls and roller skates.

When asked about a personal philosophy, Mr. Dunham answers: "To endeavor to achieve—without any thought of public recognition —whatever goal I set for myself." That means that one day "Lee" Dunham will have that plush restaurant.

Nelson Jack Edwards

Labor Union Official

Nelson Jack Edwards holds national contract negotiations with representatives of Alcoa aluminum firm.

He Is a Firm Believer
That 'Labor Disgraces No Man'

"I think that old President Ulysses S. Grant had the right idea back in 1877 when he said that labor disgraces no man."

Nelson Jack Edwards has come a very long way—from a one-room shack in rural Lowndes County, Alabama, to an elegant executive suite in Detroit, Michigan. As an international vice president of United Auto Workers (International Union, United Automobile, Aerospace and Agriculture Implement Workers of America), representing eighty-five thousand workers in collective bargaining negotiations and another three hundred thousand workers in the various councils he heads, he is one of the most powerful men in the labor movement today. He is also the first black member of UAW's powerful International Executive Board.

During his climb from shoveling sand at the Dodge Foundry to his present position, Mr. Edwards paid his dues many times over. Born in an Alabama sharecropper's shack on August 3, 1917, he spent his boyhood in the deep backwoods of Lowndes County. "We

68

*Nelson Jack Edwards,
international vice president,
United Auto Workers; born
Aug. 3, 1917 in Montgomery,
Ala.; high school graduate;
negotiates and administers
collective bargaining contracts
with major corporations. Wife:
Laura Edwards. Children:
Lorraine and Nelson Jack Jr.
Address: 8000 E. Jefferson
Ave., Detroit, MI 48214
(See full biographical
sketch in Volume I.)*

Mr. Edwards chats with Michigan Governor G. Mennen Williams (c.) and UAW
President Walter Reuther during 1966 civil rights rally at Detroit's Cobo Hall.

UAW Vice President Edwards
and Mrs. Walter Reuther
participate in historic Selma,
Ala., civil rights march.

sharecropped and I had a robust farm life as a youngster," he recalls.
"I was the youngest in a family of three boys (his brothers, Garfield and
John, are five and seven years older, respectively). My father was
always optimistic that next year's crop would put us out of debt and
over the top. Unfortunately, he was always short-penciled at
crop-payment time and we kept slipping deeper in debt."

Mr. Edwards attended the Old Pleasant Valley AMEZ Church
School until he was ten years old, then transferred to Marblestone High
School which at the time was, he says, "one of the best Negro schools
in Alabama." Mr. Edwards, who worked the fields while keeping
up with his classes, still prides himself at having been considered one
of the best plowhands in Lowndes County, although admits that
"gazing at the rear end of a mule from sunup to sundown wasn't too
much fun."

After getting married at seventeen to his childhood sweetheart,
Laura Logan, Mr. Edwards left sharecropping and moved to
Montgomery where he was hired by the Southern Oil Company, earning
"the princely sum of fifteen cents an hour for twelve hours a
day—$10.80 for a six-day week." Around that time, his brother
John—with $2.50 in his pocket—hoboed to Detroit where he got a job
at the Dodge main plant. "Two years later," Mr. Edwards remembers,

During 1968 presidential campaign, Mr. Edwards was a fervent backer of candidate Hubert H. Humphrey.

"John came down in his car for a visit and I could hardly wait for him to leave again so that I could go back with him. I was broke as a man could be, so I had to leave my wife in Alabama until I was able to save enough to send for her."

Unable at first to find a job in any of the auto plants, he took odd construction jobs until a sweeping and sand-shoveling job opened up at the Dodge main foundry. "Smoke, dust and fumes were so heavy that you could hardly see a fellow worker five feet away," he recalls. "But I was making sixty cents an hour and was one more happy soul. Within seven months after coming to Detroit, I was able to bring up my wife and my newborn son."

He was first told about unions by his brother John. "I couldn't go along with the union line before then because so many unions had a color bar in their constitutions. My brother explained that the UAW was a new, democratic and forward-looking union and that Negroes were welcome to join. So I did and have not had a single regret for doing this back in 1937. We had a strike back then and once I felt the power of this union, there was no turning back." After a layoff at Chrysler in 1941 due to a changeover to war production, Mr. Edwards took a job at the Ford Lincoln plant. He immediately became active in his new union—UAW Local 900—which had just obtained recognition to represent the workers at the plant, serving on the education, citizenship, and by-laws committees. Mr. Edwards' abilities were quickly recognized. In 1944, he was elected by his fellow unionists to the Local 900 bargaining committee. A year later, he was elected chairman, the top post on the most important committee of a local union. The membership was overwhelmingly white at the time. In 1948, his active unionism was recognized by the UAW brass and Mr. Edwards was called from plant work and appointed to the staff of the International Union as an international representative to service UAW local unions in Region 1A—the UAW region that covers the west side of Detroit (UAW is divided into eighteen regions covering all of the United States and Canada). Mr. Edwards worked as a representative for fourteen years during which time he helped negotiate hundreds of contracts providing for increased benefits and security for the workers. He also traveled to other parts of the country to help with organizing chores.

Since being elected to UAW's International Executive Board as a member-at-large in 1962, he has been re-elected to that position in 1964, 1966 and 1968, and was elevated to a vice presidency of the UAW in 1970 when the board member-at-large positions were eliminated. As a board member-at-large, Mr. Edwards became director of the UAW Councils at Alcoa, Budd, Allen Industries, Briggs, Electric Storage Battery and Kelsey-Hayes.

70

Urging minumum federal standards for private pension plans, Mr. Edwards testifies (right) before U.S. Senate Committee on Aging in Washington, D.C.

Shortly before his death in a 1970 plane crash, Mr. Reuther (above, c.) conferred with UAW Vice Presidents Edwards and Ken Bannon.

U.S. Sen. Edmund Muskie and Mr. Edwards huddle (above) during 1970 UAW Skilled Trades Conference in Atlantic City, N.J.

In May 1963, during the height of the civil rights drive, Mr. Edwards went to Birmingham, Alabama, working as the official representative of the UAW. His moving account of his experiences alongside Dr. Martin Luther King Jr. was published in the *Free Labor World*, the official organ of the International Confederation of Free Trade Unions, and was also published in four languages in Brussels, Belgium, for distribution throughout the world.

In 1970, during the 22nd Constitutional Convention of the UAW, delegates gave him the highest plurality of any UAW officer in electing him as one of their then six vice presidents (now there are seven) of the union—another black "first". He was reelected to the vice presidency in the 1972 UAW elections and presently serves on the education, fair practices, retired workers, skilled trades, and appeals committees of the UAW Executive Board. He is director or chairman of thirty different departments and councils. In addition, he is co-director of the manpower training and development department, created in 1967.

Although poverty in Alabama caused Mr. Edwards to leave high school before completing all requirements for graduation, he is well educated, having attended and graduated from numerous labor seminars, courses and classes conducted by various colleges and universities as well as those conducted by the UAW.

Mr. Edwards credits hard work and the support of his wife with much of his success. Mr. and Mrs. Edwards are the parents of Nelson Jr. and Mrs. Lorraine Harris. "I think," he concludes in summing up the reasons for his accomplishments, "that old President Ulysses S. Grant had the right idea back in 1877 when he said that labor disgraces no man."

Mr. Edwards listens intently (right) to arguments during contract negotiations before presenting his views.

Clarence C. Finley

Corporation Executive

Clarence C. Finley, executive vice president since 1972 of Burlington House Products Group, subsidiary of Burlington Industries in New York, N.Y.; born Aug. 24, 1922 in Chicago, Ill; Northwestern University (B.S., accounting, 1951) and attended John Marshall Law School. Wife: Emma. Daughter: Beth. Address: 1345 Avenue of the Americas, New York, NY 10019
(See full biographical sketch in Volume I.)

Mr. Finley stands in front of the New York City headquarters of Burlington Industries.

Mr. Finley (c.) reviews weekly sales figures with Burlington executives (l. to r.) Chester Miles, Peter Fancher, Frank Greenberg and John Spezzo.

He Rose from File Clerk to a Top Position in American Industry

"Race was never a factor in my rise. [It] worked neither for me nor against me."

In 1942, Clarence C. Finley was a $12-a-week file clerk with the Charm-Tred Co., a medium-size, family-owned carpet business in Chicago, Illinois, his hometown. Since then, both he and the company have moved on to bigger and better things. Charm-Tred has become a major subsidiary of the huge Burlington Industries combine, while Mr. Finley is now executive vice president of the combine's Burlington House Products Group. He is second in command of a division that accounted for $235 million in carpet sales in 1972. The group consists of six subsidiaries (with 6,500 employees) in the United States, Canada, Japan and West Germany, and Mr. Finley played a major role in establishing the latter two.

Mr. Finley holds the highest, most important position ever held by a black man in a major American firm. Burlington Industries, whose

73

yearly sales are more than $2 billion, is the world's largest manufacturer of textiles and related products. It is almost twice the size of its nearest United States competitor. As a highly diversified producer of textiles, home furnishings and industrial products, it has thirty-two operating divisions, all basically autonomous—a factor that is, Mr. Finley believes, one of the key reasons for the company's great success. Clarence Finley's job is to oversee all the carpet divisions, and he takes care of business with efficiency and aplomb.

It is a long way from Clarence Finley's earlier years, which were filled with hard work and struggle. As a youngster he had to interrupt his education to help support his family. This originally led him to Charm-Tred, whose owner, Ben Greenberg, he praises for helping him throughout his career. "Even as a file clerk," he says, "I used to watch what everyone was doing. By the time I was drafted into the military service in 1943, I had performed almost every job in the office. My official job by then was paymaster." After the war, Mr. Finley went back to Charm-Tred because "Mr. Greenberg had assured me that, if I came

Inspecting various operations of his division, Mr. Finley tours (above) with Everett Gowan; checks factory equipment (at right, top), and discusses carpet quality (right).

En route to his office, Mr. Finley goes over company business with Frank Greenberg, a Burlington vice president.

back, there would be no holds barred and I would progress as I qualified." In 1951, he was appointed controller, a position he kept when Charm-Tred was acquired by Burlington Industries in 1959. (Meanwhile, he had attended night school for eight years, earning a degree in accounting at Northwestern University. He also attended Chicago's John Marshall Law School.) In 1961, Mr. Finley became a BI vice president. "Race was never a factor in my rise," he insists. "From the beginning, Mr. Greenberg's commitment eliminated the job as a racial one. My race worked neither for me nor against me." His unprecedented success, he maintains, is "really a colorless story—more the career of an executive who happens to be black than one of a black executive."

Though he has gone about it quietly, and without fanfare, since the late 1960s Mr. Finley has been active in Westchester Clubmen, Inc., a group of business and professional men who provide scholarships for needy students, and the Interracial Council of Business Organizations, which provides capital and administrative expertise to aspiring businessmen who have sound ideas but limited resources.

George Foreman
World Heavyweight Boxing Champion

He Decided to Become Heavyweight Champion of the World . . . and Did

"I just fight to earn a living and to win. . . . To make statements, I think, is the job of intellectuals, not athletes."

The first time the world took notice of heavyweight boxer George Foreman was in 1968 during the Olympics in Mexico City, Mexico. He was jumping around the ring, waving a small United States flag. The fact that he had just won a Gold Medal by scoring a second-round knockout over Russia's Ionas Chepulis seemed somewhat incidental to his fame. Later, Mr. Foreman emphatically denied that his flag-waving was calculated to offset an earlier demonstration of defiance by two black United States athletes, Tommie Smith and Don Carlos, who had mounted the victors' stands clenching black-gloved fists. Asked what

George Foreman, world heavyweight boxing champion; born Jan. 22, 1948 in Marshall, Tex.; won Olympic Gold Medal in 1968 by knockout over Russia's Ionas Chepulis; won world title by technical knockout over Joe Frazier in 1973. Wife: Adrienne Foreman. Daughter: Michi. Address: 23900 Medeiros Ave., Hayward, CA 94541 (See full biographical sketch in Volume I.)

As Olympics champion, George Foreman presents plaque to President Lyndon B. Johnson at the White House, honoring the president as "father of the Job Corps program" which gave the boxer his educational training and a high school equivalency diploma at Parks Job Corps Center in Pleasanton, Calif.

In the photo which made him famous, Mr. Foreman waves American flag after defeating Russia's Ionas Chepulis in 1968 Olympics.

prompted him—a black man—to such an exuberant show of patriotism, Mr. Foreman simply said: "I did it because it's my flag. I'm proud to be an American."

On that memorable day in Mexico City, George Foreman set his mind on one day becoming the heavyweight champion of the world. He took the first step toward that end a year later, in July, 1969, when he turned professional, ending a two-year career as an amateur during which he fought twenty-two bouts, winning all but three. Under the careful tutelage of his trainer-manager, Dick Sadler, a ring-corner veteran who, at one time or other during his career, had handled such well-known fighters as Archie Moore, Sonny Liston and even the championship-bound Cassius Clay (Muhammad Ali), Sadler matched Foreman with a string of carefully hand-picked, unrated and obscure heavyweights to gain experience. While winning these little-publicized bouts did nothing to enhance Mr. Foreman's reputation as a fighter nor to substantially increase his bank account, Mr. Sadler considered them invaluable "on-the-job training." Not until 1970, after Foreman had fought and won twenty-one professional matches, did his trainer permit him to meet a fighter of some prominence. That fighter was George Chuvalo of Toronto, Canada, who had already done battle with Muhammad Ali and Joe Frazier. Chuvalo had lost a fifteen-round decision to Ali in 1967, and was stopped in the fourth round a year later by Frazier. Perhaps there was a message in the fact that it took Foreman only three rounds to incapacitate Chuvalo. If there was, nobody paid any attention, least of all "Smokin' Joe."

Less than three and a half years after his Olympic victory, with an uninterrupted winning streak in thirty-seven professional bouts—thirty-four of which he won by knockout—twenty-four-year-old, six-foot-three-and-a-half-inch, 217-pound George Foreman was given a shot at the heavyweight crown. To the majority of fight fans the outcome of the encounter was as predictable as that between a lion and a Christian in ancient Rome. Joe would send the kid back to the minor leagues after teaching him and his trainer that you never send a boy to do a man's job.

The fans couldn't have been more wrong. Before the unbelieving eyes of some forty-two thousand ringsiders at the National Stadium in Kingston, Jamaica, and hundreds of thousands of closed-circuit television viewers in the United States, the challenger scored the most spectacular upset since Ali took the crown from Liston in 1964. In a matter of four minutes and thirty-five seconds, Foreman demolished the incumbent champion by battering him three times to the canvas in each of the fight's two rounds. After stopping the fight, the referee declared George Foreman the new heavyweight champion of the world. The humiliating defeat was the first in Frazier's professional ring career.

George Foreman's spectacular rise to the top of his profession traces, with only minor variations, the classic rags-to-riches ring success stories of other black heavyweight champions, such as Jack Johnson, Joe Louis, Ezzard Charles, Floyd Patterson, Sonny Liston, Muhammad Ali and Joe Frazier. The fifth of seven children of a railroad construction worker, he was born January 22, 1948 in Marshall, Texas, but grew up in nearby Houston. When he was still quite young, his parents were divorced, leaving his mother, Mrs. Nancy Ree Foreman, alone to fend for her brood. "I came from a matriarchal family," says Mr. Foreman. "My mother raised us by working as a cook."

Finding school less than inspiring, George dropped out of the seventh grade at thirteen. The reason for quitting, he explained, was that "I never saw anybody in my neighborhood using the education they got from the school. Most of my peers didn't even go as far in school as I did." Hanging around on the block, George joined the ranks of that vast army of undereducated and unemployable black youths produced by inadequate metropolitan educational systems. "The cops were always after me," recalls Mr. Foreman. "One day, I broke two hundred windows, but I never got caught." The youth got tired of his precarious, aimless existence and in 1965, when he was sixteen, he signed up with the Job Corps, which sent him to a conservation camp at Grants Pass, Oregon. There, he received training as a carpenter, bricklayer and electronics assembler. Introduced to the camp's recreational boxing program, he soon impressed the athletic director and fellow corpsmen with his punching power. After being transferred to another Job Corps center at Pleasanton, California, he continued to box and eventually won the Corps' Diamond Belt Tournament. In 1967, he was hired as an OEO avocation instructor, earning $125 a week. As far as George Foreman was concerned, he never had it so good. Like so many champions before him, he entered the Golden Gloves and slugged his way to the finals before losing on a split decision. Although still far from being a polished fighter, he impressed United States Olympic Committee officials with his fire power, thus assuring himself a berth on the United States Olympic boxing squad.

Living quietly with his attractive wife, Adrienne, and their infant daughter, Michi, who was born while he was in Jamaica preparing for the Frazier fight, Mr. Foreman hopes to be as successful in business as he has been in the ring. Consequently, he and his trainer-manager Sadler have acquired Minority Enterprises, Inc., a venture aimed at training minority youths to run businesses. Although he hopes to help young blacks get ahead, the new heavyweight champion—like his

George Foreman keeps in shape by hauling gravel in Haywood, Calif., while his manager, Dick Sadler keeps a watchful eye on him.

Mr. Foreman arrives in Kingston, Jamaica for his February, 1973, fight with Joe Frazier.

Relaxing outside his hotel in Jamaica, the boxer drinks a Jamaican fruit punch with his brother Roy (l.), and cousin, Willie Carpenter.

Gunning for a quick knockout, Mr. Foreman lands right against Mr. Frazier (above) and continues to batter the champion until he goes down for the final count (center). At his home in Haywood, Calif., the new champion chats on the phone as he holds his daughter, Michi.

immediate predecessor—has served notice that he has no ambition to be a spokesman for anybody or any group. "I just fight to earn a living and to win. There's none of that fighting for the black man or the white man. I just want to represent myself properly in my profession," he says. Discussing former-champion Muhammad Ali's penchant for making speeches, Mr. Foreman says, "Ali is well qualified to explain physical fitness, but not philosophy. To make statements, I think, is the job of intellectuals, not athletes."

79

Redd Foxx

Comedian

Redd Foxx (John Elroy Sanford), comedian; born Dec. 9, 1922 in St. Louis, Mo.; attended Catholic and public schools in St. Louis and Chicago, Ill.; began his entertainment career by playing in a washtub band in Chicago; in 1972 became star of successful TV series, "Sanford and Son." Wife: the former Betty Jean Harris. Daughter: Debraca. Address: c/o NBC-TV, 3000 W. Alameda, Burbank, CA 91505 (See full biographical sketch in Volume I.)

He's Called 'The Funniest Man Alive'

"I knew that this all had to happen one day. I have worked hard and paid my dues and the rewards are now coming."

Although for many years nightclub audiences have hailed Redd Foxx as "the funniest man alive," it was not until recently that the veteran entertainer received the national exposure and recognition he has sought during his long career.

Born John Elroy Sanford, Redd achieved his long-awaited stardom early in 1972 when he first appeared as an aging Los Angeles junk dealer in the NBC-TV show "Sanford and Son." Since its premiere, the comedy program, which stars Redd and Demond Wilson (who plays the part of Sanford's son, Lamont) consistently has been in the top-ten television ratings. Born December 9, 1922 in St. Louis, Missouri, Redd was the second son of Mr. and Mrs. Fred Sanford. His brother, Fred Jr., was four years older, and two sisters had died before he was born. His maternal grandmother was a full-blooded Indian; his paternal great-great grandfather had been brought from Africa. When Redd was only four years old, his father deserted the home. "Things were tough for us for many years after that," the comedian recalls. The first school he attended was St. Benedict the Moor Mission, a Catholic school in Milwaukee, Wisconsin. Later, he attended Banneker School in St. Louis but was expelled when he threw a book back at a teacher who had thrown it at him.

80

As star of his own television series, "Sanford and Son," Redd Foxx plays screen father of co-star Demond Wilson.

"Sanford and Son" producer Aaron Ruben (c.) congratulates Redd and co-star Demond Wilson after completing successful show season.

Redd moved to Chicago with his mother (who worked as a domestic for a vice president of the Chicago White Sox baseball team) and finished his grammar school education at the Carter School. His first year of high school was spent at DuSable High School on the city's South Side but he quit in order to devote more time to playing in the washtub band that he and two friends, Lamont Ousley and Steve Trimel, had formed. In 1939, the trio ran away from home in search of fame as musicians. They almost found it in another way, however, when police found them aboard a freight train they had hopped to Weehawken, New Jersey. Redd escaped; his friends were released from jail thirty days later. The trio reunited and began performing on Harlem street-corners and subways, each of them earning as much as $50 a night.

When World War II came, the group, called the Bon-Bons, again was split and, again, it was only Redd Foxx who remained on the streets. It was during this period, while working as a busboy and sleeping on a Harlem rooftop, that he first came to know Malcolm Little, the man who became famous as Malcolm X. The two played pool together, and because both were light complexioned and had red hair, Mr. Foxx was nicknamed "Chicago Red" and Malcolm X was called "Detroit Red." Around the same time, the name Redd Foxx was born. John Elroy Sanford decided he needed a name that would attract talent scouts as well as patrons, so he added a second "d" to his nickname and an extra "x" to his new name of Fox (which came about "because I'm such a foxy and cool dude"). Recalling Redd in his autobiography, which was written just before he was assassinated in 1965, Malcolm X

At Los Angeles premiere of *Wattstax*, Redd and his wife, Betty Jean, chat with city councilman Thomas Bradley.

During the early days of his career, Redd shared stage billing with such stars as Bob Hope (above) and singer-actress Abbey Lincoln (below), a close friend.

stated: "Chicago Red was the funniest dishwasher on this earth."

One of Redd's first nightclub jobs came in the 1940s when he was allowed to clown, mime and sing funny songs at Mimo's, a club on Seventh Avenue in Harlem. A friend later told him that Gamby's, a Baltimore club, needed a master of ceremonies. Redd got the job and stayed for three years. After developing his standup comic routine, he returned to New York. In 1947, he teamed with comedian Slappy White and the two hit the black vaudeville circuit, where they played for nearly five years, earning as much as $450 a week.

Redd and Slappy split up in 1952 and Redd moved to Hollywood, where he alternated nightclub engagements with a part-time job as a sign painter. While playing at the Brass Rail, a downtown Los Angeles club, he met Dootsie Williams, owner of Dooto Records, who persuaded him to begin recording "party records." The material, like almost all of the Redd Foxx routines, was risqué—but funny. During a fifteen-year period, more than ten million copies of forty-nine Redd Foxx recordings were sold.

Many persons contend that it was the comedian's "blue" humor which denied him the acceptance and exposure that was enjoyed by a number of younger comedians such as Dick Gregory, George Kirby and Flip Wilson. The tide began to turn for Redd in 1964 when Hugh Downs, then the host of "The Today Show," saw him in a San Francisco nightclub and invited him to appear on the network television program. Shortly thereafter, he was asked to perform on Johnny Carson's "The Tonight Show" and, since that time, has appeared on virtually every network variety program, including the Steve Allen, Merv Griffin, Mike Douglas, Virginia Graham and Flip Wilson shows.

Another rewarding break came for Redd in 1968 at Caesars Palace in Las Vegas. Signed to appear on the same bill with singer Aretha Franklin for the club's opening night, he had to take over the entire three-hour show when Miss Franklin failed to appear. Bookers noted his audience appeal and, in August, 1970, signed him to a contract paying $960,000 for a minimum of thirty-two performing weeks a year.

The event which is credited with paving the road to Redd's television stardom was his acceptance in 1970 of a role in the movie *Cotton Comes to Harlem*. Although the role of the aging junk dealer was small, it was noticed by Cleavon Little, another performer in the film, who convinced television producers Bud Yorkin and Norman Lear that Redd Foxx was the man they wanted for the part of an old junkman in a series they planned to introduce.

"Sanford and Son" premiered on January 14, 1972. Redd named the lead character Fred Sanford, in honor of his brother, who died in 1967. He also named his television son Lamont, and another character on the

Always one for laughter, Redd
stages a zany motorcycle ride
(above) for the sheer fun of it.

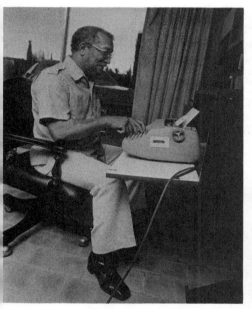

Typing his own jokes (above),
Redd makes certain his material
is up to par. Later (r.), he takes
his wife for a spin in their
custom-built auto.

show Reverend Trimel, as a tribute to the two friends who had run away
from home with him and helped start his career. The program, which
appeals to a general audience, has episodes which deal mainly with the
generation gap between Sanford and his son. Although the father-son
dialogue often is abrasive, the two are very close and manage to
overcome all efforts to separate them.

Following an unsuccessful marriage during the 1940s, Redd met
Betty Jean Harris in 1955 when the Harris Sisters singing group
appeared on a bill with him at a Hollywood nightclub.

"I would see Redd backstage and he would never pay any
attention to me," Mrs. Foxx recalls. "For some reason, he would laugh
and talk with my sisters. I didn't like him because he would be loud in
the dressing room. A year passed, and during all this time if someone
had told me I would marry Redd, I would have made a bet against it.
Redd later told me, however, that he would watch me with my sisters
when we were on stage and, from the first time he saw me, he knew
someday I would be the one for him. It was love at first sight with him.
He waited a year to make his bid." The couple eloped in 1956 and were
married in Las Vegas. Redd later adopted Debraca, a daughter by his
wife's previous marriage, and the family now has homes in Las Vegas
and Hollywood.

Speaking of his long trek to success, Redd Foxx says, "I knew that
this all had to happen one day. I have worked hard and paid my dues
and the rewards are now coming."

Arthur George Gaston Sr.

Businessman

Arthur George Gaston Sr., business executive; chairman of the board, president and treasurer of Smith & Gaston Interests and Citizens Federal Savings and Loan Association, and has various other business enterprises—Booker T. Washington Insurance Company, Booker T. Washington Business College, Smith & Gaston Funeral Home, A. G. Gaston Motel, A. G. Gaston Home for Senior Citizens, etc.— in Birmingham, Ala.; born July 4, 1892 in Demopolis, Ala.; graduate of Tuggle Institute in Birmingham. Wife: Minnie L. Gaston. Son: Arthur G. Gaston Jr. Address: 1728 Third Ave., North, Birmingham, AL 35233 (See full biographical sketch in Volume I.)

Starting with a Mere 'Plan to Make Money,' He Became a Multi-Millionaire

"How does a poor man become a businessman? By accumulating money and keeping his eyes open for the main chance."

When Arthur George Gaston first decided that he wanted to be "somebody," he was just a common laborer making thirty-one cents an hour in a Birmingham, Alabama, steel mill. But he had a plan to make money and later started a burial society with his father-in-law, A. L. Smith. The Smith and Gaston Burial Society, which grew into the Booker T. Washington Insurance Company, eventually became the hub of a network of businesses that rocketed Mr. Gaston's 1972 holdings to an estimated $24 million. Today, his main offices are in a modern

84

Mr. Gaston and Birmingham mayor George S. Seibels Jr. stand in front of Mr. Gaston's new Citizens Federal Savings & Loan Association Building in downtown Birmingham. Below (l. to r.), M. E. Wiggins, Mr. Gaston, L. J. Willie, Cooper Green and Mrs. A. G. Gaston cut ribbon at opening of building in 1969.

building, which he owns, in downtown Birmingham.

The road was not easy. "As far back as I can remember," Mr. Gaston says, "I had determination. I guess I was born to be a businessman. In Demopolis, Alabama, my hometown, there wasn't much to inspire a black boy, but somehow I found the inspiration I needed. My family was poor. My father died when I was young and my mother went off to Birmingham to work in the white folks' kitchens. I stayed in Demopolis with my grandmother. We had an old swing in our yard and all the kids used to come to our house to swing. Right then and there I started the first Gaston business." It was founded on a principle which remained with him throughout his career: find a need and fill it. He charged the kids in the neighborhood a pin or a button to swing. Once he had a cigar box full of buttons and pins, he sold them to women in the community when their buttons and pins disappeared.

After graduating from Birmingham's Tuggle Institute and serving in the army during World War I, young Gaston set out to make his fortune. "Day in and day out, I dug holes and painted boxcars for the Tennessee Coal, Iron and Steel Company. While I worked, I planned my next move. I had decided what I wanted to do with my life: I was going to be a businessman. How does a poor man become a businessman? By accumulating money and keeping his eyes open for the main chance."

Mr. Gaston, who was earning $3.50 a day, put himself on a tight budget—$10 a pay period (every two weeks). Five dollars were for living expenses, the other five dollars were for social activities—"for spending on the girls and so forth." But he earned a reputation for being cheap and the girls began to avoid him—"so I had another five dollars to save." He also found a way to make more than the thirty-one cents an hour the steel mill was paying him. He sold peanuts. He also started lending money to fellow workers for "twenty-five cents on the dollar."

Before long, Arthur Gaston and his father-in-law started the burial society which rapidly grew into the insurance company and other firms. As his holdings increased, Mr. Gaston turned the money back into the business. He also started a chain of funeral homes throughout Alabama. When he found that there were not enough clerks and typists to service the businesses, he started the Booker T. Washington Business College, which offered courses in business administration, bookkeeping, accounting and eventually in IBM machine accounting and computer technology.

Meanwhile, many blacks found it difficult to get financing for houses. So Mr. Gaston founded the Citizens Federal Savings and Loan Association. Again, he turned all of his profits back into the

85

At right is a full view of new building housing two of Mr. Gaston's enterprises in downtown Birmingham. Below is another Gaston business.

institution that was founded "to fill a social need."

Actually, none of the Smith and Gaston businesses were founded to make a great deal of money. As a matter of fact, the only time Mr. Gaston ever lost money was when he went into business "to make a killing." He says: "Back in 1938 or 1939, we got a Joe Louis Punch franchise and started the Brown Belle Bottling Company. I bought machinery and sat down and waited for money to roll in. I lost more than $60,000 in the venture."

Among the corporations which Mr. Gaston has served as board chairman and president are the Booker T. Washington Insurance Company, the Booker T. Washington Business College, the A. G. Gaston Home for Senior Citizens, the A. G. Gaston Motels, Inc. (including a 65-unit, modern, air-conditioned motel), New Grace Hill Cemetery, Vulcan Realty and Investment Corporation, Smith and Gaston Funeral Directors, and the Citizens Federal Savings and Loan Association.

The secret of Mr. Gaston's success is obviously due to a combination of many factors. His own rules for success are:

1. Pay yourself first. Take yours off the top. Pay yourself a salary. Set aside a specific amount of each paycheck as your money. Take that money out first and bank it. You'll be surprised how fast the money builds up. If you have two or three thousand dollars in the bank, sooner or later somebody will come along and show you how to double it.

Mr. and Mrs. Gaston (seated) receive congratulations and citations from employees and friends during his 80th birthday celebration. Below, he receives a 1972 Certificate of Appreciation from Birmingham's Ferd Weil, president of the Downtown Action Committee.

Money doesn't spoil. It keeps.

2. Establish a reputation at a bank or a savings and loan association. Save at an established institution and borrow there. *Stay away from loan sharks.*

3. Take no chances with your money. Play the safe number, the good one. Take your time. A man who can't afford to lose has no business gambling. When you can afford to lose you seldom do.

4. Never borrow anything that, if forced to, you can't repay.

5. Don't get big headed. Never forget "the little fellows." That's where the money is. If you stick with the "little fellows," if you give them your devotion, they'll make you big.

6. Don't have so much pride. Wear the same suit for a year or two. It doesn't make any difference what kind of suit the pocket is in, if there is money in the pocket.

7. Find a need and fulfill it. Successful businesses are founded on the needs of people. Once in business, keep good books. Everything that goes in the cash register doesn't belong to you. Also hire the best people you can find. Try to find a person who is worth more than you can afford to pay and pay him.

8. Stay in your own class. Never run around with people you can't afford to compete with.

9. Once you get money or a reputation for having money, which is the same thing, people will give you money.

10. Once you reach a certain bracket, it is very difficult to make more money.

87

Berry Gordy Jr.

Chairman and President, Motown Industries, Inc.

Berry Gordy Jr., chairman of the board and president of Motown Industries, Inc.; born in Detroit, Mich.; attended Detroit's Northeastern High School; had 15 fights as a Golden Gloves featherweight; began business career as owner of a record store and songwriter, now heads one of the nation's most successful business conglomerates. Single. Children: T. James, Berry and Hazel Joy. Address: 6464 Sunset Blvd., Hollywood, CA 90028 (See full biographical sketch in Volume I.)

From Auto Plant Laborer to Head Of the Motown Industries Empire

"I felt that if I built a company on the philosophy of having a close relationship with writers, producers and artists, the company would be stronger and more productive."

In 1959, Berry Gordy Jr. quit a secure $85-a-week job as a laborer at an automobile plant in Detroit, Michigan to take a chance on his lifetime dream of becoming a successful songwriter. In less than five years, he had built Motown Record Corporation, now a part of one of the greatest of entertainment empires.

Born on Detroit's lower East Side to Berry Sr. and Bertha I. Gordy, Berry (he was one of eight children) came out of Northeastern High School in 1948 to try for success in the same way that Joe Louis had done—with his fists. He had fifteen fights as a Golden Gloves featherweight, then the United States Army sent him to try another form of fighting—in Korea. When he was discharged in 1953, Mr. Gordy opened the 3-D Record Mart in Detroit but went bankrupt in the two years it took him to find out that there wasn't much of a market for jazz

The extraordinary success of Berry Gordy Jr. (above) is cited (opposite page) by Mayor Jerome P. Cavanagh of Detroit, Mich., the city in which Motown began. At right above are two of Motown's most successful acts early in their careers—(top) Stevie Wonder in Mr. Gordy's old Detroit office and the original Supremes (l. to r. Florence Ballard, Diana Ross and Mary Wilson) with Mr. Gordy and former U.S. Vice President Hubert Humphrey in Washington, D.C.

in the black community at that time. Then he went to work on an assembly line—nailing the upholstery in Lincoln automobiles.

But Mr. Gordy retained his first love, writing songs. His first hit was "Reet Petite," which he and his sister, Mrs. Gwen Fuqua, wrote for Jackie Wilson. They also wrote Mr. Wilson's early hits: "To Be Loved," "I'll Be Satisfied," "That's Why" and "Lonely Teardrops."

Mr. Gordy then became an independent producer, establishing himself with two songs he wrote for Marv Johnson, "I Love the Way You Love" and "You Got What It Takes." The records were sold to United Artists for distribution and became hits. Then Mr. Gordy decided that he wanted to distribute and promote his records himself. "I had a certain business philosophy that I wanted to develop. As a writer, I had problems getting money at the time that I needed it. I was broke even with hit records in certain cases. When the companies paid me, it was three months later and I owed money out to the family. So I felt that if I built a company with the philosophy of having a close relationship with writers, producers and artists, the company would be stronger and more productive."

He borrowed $800 from his family and started the Tamla record label, signing as his first artist a teenager named William "Smokey" Robinson, who had a group called the Miracles. Although Mr. Gordy

89

rejected more than one hundred songs that Smokey had written, he recorded the group, and a song called "Way Over There" sold 60,000 copies and became Berry Gordy's first national hit. It was followed by a successful tune called "Money," and by another hit by the Miracles, "Shop Around," which sold more than a million copies and which spurred Mr. Gordy upward in the record industry. Meanwhile, he borrowed from Detroit's nickname, "Motor Town," and formed Motown Record Corporation. He signed a stable of little known singers—the Temptations, the Four Tops, the Supremes, the Marvelletes, Martha Reeves and the Vandellas, the Velvettes, Brenda Holloway, Mary Wells—who eventually became top recording artists around the world.

Eventually occupying eight former residences on Detroit's West Grand Boulevard, Motown began recording on a number of labels, including Gordy, VIP, Soul and, of course, Tamla and Motown. Added later were Ecology, Rare Earth, Weed, Natural Resources and Black Forum, and the company distributed the Chisa releases. Though an independent record producer (unlike such conglomerates as Columbia Records, ABC Records, etc.), Motown has been among the top three companies in sales volume for a number of years, and is number one in sales in the United Kingdom. Motown artists have won just about every award the industry has to offer.

As a businessman, Berry Gordy Jr. has proved to be among the very best in the entertainment industry. Though he was achieving extraordinary success in Detroit, he decided in 1970 to move his company's headquarters to the very heart of the American entertainment industry—Hollywood, California. Thus today, as chairman

Mr. Gordy has given consistent support to such black activist groups as SCLC and Operation PUSH. At left, Mrs. Coretta S. King and the Rev. Ralph D. Abernathy present him with awards for flying to Atlanta with top Motown acts for a benefit performance on behalf of SCLC's Poor People's Campaign.

At premiere of his first movie production, *Lady Sings the Blues*, in New York City in October 1972, Mr. Gordy greets NAACP Executive Director Roy Wilkins (above) and chats with friends, including one of film's stars, Billy Dee Williams (c.). Below, Mr. Gordy congratulates his father, William Gordy Sr., on the elder Gordy's 50th wedding anniversary.

of the board and president of Motown Industries, Inc., he not only controls Motown Record Corporation (which still maintains offices and recording studios in Detroit) but other subsidiary companies which include Jobete Music, Stone Diamond Music Corporation and Stein & Van Stock, Inc.—all music publishing firms; Motown Productions, Inc.; Multimedia Management Co.; Motown, Inc., a New York City production office, and Motown-Weston-Furre Productions, which was formed to produce the movie, *Lady Sings the Blues*. Multimedia Management evolved from one of Mr. Gordy's first subsidiaries, International Talent Management Corporation (later International Management Corporation), which groomed some of Motown's most famous acts and supervised their careers.

With the aggressiveness which characterized his development of Motown, Mr. Gordy has also moved into other aspects of entertainment. *Lady Sings the Blues*, based on the life of Billie Holiday and starring Diana Ross, was his first film—one which brought Miss Ross a 1973 Academy Awards nomination as Best Actress. He has also produced television specials and the Broadway play, *Pippin*.

Berry Gordy's continued development, expansion and diversification of his giant firm—which grossed an estimated $50 million in 1972—was built on what he calls "love and character." Its success has been due, in large measure, to its founder's extraordinary business sense and his determination to succeed—a determination that simply refused to be frustrated.

91

Rear Admiral Samuel L. Gravely Jr.
United States Naval Officer

Navy's First Black Admiral
Climbed Every Step of the Way

"If something is worth doing, it is worth your best effort."

After he enlisted in the United States Naval Reserve on September 15, 1942, Samuel Lee Gravely's wife, Alma, recalls, "They were not letting Negroes do anything. He used to clean up the pool hall." Admiral Gravely for twenty-nine years has been climbing from the pool hall up through the ranks of the navy. During that time he never dreamed his climb was toward the rank of the navy's first black admiral.

He was born on June 4, 1922 in Richmond, Virginia, the son of Samuel Gravely, a Pullman porter and his wife, Mary. Young Samuel raised pigeons in the back yard, a hobby which carried over into his adult life. "Now that I'm commander of the Naval Communications Command," he says with a laugh, "some people claim I'm going to use my pigeons to carry messages. The truth is, I'm a pigeon fancier who raises them to eat."

Samuel Gravely attended Armstrong High School in Richmond, and Virginia Union University, from which he graduated with a bachelor of

Samuel L. Gravely Jr., rear admiral in U.S. Navy, director of Naval Communications and commander of Naval Communications Command; born June 4, 1922 in Richmond, Va.; Virginia Union University (A.B., 1948). Midshipmen's School of Columbia University. Wife: Alma Bernice Gravely. Children: Robert, David and Tracey. Address: Chief of Naval Operations, The Pentagon, Washington, DC 20530 (See full biographical sketch in Volume I.)

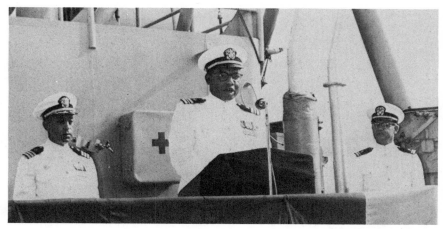

In 1961 at Pearl Harbor, Lt. Cmdr. Gravely is shown taking command of the escort ship, U.S.S. *Falgout*, becoming the first black man to command a warship in the navy.

arts degree in history in 1948. It was while he was at Virginia Union that he met his wife, Alma Clark, who was a student at Virginia State College at Petersburg. After boot training at the Naval Training Center in Great Lakes, Illinois, he reported in January, 1943 as a student at the Service School in Hampton (Va.) Institute. In May of that year, he was assigned to the Section Base, San Diego, California. From November, 1943 to June, 1944, he was a member of the V-12 Unit at the University of California at Los Angeles and later attended the Pre-Midshipmen School in Asbury Park, New Jersey.

Appointed midshipman in the United States Naval Reserve in August, 1944, he attended the midshipmen school at Columbia University in New York City and graduated in December of that year, the first black to do so. He was commissioned an ensign and his climb through the naval ranks began. He advanced to the rank of captain in 1967, having transferred from the United States Naval Reserve to the United States Navy on August 16, 1955.

After being commissioned an ensign in December, 1944, he reported as assistant battalion commander at the Naval Training Center in Great Lakes Naval Base near Chicago, Ill., where he remained until February, 1945. Following instruction at the Sub-Chaser Training Center in Miami, Florida, Ensign Gravely was assigned to the submarine chaser, USS *PC 1264*. He served on that vessel as communications officer, electronics officer and finally as executive officer and personnel officer. Released from active duty in 1946, he went back to Virginia Union to complete his education.

Ordered back to active naval service, he reported on August 30, 1949 as assistant to the officer in charge of recruiting at the Naval Recruiting Station and Office of Naval Officer Procurement in Washington, D.C. From October, 1951 to February, 1952, he had instruction in a short communications course at the Naval Postgraduate School in Monterey, California—after which he served as radio officer aboard the battleship USS *Iowa*. In June, 1953, he transferred to the heavy cruiser USS *Toledo*, on which he served as communications officer and in various other capacities, including that of assistant operations officer during the two following years. While serving on the *Toledo*, he learned a lesson from the ship's executive officer's apparently harsh treatment of him: "If

93

Adm. Gravely's daughter,
Tracey, welcomes him home
after promotion.

The new admiral leaves his ship
for the last time upon arrival at
San Diego, Cal. At right (below),
he talks with fellow officers on
grounds of naval base.

something is worth doing, it is worth your best effort.'' On both vessels he saw action in the Korean area for which he was awarded the Korean Presidential Unit Citation Ribbon given those ships.

Detached from the *Toledo* in July 1955, officer Gravely was assigned to Headquarters, Third Naval District, New York, where he served for two years as assistant district security officer. Between September and November, 1957, he had instruction in amphibious warfare attached to the Amphibious Training Command, Pacific Fleet which was headquartered at Coronado, California. He then joined the attack transport USS *Seminole* as operations officer. He had temporary duty while training for executive officer of a destroyer of the Staff of Commander Destroyer Squadron Seven and Five during the period August, 1959 to January, 1960. However, he became executive officer of the destroyer USS *Theodore E. Chandler*. On February 15, 1961, he was named commanding officer, relieving Commander G. C. Brown, and remained in command of that destroyer until October 21, 1961 when he again became her executive officer.

On January 31, 1962, he assumed command of the radar picket destroyer escort, USS *Falgout*, becoming the first black man ever to command a United States warship. The *Falgout*, based at Pearl Harbor, patrolled the Pacific Early Warning Barrier. From August, 1963 to June, 1964, he attended a senior course in naval warfare at the Naval College, Newport, Rhode Island, after which he served as national emergency airborne command post program manager at the Defense Communications Agency, Arlington, Virginia he was given command of the destroyer USS *Taussig* from January, 1966 to August, 1968, then reported as coordinator of the Navy Satellite Communications Program to the Office of the Chief of Naval Operations in Washington, D.C. In May, 1970, he assumed command of the USS *Jouett*, one of the navy's most modern guided-missile frigates.

At reception in his honor, Adm. Gravely and Mrs. Gravely greet a young Navy officer and (above, right) stand in receiving line with their children.

In April, 1971, at the age of forty-eight, Samuel Gravely, commanding officer of the USS *Jouett*, was sailing home to San Diego after seven months patrolling the waters off Vietnam when the announcement came that—along with astronaunt Alan Shepard and forty-seven other navy captains from a field of some two thousand candidates—he had been tapped for promotion to rear admiral.

"I will not be the last," he radioed back.

Admiral Gravely was not only the first black to be assigned to the Naval War College, and the first black to command a ship, he was now the first black admiral.

"I feel personally that since 1948 (the year the military services were ordered integrated by President Harry S Truman), my opportunities have been greater in the military than they would have been in civilian life." Admiral Gravely says, "But a guy who really wants to work and do a job can be a success anywhere. I think I would have been a success even in the post office."

The Gravelys spend an evening out with film star Joseph Cotton and Mrs. Cotton at the Virginia Museum in Richmond, Va.

Fannie Lou Hamer

Black Activist

Fannie Lou Hamer, black rights activist and founder of the Freedom Farm Cooperative and a garment factory in Ruleville, Miss.; vice chairman, Mississippi Freedom Democratic Party, born Oct. 6, 1917 in Ruleville. Husband: Perry Hamer. Address: 626 E. Lafayette St., Ruleville, MS 38771 (See full biographical sketch in Volume I.)

Mrs. Hamer is shown with an associate, Mrs. Ella Baker, during a meeting of the Mississippi Freedom Democratic Party in 1966.

At her Ruleville home, Mrs. Hamer and neighbors confer in yard with an agent of the U.S. Civil Rights Commission. Below, she is shown with Dr. Martin Luther King Jr. in march from Selma, Ala. in 1965.

Success for Her Is Measured by the Strides She Has Helped Blacks Make

"We'll be back. We won't give up the fight."

Fannie Lou Hamer first saw the light of day on October 6, 1917, on a tenant farm in Ruleville, Mississippi. She was the youngest of twenty children in a poverty-stricken family. By the time she was fifty, Mrs. Hamer had challenged the conscience of white America by waging a victorious battle against racism in her native state—a battle which won her the esteem and high regard of blacks all over the United States.

"We'll be back. We won't give up the fight," Mrs. Hamer vowed in 1964 when the Mississippi Freedom Democratic Party failed to be seated at the Democratic National Convention in Atlantic City, New Jersey. In 1968 she lived up to her words: she was one of twenty-two blacks in the forty-four-member group that unseated the regular (white)

97

Mississippi delegation at the Democratic convention in Chicago.

The road from Ruleville to the floor of a major party convention was not easy for Mrs. Hamer. When she was only six years old, she had to work in the cotton fields, toiling from sunup to sundown. "The family would pick fifty to sixty bales of cotton a year, so my father decided to rent some land," Mrs. Hamer recalled many years later. "He bought some mules and a cultivator. We were doing pretty well. He even started to fix up the house real nice and had bought a car. Then our stock got poisoned. We knew this white man had done it. He stirred up a gallon of Paris Green with the feed. When we got out there, one mule was already dead. The other two mules and the cow had their stomachs all swelled up. It was too late to save them. That poisoning knocked us right back down flat. We never did get back up again. That white man did it just because we were getting somewhere. White people never like to see Negroes get a little success. All of this stuff is no secret in the state of Mississippi."

The poisoning of her family's mules was but the first in a long series of tragic incidents that followed Fannie Lou Hamer for the rest of her life. She had to drop out of school to help with the family chores. She recalls having her feet wrapped in rags to take the place of shoes she could not afford. She remembers trudging across the bleak Mississippi landscape scavenging the cotton fields after the harvest for enough of the leftovers to make into a bale to buy food—which usually consisted of bread and a slice of onion with salt on it. And a limp, caused by a fall as an infant, has stayed with her all her life; her family could not afford proper medical care.

On August 31, 1962, Mrs. Hamer faced the first of a string of intimidations. That was the day when she and seventeen others went down to the county courthouse in Indianola, Mississippi, to try to register to vote. The police began to harass them the moment they arrived. "I wonder what they'll do?" the bus driver had asked Mrs. Hamer. Halfway back to Ruleville, he got his answer. Police stopped the bus and arrested everyone. The bus was "painted the wrong color," the police claimed.

When Mrs. Hamer returned to the plantation where she had lived for eighteen years, her oldest daughter met her and told her that the plantation owner was "mad and raisin' Cain." He had heard that Mrs. Hamer had tried to register. She had to move elsewhere. Less than two weeks later, night riders fired sixteen times into the home of one of the persons who had given her a place to stay.

Refusing to be intimidated, Mrs. Hamer began working in a voter registration movement. However, on June 3, 1963, while returning from a voter workshop in Charleston, South Carolina, she was arrested in

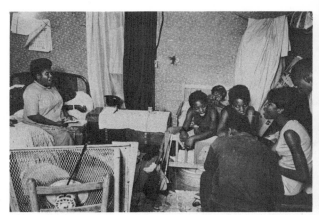

Mrs. Hamer is shown in her Ruleville home with neighborhood children. She is foster mother to two in the group. At right, she speaks before the 1968 Democratic National Convention in Chicago.

Winona, Mississippi, when she stepped off a bus to see what was happening to five blacks who had tried to use the rest room at the bus station. At the jail, she later remembered, "We could hear sounds of licks, and there was screaming in the back room, but we couldn't see. I could hear a man saying 'Can't you say "Yes sir," nigger?' " Later, three men took Mrs. Hamer into a cell along with two black men. "They made me lay down on the bunk and they gave one of the Negro men a long leather blackjack and told him to beat me—or else he knew what would happen to him. I was beat by that Negro man 'til he was exhausted. Then they had the second one beat me. . . . After I got out of jail, half dead, I found out that Medgar Evers had been shot down in his own yard."

But the countless threatening phone calls, the abusive letters and the reprisals taken against her husband, Perry, who was unable to find work for a long time because of her activities, did little to discourage Mrs. Hamer from continuing her fight against racist oppression. In fact, it fired her enthusiasm and gave her the determination to intensify her fight for justice. In addition to defeating the Mississippi political structure at the national party level, she embarked on two ambitious projects—a garment factory that provided jobs for residents of Ruleville, and a day-care center. She also launched the Freedom Farm Cooperative, a land development complex for raising and storing vegetables.

Housing, jobs, a new security, a new dignity for many in Mississippi are the fruits that have grown from Fannie Lou Hamer's determination to better the lives of black people.

Fannie Lou Hamer had a broad vision that neither she nor those to come after her would be trapped by the same exploitative system that had kept her parents impoverished. She continues hoping that she will live to see that broad vision become a reality.

99

Patricia Roberts Harris

Lawyer, Diplomat, Politician

Patricia Roberts Harris, attorney; born May 31, 1924 in Mattoon, Ill.; Howard University (B.A., 1945), George Washington University Law School (J.D., 1960). Husband: William Beasley Harris. Address: 600 New Hampshire Ave., N.W., Washington, DC 20037 (See full biography in Volume I.)

"If there is one thing that gives me satisfaction, it is law, the last refuge of the generalist, of which there are too few these days."

She Has Succeeded As Lawyer, Politician, Educator, Diplomat

Patricia Roberts Harris is a woman whose story is one of brilliant achievement as lawyer, educator, administrator, diplomat and politician.

Patricia Roberts was born May 31, 1924 in Mattoon, Illinois, the daughter of a railroad waiter. Her family descended from slaves who moved from Virginia to Illinois, then bought their freedom through indentured servitude. Patricia grew up in the flatland of Mattoon and later in Chicago. When she graduated from high school, she had the choice of five college scholarships. She decided on Howard University in Washington, D.C., and began an association with the institution that was to span many years. She established a distinguished academic record at Howard and, with the aid of two research assistantships,

Mrs. Harris is sworn in as U.S. ambassador to Luxembourg by Norman Armour Jr. as U.S. Secretary of State Dean Rusk looks on. Appointed in 1965 by President Lyndon Johnson, Mrs. Harris was the nation's first black woman ambassador.

Mrs. Harris is congratulated by President Johnson after her appointment as ambassador.

obtained her B.A. degree *summa cum laude* in 1945, following her election to Phi Beta Kappa.

At Howard, the future diplomat began her involvement in civil rights, openly denouncing racism in the United States. As the vice chairman of a student chapter of the National Association for the Advancement of Colored People (NAACP), she joined students in one of the earliest sit-ins—at a white restaurant in the heart of the black ghetto in Washington. During those early college days, she formed her belief in non-violent protest—a philosophy to which she has adhered throughout her life.

Patricia Roberts returned to Illinois in 1945 for two years of graduate work in industrial relations at the University of Chicago. Between 1946 and 1949, she was program director of the Chicago YWCA before returning to the nation's capital in 1949 to enroll in American University for further graduate study while serving as assistant director of the American Council on Human Rights. In 1953, she accepted the post of executive director of Delta Sigma Theta, a black sorority, at its national headquarters in Washington. She held that position until 1959 meanwhile marrying (in 1955) William Beasley Harris, a Washington attorney.

Knowing that the study of law was excellent training for many activities, Mrs. Harris obtained her law degree in 1960 at George Washington University. She was the first scholar in her class to receive the John Bell Larner Prize as well as membership in the Order of the Coif. "If there is one thing that gives me satisfaction," she says "it is law, the last refuge of the generalist, of which there are too few these days."

As an attorney for the United States government from 1960 to 1961, she worked in the appeals and research section of the criminal division of the Justice Department where she met Robert Kennedy, who became attorney general in 1961. After a year, Mrs. Harris left the department to become an associate dean of students and

In Luxembourg (from top, right), Mrs. Harris receives Council of State President Felix Welter; is saluted by Embassy's Marine guard; calls at home of prime minister; with her husband (l.), gives instructions to a servant.

lecturer in law at Howard University. In 1963, she resigned as dean but continued to teach as assistant professor of law. She was promoted to associate professor in 1965 and taught courses in constitutional law, torts, and government regulation of business.

In July, 1963, Mrs. Harris resigned as associate dean at Howard with the intention of joining her jusband's law practice in Washington, but President John F. Kennedy changed her plans by appointing her co-chairman of the National Women's Committee for Civil Rights. In that capacity, Mrs. Harris helped coordinate the activities of nearly one hundred national women's organizations.

After President Kennedy's assassination, President Johnson announced that he would appoint some fifty women to important government posts. Mrs. Harris was one of the first. In March, 1964, the president named her to the newly created Commission on the Status of Puerto Rico.

Impressed with her diplomatic skills, President Johnson on May 19, 1965 named her ambassador to Luxembourg. Her appointment won immediate approval from the United States Senate and she became the first black woman ambassador in the history of the United States. "I feel deeply proud and grateful that the president chose me to knock down this barrier, but also a little sad about being the first Negro woman because it implies we were not considered before," Mrs. Harris commented on her appointment.

Immediately upon taking her assignment, headlines splashed around the world concerning the black woman who charmed the Grand

102

Duchy of Luxembourg with her diplomacy, tact and wit. For two years, Ambassador Harris was the White House's link to Luxembourg. Resigning in 1967, she explained: "I have been on leave from Howard University too long, My heart has always been with teaching and law."

Mrs. Harris resumed her professorship of law at Howard, and was also appointed alternate delegate to the United Nations. In debate, the Harris style in the United Nations was characterized by confident and precise argument, reflecting careful homework on government policies and touches of personal experience.

In the late 1960s, Patricia Harris became well-known on national television. An ardent Democrat, she seconded the nomination of President Johnson for his second term. Her appearance on the Democratic platform committee again gave her nationwide exposure. On October 12, 1971, the Democratic National Committee's executive committee voted 9–3 to ask her to serve as temporary chairperson of the Credentials Committee for the Democratic party's 1972 convention in Miami, Florida. Mrs. Harris wielded a tough gavel during those tense meetings and won a further measure of respect. Today she is a partner in Fried, Frank, Harris, Shriver, and Kampelman, a distinguished law firm with offices in Washington, New York and London.

In her political activities, Mrs. Harris (from top, right) hosts a press conference to explain her role as chairman of the Credentials Committee of the 1972 Democratic National Convention; meets with Democratic Party Chairman Lawrence O'Brien; meets later with new chairman Robert Strauss; leaves her office at Party headquarters.

Mrs. Harris and her husband, William Beasley Harris, also an attorney, spend a moment together in their Washington, D.C. home.

Jerome Heartwell Holland

New York Stock Exchange Director

*Jerome H. Holland, director,
New York Stock Exchange;
born Jan. 9, 1916 in Auburn,
N.Y.; Cornell University (B.S.,
1939; M.S., 1941), University of
Pennsylvania (Ph.D, 1950);
wife: Laura Mitchell Holland;
children: Lucy, Joseph,
Jerome Jr. and Pamela.
Address: 270 Park Ave.,
New York, NY 10017
(See full biographical
sketch in Volume I.)*

Noted Educator Succeeds In World of Business and Finance

"Obstacles are no obstacles. There's always a way of getting something done."

In a capitalistic system such as that in the United States, any citizen who has money to invest can own an interest in the tools of production by buying stock in any of hundreds of firms. And an estimated thirty-two million persons do just that. The leading marketplace in which citizens' money and business securities come together is on the vast trading floor of the New York Stock Exchange. Each day, scores of member brokers of the exchange buy and sell, for thousands of investors, the stocks and bonds of the nation's leading corporations. The policy-making body of the exchange is a Board of Directors composed of ten representatives of the public, ten representatives of the securities industry, and a chairman. In 1972, Dr. Jerome Heartwell Holland became the first black man ever elected to the board. The distinguished former president of Hampton Institute and former United States Ambassador to Sweden was elected as a representative of the public for a two-year term.

Dr. Holland was born January 9, 1916 in Auburn, New York. The only one of five children to go to college (there were originally twelve but seven of them died), young Jerome was a high school football star and was encouraged by his parents—Robert Holland, who was a gardener and houseman for several families, and Viola Bagby Holland, a factory worker—and his teachers to get as much education as he could. "My parents were very religious people, strong in church memberships, and they belonged to many of the fraternal organizations, which in those days were extremely popular in the Negro community," Dr. Holland recalls.

Although blacks were a very small minority in Auburn—only about five hundred in a total population of some thirty-eight thousand—young Jerome experienced little racial discrimination. "Our family lived in the ninth ward, and most people there were first generation Italian, Polish and second and third generation Irish," he remembers. "No, there were no tensions then. Everyone was poor and you cooperated. It was the only means of survival. We helped one another. People weren't affluent then. Everybody backed the local baseball team, and if one person got into trouble the whole town turned out to help. You weren't conscious of racial prejudice as such, but you were conscious of race. There was the *Negro* church and the *Negro* fraternal orders, but the

An All-American end at Cornell University in Ithaca, N.Y., Jerome Holland was known as an excellent blocker and pass receiver.

Ambassador Holland greets touring Hampton Institute choir during its visit to Stockholm, Sweden.

schools were integrated."

After completing his public school education in Auburn, Jerome Holland entered the college of agriculture at Cornell University on a scholarship. He achieved an outstanding record as a student and as a football player. During his undergraduate and graduate years at Cornell, where he earned a master's degree in sociology, he was twice chosen (1937 and 1938) as an All-American end and was known as a superior blocker and defensive performer. (He was inducted into the College Football Hall of Fame in 1965 and was the recipient of the National Football Foundation's Distinguished American Award for 1972.)

He later enrolled at the University of Pennsylvania, where he earned a doctorate in sociology in 1950. His dissertation was on the wartime integration of blacks into the shipbuilding industry, a subject on which he gained first-hand insight in World War II as industry personnel director for a shipbuilding and dry dock company. While completing his doctoral requirements, he also taught sociology and physical education at Lincoln University in Pennsylvania.

At about this time, Dr. Holland, who had married shortly after he left Cornell and was the father of two children (Jerome Jr. and Pamela), divorced his first wife and went to Tennessee A & I State University where he became director of the division of social sciences and served as a coach on the football team. While there, he met Laura Mitchell, a psychology professor at Fisk University. The two married and have two children, Lucy and Joseph.

It was not long before word spread through academic circles that Dr. Holland was a very capable administrator, and when Delaware State College sought a new president in 1953, he was asked to assume the post—because, he says, "No one else wanted it. The school was in a hopeless state and I was told by the governor to either build it up or close it."

When Dr. Holland left the college in 1961 to become president of Hampton (Va.) Institute, he had set Delaware State on a decidedly upward course. The school had been accredited, saved from bankruptcy and had attracted about one hundred white students to the formerly all-black institution whose enrollment had risen to about eight hundred.

During his career at Hampton, which spanned ten years, Dr. Holland recorded one impressive achievement after another. In less than five years, the dynamic educator constructed three new buildings, the first since 1928, on the school's ailing campus. Moreover, he developed flexible and innovative educational programs such as internships with business and industry for students in commercial

106

Dr. Holland cuts ribbon to formally open electronics trade show for Scandinavian countries in Stockholm.

sciences, and a foreign student exchange program. In addition, he shifted the school's emphasis from teacher training to liberal arts, thus affording students the opportunity to acquire preparation for many jobs that traditionally had been somewhat inaccessible to blacks. Most notably, Dr. Holland continued at Hampton the strong efforts he had made at Delaware State to attract more white students to the institution.

Dr. Holland had acquired a distinguished reputation as an administrator and educator, and big business—including the nation's largest employer, the federal government—realized that he was a man of valuable talents. In January, 1970, President Richard M. Nixon appointed him United States ambassador to Sweden, hoping that the educator could resolve some of the tensions that existed between the two countries because of United States policy in Vietnam. When Dr. Holland arrived in Sweden a few months later to assume his post as a diplomat, he was the focus of demonstrations, physical threats and racist insults from anti-war demonstrators.

But while Dr. Holland was faced with anti-American sentiment throughout the two and one half years that he served as ambassador (he retired from the post in 1972 to join the board of directors of the New York Stock Exchange), few could deny his abilities as a diplomat. For example, there was improved cooperation between the two countries in business, science and government projects—all attributed to the ambassador.

No sooner had he joined the stock exchange than several American companies, subjected to criticism for failing to place blacks on their boards, also sought his expertise and competence as an executive, and he soon found himself on the boards of a number of major American businesses—unprecedented for a black person. Among the boards he joined were the General Cigar Company, Inc., American Telephone & Telegraph Company, General Foods Corporation, Manufacturers Hanover Trust Company, Union Carbide Corporation, Chrysler Corporation, Federated Department Stores, Fireman's Insurance Company, and the Continental Corporation.

Looking back over his life, Dr. Holland firmly believes: "Obstacles are no obstacles. There's always a way of getting something done."

A New York Stock Exchange director, Dr. Holland talks with fellow director Walter N. Frank on floor of the Exchange.

107

Richard Hunt

Sculptor

An Artist Who Feels the Responsibility to 'Locate Truth'

"I must work fast. Any artist, particularly a Negro, has a responsibility to locate the truth."

Richard Hunt, internationally known sculptor, has been working fast since he was fifteen years old to fulfill that responsibility to his art.

Richard Howard Hunt was born September 12, 1935 in Chicago,

Richard Hunt discusses his work in his spacious studio in Chicago, Ill.

Ill. to Howard Hunt, a barber, and his wife, Inez, a librarian.

What began as a series of informal classes at the Art Institute of Chicago in 1948 developed with the years into a brilliant art career, and Mr. Hunt today is widely considered one of the best young practitioners of what is called the "direct open-form medium." Much of his work is welded metal.

"When I was fifteen," he says, "I did a couple of clay and plaster sculptures and I got to liking that better than painting or drawing, so I started taking sculpture with a teacher at the Art Institute. She was my first big influence." The instructor in question was Nelli Bar, and it was not very long before her talented young pupil had established himself as a promising sculptor.

In June, 1953, Mr. Hunt graduated from Chicago's Englewood High School and entered the Art Institute on a scholarship provided by the Chicago Public School Art Society. He majored in art education. He later attended classes at the University of Chicago.

In 1956, at the age of twenty-one, Mr. Hunt received his first major award, the Mr. and Mrs. Frank G. Logan Prize, for his *Construction D.* The following year, in his senior term at the Art Institute, he was awarded a James Nelson Raymond Foreign Travel Fellowship and, upon graduating from the school, traveled and studied in England, France, Spain and Italy.

On November 18, 1957, while in Rome, he married Betty Scott, a former art student at the Chicago insitute. The Hunts returned home in the spring of 1958 and settled in Chicago.

Mr. Hunt was drafted into the army in September and did basic training at Fort Leonard Wood, Missouri, before reassignment to the Brooke Army Medical Training Center at Fort Sam Houston in San Antonio, Texas. He was discharged in June, 1960, as a private first class.

After discharge from the army he returned to Chicago, where he was an instructor at the Art Institute until mid-1961. Shortly after his return, he again was the recipient of the Logan Prize. He taught in the department of architecture and art at the University of Illinois' Chicago campus until mid-1962 and was later the winner of still another Logan Prize, the Walter H. Campana Memorial Prize and a John Simon Guggenheim Fellowship. On September 10, 1962 a daughter, Cecilia Elizabeth, was born.

In 1964, Mr. Hunt joined the teaching staff at Chouinard Art School in Los Angeles as a visiting professor. During 1965, he was visiting artist at Yale and Purdue universities. He received a fellowship to work at the Tamarind Lithography Workshop in Los Angeles, California in 1965. The program was funded by the Program in Humanities and

Richard Howard Hunt, sculptor; born Sept. 12, 1935 in Chicago, Ill.; studied sculpture with Nelli Bar (1950–53), studied at the University of Chicago (1953–55), graduate of the School of The Art Institute of Chicago (B.A.E., 1957); has participated in numerous exhibitions; has won numerous prizes; John Simon Guggenheim Fellow (1962–63). Wife: Betty. Daughter: Cecilia. Address: 1503 N. Cleveland Ave., Chicago, IL 60610 (See full biographical sketch in Volume I.)

the Arts of the Ford Foundation, and the entire lithographic production during his association with the workshop was given to the Museum of Modern Art in New York City.

The following year, Mr. Hunt was included among *Ten Negro Artist from the United States*, organized as a part of the First World Festival of Negro Arts in Dakar, Senegal.

During 1966, Mr. Hunt was visiting professor at Northern Illinois and Northwestern universities and was later appointed a member of the National Council of Arts by President Lyndon B. Johnson. The following year he returned to academic work as visiting artist at Wisconsin State University and Southern Illinois University.

With few exceptions, Mr. Hunt has worked in expressionist sculpture using metal materials, although he refuses to assign a label to his preferred medium. His works may be viewed in the permanent collections museums in Chicago, New York, Cleveland, Milwaukee, Buffalo and Israel.

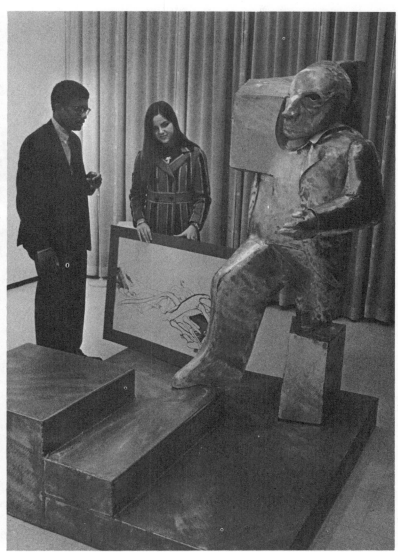

A dedicated craftsman, Mr. Hunt, who frequently works in sheet metal, uses some of the skills, including welding, which are involved in his work. Among his works is a stylistic study of an early black leader in Cook County, Ill. He discusses the work with Anne Louise Howard, a niece of Sen. Hubert H. Humphrey.

111

Jesse L. Jackson

Clergyman and Black Activist

He Succeeds in Leading Thousands Under the Banner of Operation PUSH

The Reverend Jesse L. Jackson, national president of Operation PUSH (People United to Save Humanity); born Oct. 8, 1941 in Greenville, S.C.; North Carolina A & T University (B.A., sociology, 1964), studied at Chicago Theological Seminary on a Rockefeller Foundation grant; ordained as a Baptist minister (1968). Wife: Jacqueline Brown Jackson. Children: Santita, Jesse Jr., Jonathan Luther and Yusef DuBois. Address: 930 E. 50th St., Chicago, IL 60615 (See full biographical sketch in Volume I.)

"It ain't nothing new for God to speak through imperfect people."

He calls himself "The Country Preacher," and since the murder in 1968 of Dr. Martin L. King Jr. in Memphis, Tennessee, the Reverend Jesse Louis Jackson is the person who has emerged as the most likely heir to Dr. King's pre-eminent position in the civil rights movement.

Born October 8, 1941 in Greenville, South Carolina, Jesse Jackson declined a baseball contract with the Chicago White Sox team to attend college after starring in football, baskeball and baseball at Greenville's all-black Sterling High School.

He accepted an athletic scholarship to attend the University of Illinois in 1959 but transferred to North Carolina A & T University a year later after being informed by a coach at Illinois that, ability notwithstanding, blacks were supposed to be linemen and not quarterbacks on the school's football team.

Rev. Jackson and Stax Records president Al Bell salute as the Black National Anthem, "Lift Ev'ry Voice and Sing," is played at the 1972 Wattstax festival in Los Angeles, Cal. Below, after speaking at the 1972 NAACP convention in Detroit, Mich., Rev. Jackson hugs NAACP Executive Director Roy Wilkins.

Jesse Jackson continued to distinguish himself as an athlete at North Carolina A & T, but the events which did most to determine his future course occurred in 1963 when he became leader of the student sit-in campaign in downtown Greensboro. He led the almost daily protest marches for ten months before integration came to the city's theaters, restaurants and other public facilities. In recognition of his efforts, Mr. Jackson was elected president of the newly created North Carolina Intercollegiate Council on Human Rights.

Following his graduation from college in 1964 with a bachelor's degree in sociology, Mr. Jackson was named field representative of the Congress of Racial Equality for the southeastern United States, a post he held until he accepted a grant from the Rockefeller Foundation to attend the Chicago Theological Seminary. In Chicago, Mr. Jackson became active in the Coordinating Council of Community Organizations, a coalition of civil rights and civic organizations working with Dr. Martin Luther King Jr.

In 1966, at the behest of local leaders, Dr. King, president of the Southern Christian Leadership Conference, named Mr. Jackson Chicago director of SCLC's Operation Breadbasket, an organization which had been established in 1962 to change, through economic boycotts, racist hiring and promotion policies at business concerns. Although he left his studies at the seminary to work full time with Operation Breadbasket, Jesse Jackson was ordained as a Baptist minister on June 30, 1968, almost a year after he was named national director of Operation Breadbasket.

On April 4, 1968, when Dr. King's life was snuffed out by the bullet of an assassin, the Reverend Jackson, by now a protégé of Dr. King, was among those standing with him on the balcony of the Lorraine Motel in Memphis.

113

As the first national director of SCLC's Operation Breadbasket, Rev. Jackson leads a boycott of A & P supermarkets in Chicago (left), and signs a jobs agreement with Norman A. Stepelton, president of the National Tea Co., as Breadbasket and National Tea officials look on.

The day following Dr. King's death, Chicago Mayor Richard J. Daley pledged, at a City Council meeting, a "commitment to the goals for which Dr. King stood." Arriving at the meeting from Memphis, the Reverend Jackson stood in a sweater stained with Dr. King's blood and shouted to the politicians present: "His blood is on the hands of you who would not have welcomed him here yesterday."

The gesture was but one example of "The Country Preacher's" impatience with injustice and of his determination to expose those who, he says, "seek to brutalize and violate black humanity."

The Reverend Jackson's prominence began to increase as he led Operation Breadbasket. With his brash and persuasive style, he made Breadbasket a household word. Thousands attended his regular Saturday morning rallies in Chicago, and the meeting place was moved several times to accommodate the large crowds.

One of the Reverend Jackson's first major victories as director of Operation Breadbasket came in July, 1968 after Breadbasket staff members found that A & P food stores in Chicago's black community were not complying with a pledge made a year earlier to hire 770 blacks.

Cited for his work in Chicago, Rev. Jackson receives the 1972 Gold Oilcan Award of the Chicago Economic Development Corporation from Alvin Boutte, president of Chicago's Independence National Bank, and CEDC Executive Director Garland Guice. At right, during a 1972 visit to Liberia, he is given a watch by the country's president, William R. Tolbert Jr.

When further negotiations between A & P and Breadbasket broke down, a boycott was called. Within a couple of weeks, all of the forty A & P stores in black areas were being picketed. "It was a process," the Reverend Jackson recalls, "of squeezing a company's vitals, and a company's vitals is its profit margin."

Indeed, after fourteen weeks, A & P capitulated and signed a "covenant" with Breadbasket calling for a variety of changes ranging from the use of black janitorial and extermination services and letting of building contracts to blacks to the use of black media to advertise and the promise of investment of funds in black banks.

While under the direction of the Reverend Jackson, Operation Breadbasket also sponsored Black Expo—the first of a series of massive expositions—where black businessmen were given an opportunity to sell and display their wares; youngsters were given an opportunity to see top-drawer entertainment acts at reduced prices, and black artists were able to receive exposure the likes of which they had never experienced.

In December, 1971, after four years as head of Operation

While leading "Black Solidarity Week" in Pittsburgh, Pa. in 1972, Rev. Jackson meets in Pennsylvania state capital with (l. to r.) Secretary of State Mrs. C. Delores Tucker, Pennsylvania House of Representatives Majority Leader K. Leroy Irvis, labor activist Nate Smith (chairman of Black Solidarity Week) and Gov. Milton Shapp. At right, above (top photo), he and Mrs. Jackson greet guests at a party in their home: attorney A. Benjamin Johnson of Philadelphia, Pa. (l.), Howard University president James E. Cheek and Chicago mortgage broker Dempsey Travis. In bottom photo, Rev. Jackson and his children shop for shoes.

Breadbasket, the Reverend Jackson resigned the post following a number of disputes with the Reverend Ralph D. Abernathy, who succeeded Dr. King as president of SCLC. On Christmas Day, the Reverend Jackson announced the birth of his new organization, Operation PUSH (People United to Save Humanity).

As president of the new economic organization, he has continued to press large white business concerns to deal more equitably with blacks. He established covenants in 1972 with two major companies—General Foods, Inc. and Schlitz Brewers of St. Louis—totaling more than $150 million.

Operation PUSH has opened offices in New York City, Los Angeles, Memphis, Columbus (Ohio), and in a number of other cities. It intends to establish a network of PUSH operations in key cities throughout the United States.

In another effort to further black economic independence, the Reverend Jackson visited Liberia in 1972 and discussed with leaders, including President William R. Tolbert Jr., the possibility of American blacks establishing dual citizenship with the African nation. The Reverend Jackson noted that the move would further "concretize" the historic ties between American blacks and Africans and also would serve to increase the political power of blacks.

116

During an Operation PUSH fund-raising party in the Playboy Mansion in Chicago, Rev. Jackson talks with one of his staunchest supporters, Hugh M. Hefner, editor and publisher of *Playboy* magazine.

As a leader of a "reform delegation" from Illinois to the 1972 Democratic National Convention, Rev. Jackson leaps with joy as a delegation led by Chicago Mayor Richard J. Daley is denied seats.

Through all his efforts, the Reverend Jackson has become one of the top black civil rights leaders in the country and has attracted a following which includes top businessmen and entertainers as well as the "common folks" who form the nucleus of his support group.

The handsome and charismatic activist often has been accused of ignoring the advice of his colleagues and of refusing to recognize and deal with his faults, but he responds, "It ain't nothing new for God to speak through imperfect people. Too many people concentrate on my charisma. They never seem to realize that I also have some intelligence, some brainpower, too."

The Reverend Jackson lives on Chicago's South Side with his wife, the former Jacqueline Lavinia Brown, whom he married while a senior in college, and their four children, Santita, Jesse Jr., Jonathan Luther and Yusef DuBois.

117

Michael Jackson

Lead Singer, the Jackson Five

Michael Jackson, lead singer of the Jackson Five; born Aug. 29, 1958 in Gary, Ind.; introduced to Motown recording star Diana Ross by Gary's Mayor Richard G. Hatcher, the Jackson Five became the biggest act in Motown Records history; the brothers now live in Los Angeles where Michael attends school. Address: Motown Record Corp., 6464 Sunset Blvd., Los Angeles, CA 90028 (See full biographical sketch in Volume I.)

Michael displays flair which made fans dub him the "little prince of soul."

A Pop Culture Hero Before He Was Thirteen

". . . we practiced a lot, and then we started entering talent shows and we won every one we entered."

Michael Jackson, the lead singer and youngest of the Jackson Five, emerged as a pop culture hero before he was twelve years old. At airports, teenagers chase him. In homes, posters featuring his famous smile are tacked on the walls of his fans' rooms. "Michael-mania" is a phenomenon which captures not only the young but the old. Young Michael, dressed in a burst of pastel colors during his concerts, sings and dances, and teeny-boppers and older ladies alike are caught up in the frenzy.

How, an unbelieving observer of "Michael-mania" may ask, did it all begin?

"We started singing together after Tito (one of his brothers) started messin' with Dad's guitar and singin' with the radio," Michael recalls. "It was Tito who decided we should form a group and we did, and we practiced a lot, and then we started entering talent shows and we won

118

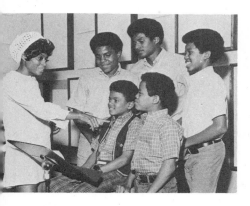

The Jackson Five are (front) Michael and Marlon and (back row) Tito, Jackie and Jermaine. At left, Michael takes charge during a show. Below, Diana Ross coaches the group shortly after she discovered them. In bottom photo, Motown president Berry Gordy Jr. supervises a TV show.

every one we entered."

Dubbed the "little prince of soul," Michael—with his four brothers, Sigmund (Jackie), Marlon, Jermaine and Toriano (Tito)—has become part of the biggest money-making team in the history of Motown Record Corporation, the recording organization which gave the world the Supremes, the Temptations and other famous groups.

Many critics braved the Jackson Five concert trail, littered with pre-teen screamers, and survived the ordeal to praise the dynamic group. One remarked: "The Jackson Five, led by young Michael Jackson, is undoubtedly the most popular act in show business and, in general appeal, second only to the Rolling Stones in current concert business."

Those persons who have followed the Jackson Five career know the story of the young men's discovery.

Motown recording star Diana Ross was appearing in Gary, Indiana, when the city's black mayor, Richard G. Hatcher, brought the youngsters to her attention. Miss Ross heard the super-charged group and was impressed. So captivated was she by young Michael in particular that she called her boss, Berry Gordy Jr., at Motown, and in a matter of weeks the names of Michael Jackson and the Jackson Five were being heard everywhere.

The group was soon recording both singles and albums and appearing on television in "The Ed Sullivan Show," "Hollywood Palace" and "The Andy Williams Show." "Goin' Back to Indiana" was their own popular special for ABC-TV. In 1970, the group ranked tops in single-record sales and was Number One in album sales for new artists. In the fall of 1971, young television viewers were treated to a Saturday morning television series in which the singing wonders from Indiana were featured in animated cartoons.

Michael and his brothers have adjusted well to their popularity. Though he is no longer frightened by flashing cameras and the push of admiring fans, he leads a sheltered life under the care of his parents, Joseph and Katherine Jackson.

Michael was born in Gary on August 29, 1958. He now lives in Los Angeles where the family occupies a sprawling ranch-style home. Memories of their past life in Gary, where the boys' father worked as a crane operator, are a constant reminder that "we were and still are just ordinary folks." In the old days, Mr. Jackson played the guitar and wrote songs for relaxation. As the children grew older, they would join their father in music sessions. As Mr. Jackson says: "It was fun; the kids liked it and it was one sure way of keeping them home and not roaming in the streets of Gary. The neighborhood we lived in offered a lot of ways to get into trouble."

Honored guests almost everywhere they appear, the Jackson Five are presented the Key to New York City (left) by Deputy Mayor Edward Hamilton. In front is Randy, youngest member of the group. Above (right), the group is received in London by the Queen Mother. At right, comedian Flip Wilson (r.) presents them the 1970 Image Award of the Hollywood Branch NAACP.

Michael and his brothers—there are nine Jackson children in all—are protected from trouble in some elaborate ways. There are, of course, security men with them when they travel, and their home is guarded by a special fence and watchdogs.

At home, in his private life, Michael is "just an average guy." He spends his hours away from the stage and recording studios playing baseball and basketball, swimming and studying. He attends a school near his home and a tutor accompanies him when he is on the road. All of his activities, including recording sessions and tours, are planned so that there is no interference with his education. Michael receives a small weekly allowance and usually ends his days—whether at home or traveling from city to city—playing card games, Scrabble or Monopoly, with his brothers.

Michael has now ventured out on his own and made successful solo albums. And in 1972 he sang the title song in the film *Ben*.

At their large home in Los Angeles, Cal., Michael and his brothers jog (above) and play a game of basketball (left) to keep physically fit for their strenuous performances.

England's Queen Mother praised him and his brothers during their royal command performance in London in the same year. Also in 1972, Michael and the Jackson Five drew a standing-room-only crowd at their performances at PUSH Expo in Chicago, and Michael won praise for his appearance on the Diana Ross television special, "Diana."

Michael, like each of the Jackson Five, has earned a lot of money. It is said that he could "retire at age fifteen if he wants to." However, he still believes his father's reminder: "There are no short cuts to success. It comes from hard work and constant practice. And once success is achieved it is all the more important that the successful person remembers where he came from—and acts accordingly."

Major General Daniel James Jr.
Deputy Assistant Secretary of Defense

Despite Racism, He Became One of America's Highest-Rated Flying Aces

"It's not easy to make it . . . but I do say that, in America, everything is possible."

Daniel James Jr., the youngest child in a blue-collar family of seventeen children, was born February 11, 1920 in Pensacola, Florida. Later, he would overcome U.S. armed forces racism to become the second black American promoted to the rank of general in the U.S. Air Force and the fourth in the history of the military services.

As a child, Daniel had to walk two and a half miles past three modern, beautifully equipped schools to reach the dilapidated, ill-staffed school that black children had to attend. He soon learned about inequality. Park benches, rest room doors, bus and train station waiting rooms—virtually everything in Pensacola—were labeled "colored" and "white." "Everywhere I turned I was reminded that I was different and supposedly inferior," he remembers. After graduating from Washington High School in 1937, he enrolled at Tuskegee Institute in Alabama. He earned a degree in physical education, took flying lessons and became a licensed pilot and flight instructor before entering what was then the Army Air Corps. It was at Tuskegee that he

At Ubon Royal Thai Air Force Base in 1967, then Colonel James stands (opposite page) in front of one of the F4C Phantoms he flew on 78 missions over Vietnam. At right, he reports personally to President Lyndon B. Johnson on aspects of the air war.

Maj. Gen. Daniel James Jr., U.S. deputy assistant secretary of defense; born Feb. 11, 1920 in Pensacola, Fla.; Tuskegee Institute, aviation cadet program (commissioned, 1943), Air Command and Staff School (1956). Wife: Dorothy Watkins James. Children: Danice, Daniel III and Claude. Address: The Pentagon, Washington, DC 20301 (See full biographical sketch in Volume I.)

was dubbed "Chappie" (after a nickname given his brother Charles, who was an All-American football player at Florida A & M University).

There were two important events in David James' life about this time. First, on November 3, 1942, he married the former Dorothy Watkins. (They now have three children, Danice, Daniel III and Claude.) But two months later, he grew restless watching the men he had trained go off to war. So early in 1943, he volunteered for the Army Air Corps as a cadet and received his commission as second lieutenant in July, 1943. He completed fighter pilot combat training at Selfridge Field, Michigan, and over the next six years was assigned to various fighter units in the United States.

However, during his tenure at Selfridge, Cadet James participated in what he came to regard as "the first sit-in." In 1943 he and about one hundred other black cadets refused to accept the segregated policies in effect at the air base. They were all arrested and threatened with court-martial, but they held their ground and the charges were dropped. In September, 1949, First Lieutenant James was ordered to the Philippines as a flight leader in the 12th Fighter Bomber Squadron, 18th Fighter Wing. From there, in July, 1950, he went to Korea, where he flew 101 combat missions and became known as "The Black Panther." The panther in this case symbolized the all-black 99th Pursuit Squadron that flew combat missions in Europe during World War II. Lieutenant James

123

As his wife, Dorothy, holds a Bible, and his son, Claude, looks on, Maj. Gen. James is sworn-in by U.S. Secretary of Defense Melvin R. Laird as deputy assistant secretary of defense (public affairs). At right, in his new role, he briefs the press on the status of U.S. prisoners of war in Vietnam.

instructed black pilots during the war. It was usual for Air Force units and individual pilots to adopt an insignia. Therefore, when the Air Force integrated and Lieutenant James was assigned to Korea, he adopted the black panther as his personal sign. "I wore the panther on my helmet all through Korea and in Vietnam and I still wear it," he says. "Mine started long before the infamous Black Panthers came into being."

During the next four years, "the Panther" was assigned to various military operations: first as an all-weather jet pilot and eventually as the commander of the 60th Fighter Interceptor Squadron, a post he assumed in August, 1955. During this same four-year period, Lieutenant James was promoted to captain (October, 1950), major (September, 1952) and lieutenant colonel (August, 1956). In 1956, he was assigned to the Pentagon as a staff officer in the Office of the Deputy Chief of Staff for Operations, Air Defense Division. The next ten years found him functioning in several different Air Force posts, including the Bentwaters Royal Air Force Station in England, where in February, 1961 he became Assistant Director of Operations of the 81st Fighter Wing, later moving to command of the 92nd Tactical Fighter Squadron, and ultimately becoming Deputy Wing Commander for Operations.

On his return to the U.S. in September 1964, Lieutenant Colonel James was assigned to Davis-Monthan Air Force Base, Arizona, where he was director of operational training and later deputy commander for operations of the 4453d Combat Training Wing, flying F-4Cs. In November of that year, he was promoted to the rank of colonel.

His career took a sharp upward turn in December, 1966, when he was assigned to Ubon Royal Thai Air Base in Thailand as deputy commander for operations of the 8th Tactical Fighter Wing. His work was so impressive that on June 4, 1967, he was appointed vice

124

Attending the 125th anniversary celebration of Liberian independence, Maj. Gen. James is greeted at the Liberian Embassy in Washington, D.C. by Ambassador Edward Peal (c.) and Counselor-First Officer James B. Freeman. At right, he attends a garden party in his honor and is welcomed by his host, Washington restaurateur Billy Simpson (l.)

Before speaking to students at the University of Arkansas at Pine Bluff, Maj. Gen. James "gets his Afro together" with a hair pick.

commander. As a member of the famed "Wolfpack," he flew 78 combat missions into North Vietnam, many in the Hanoi-Haiphong area. He personally led a flight in the "Bolo" MIG-sweep in which seven Communist MIGs were destroyed, the highest total one-day kill for any unit in the Vietnam war. When he returned from Southeast Asia in December, 1967, he was personally debriefed by President Lyndon B. Johnson.

He was assigned as vice commander of the 33rd Tactical Fighter Wing at Eglin Air Force Base, Florida. Despite his competence, Colonel James had rough experiences in the services. But he had what it took to survive, grow and move up. For this, he credits his parents who were, he says, "strong patriots."

"My mother taught us all the basics—love of God, love of country, love of fellow man," he once commented. "She used to say, 'Don't be part of the problem. Always contribute to the solution.' My mother was the greatest single influence in my life. She used to say things like 'always perform in such a manner and live your lives in such a way that you eliminate all the reasons they give for saying you're not ready. If they say you're dirty, make sure you're clean. If they say you're dumb, make sure you learn. If they say you're afraid, make sure you're brave, my son. And don't be so busy practicing your right to dissent that you forget your responsibility to contribute.' "

"Chappie" James, who was promoted to brigadier general on March 31, 1970, was assigned on the same day to the Pentagon as a deputy assistant secretary of defense, a position that made him the third-ranking official in the Pentagon's public affairs division. He was promoted to the rank of major general on August 1, 1972.

General James sees his career as proof that in America anyone can succeed as long as he has the commitment, the determination and the will.

"It puts the lie to the stories that you can't make it if you happen to be a member of a minority group or come from certain sections of the country," he has said. "It's not easy to make it with these handicaps, but I do say that, in America, everything is possible."

125

George E. Johnson
Cosmetics Manufacturer

From an Idea for a New Product Has Grown a Giant Cosmetics Empire

George E. Johnson, president, Johnson Products Co., Inc. in Chicago, Ill.; born June 16, 1927 in Richton, Miss.; graduated from Wendell Phillips High School in Chicago; chairman of the board, Independence Bank of Chicago; member, board of directors, Commonwealth Edison Co.; member, board of governors, U.S. Postal Service, and member of numerous civic and professional groups. Wife: Joan. Sons: Eric and John. (See full biographical sketch in Volume I.)

"No one is qualified to change the system he does not understand. Education brings that understanding."

George Ellis Johnson started making money when he was only six years old by collecting and selling old newspapers, milk and pop bottles, rags and other junk from his neighborhood. On his ninth birthday, in 1936, his mother apparently realized his potential as an entrepreneur: she proposed and financed his first real business venture by having a janitor in the building where they lived build him a shoeshine box—a "first class" one.

Early on Saturday mornings, George would get up and walk the thirty-four blocks from his home on Chicago's South Side to the

126

A view of the Johnson Products Co. headquarters in Chicago, Ill. Recent new construction added additional space to the sprawling office-plant complex.

downtown area to hustle customers for "the best spit shine in town."

Since that time, George Johnson has not been without a means of earning money. And he eventually masterminded a $500 loan into Johnson Products Company, the multi-million-dollar Ultra Sheen cosmetics firm.

Mr. Johnson was born June 16, 1927 in Richton, Mississippi. His mother moved to Chicago when he was about two. Until he was in high school, he worked on jobs ranging from selling newspapers to running errands. After graduating from Wendell Phillips High School, he began working days as a production chemist for Fuller Products (a black cosmetics concern in Chicago) and evenings as a busboy at a hotel, netting $150 a week to support his wife, Joan, and two small sons, Eric and John. (The family eventually grew to include two other children—Joan Marie and George Jr.).

It was during his employment with the Fuller organization that Mr. Johnson gained the confidence and determination to succeed as a businessman. In fact, he credits S. B. Fuller with giving him the desire to succeed.

But in the business world, it would take more than creative imagination to realize his dreams, Mr. Johnson soon discovered. Moreover, the aspiring young businessman was often a victim of racism. For example, when he went to a finance company to borrow $250 to go into partnership with a black barber, the loan officer with whom he had previously dealt, turned him down. "He said my idea was ridiculous," Mr. Johnson remembers. "So three days later, I went to another branch of the same loan company and told them I wanted to take my wife to California on vacation. In ten minutes the loan was okayed."

That experience taught Mr. Johnson a lesson. He came to understand that financial institutions in the United States had their own special kind of racism, a kind which perpetuates the system in which blacks are always consumers rather than manufacturers. A year later, in attempting to arrange a $500 loan through a bank where he then had "a small but active account," he was prepared for the situation. "The bank officer laughed at me. He wouldn't even give me an application form," Mr. Johnson says. "I immediately took my money out and put it

127

Mr. Johnson and Edwin C. Berry look over some
of the scores of applications for scholarship
assistance that came from students across the
U.S. after the announcement of the George E.
Johnson Educational Fund, established in 1972
with a personal gift of $1 million from Mr. Johnson.
Mr. Berry is administrative officer of the Fund.

The George E. Johnson family includes (front) George Jr. and Joan Marie, and (l. to r., back row) Eric, Mrs. Joan Johnson, John and George E. Johnson Sr.

in another unsympathetic bank. That's one reason that when the opportunity came in 1964 to organize a black bank, I took it.''

Mr. Johnson eventually became chairman of the board of the bank he helped organize, the Independence Bank of Chicago, and watched the firm grow, in less than ten years, from an $800,000 institution to one with assets of more than $20 million in 1972.

But the road from busboy to bank director was not easy. Getting adequate financing was only half the battle that Mr. Johnson had to wage against the corporate world. He had come up with a hair straightener for men, but he still had to find a way to market and distribute his product.

129

Mr. Johnson, who is chairman of the board of the Independence Bank of Chicago, visits the office of the bank's president, Alvin Boutte.

His wife proved the truth of the saying that behind every successful man there is an understanding woman. "In 1954 when I decided to market a hair product, most people I talked with about it said I was nuts to jeopardize my wife and two small children and a job I had held for ten years on a wild idea," Mr. Johnson says. "But Joan kept saying to me, 'George, if you believe you can do it, I know you can.' Not only did she have faith in me, she was willing to take the risk and she took a job so that I could afford to quit my evening job at a downtown restaurant. This allowed me time to pursue my idea. The faith my wife had in me was a great source of my inspiration."

Fortunately for Mr. Johnson, the men's hair straightener won immediate and widespread acceptance. In 1957, Johnson Products Company was incorporated and a product named Ultra Wave Hair Culture began to find its way onto store shelves.

"My wife took over the office," Mr. Johnson recalls. "I taught my brother, John, to produce the product, and I hit the road to build national distribution." In less than a year, the demand for the Ultra Wave product encouraged Mr. Johnson to introduce three hair-straightening and hair-conditioning products for women. These were presented to the public under the Ultra Sheen label and were distributed through beauty shops. Until this time, black women had usually straightened their hair with hot combs.

Based on his initial success, Mr. Johnson sat down and made a fifteen-year projection. He aimed for $1 million in sales by the end of 1964, at least $10 million by the end of 1969, and $50 million by 1975. The impressive record of growth his company experienced in its first decade indicated realization of that goal. For example, in 1970, annual sales were more than $12.6 million. Thus, it was not surprising that in 1971 Johnson Products Company, Inc. became the first black-owned corporation to be listed on a major stock exchange, the American Stock Exchange. While Mr. Johnson realized the advantage of "going public," he still retained the controlling interest in his company. Even after selling 300,000 shares of the stock (which netted $7,890,000) he was left with 83 percent control of the company, which employed some 250 persons in 1972.

Mr. Johnson has begun returning a substantial portion of his earnings to the black community, primarily through the George E. Johnson Foundation. In 1972, he earmarked $1 million of his personal funds for business education scholarships for minority students. The project, designated as the George E. Johnson Educational Fund, was designed "to create opportunities for inner city youths who have the potential for success in school and business, but who are excluded by most scholarship selection processes." In accepting the

Mr. Johnson receives the Humanitarian of the Year Award at a Chicago dinner in February 1972. At left is Robert Wallace, president of the Exchange National Bank of Chicago; at right is Harry Paine, president of Chicago's Abraham Lincoln Center.

Humanitarian Service Award in February, 1972, Mr. Johnson said: "No one is qualified to change the system he does not understand. Education brings that understanding."

In effect, Mr. Johnson made it possible for many blacks with an interest in business to escape many of the hardships and inequities with which he had to cope.

After Johnson Products Co. became the first black-owned firm on the American Stock Exchange, Amex Senior Floor Official James J. Maguire presents ticker tape to Mr. and Mrs. Johnson.

John H. Johnson
Magazine Publisher and Editor

John H. Johnson speaks at the 1972 dedication ceremony for his company's new headquarters building in Chicago, Ill. The building, costing more than $8 million, is the first one ever built by blacks in downtown Chicago.

A $500 Loan Started Him on the Road to Success

"I guess my formula for success is picking attainable goals, then achieving them. Once you have achieved one goal, the success will give you the confidence to reach the next."

Perhaps more than any other black man in recent time, John H. Johnson, president of Johnson Publishing Company, Inc. and publisher-editor of *Ebony*, *Jet*, *Black Stars*, *Black World* and *Ebony Jr!* magazines, personifies the truth that it *is* possible to achieve success in life despite great odds. In little more than thirty years, Mr. Johnson, whose family once was on welfare, built the largest black-owned publishing empire in the world.

John Johnson and his mother, Mrs. Gertrude Johnson Williams, moved to Chicago, Illinois in 1933 after attending the Century of Progress Exposition there. Mrs. Williams was convinced that her son's

John Harold Johnson, president of Johnson Publishing Co., Inc. in Chicago, Ill., editor and publisher of Ebony, Jet, Black Stars, Black World *and* Ebony Jr! *magazines; owner or holds controlling interest in other business enterprises; attended the University of Chicago and Northwestern University; numerous honorary degrees. Wife: Eunice. Children: John Jr. and Linda. Address: 820 S. Michigan Ave., Chicago, IL 60605 (See full biographical sketch in Volume I)*

chances for a better life would be far greater in Chicago than they ever would be in Arkansas City, Arkansas, the little Mississippi River town where he was born on January 19, 1918. His father was killed in a sawmill accident when John was six years old.

"We arrived in Chicago during the Depression," Mr. Johnson recalls, "and my most vivid memories are that we were always very, very poor. But I knew that my mother was doing all that she could do. And since just about everybody else was poor in those days, I never had any special feeling of being deprived. We were poor and we didn't like it. We had to go on welfare for about a year and we didn't like that either. Both my mother and I were determined that we weren't going to stay on welfare; we were determined to move out of that category. We worked always toward doing better, toward having a better life. We never had any doubts that we would."

John Johnson first began to distinguish himself while a student at Chicago's DuSable High School. Though he worked part-time for the National Youth Administration, he studied hard enough to graduate from DuSable with honors in 1936. And he had been president of the student council, president of his class, editor of the school newspaper and editor of the class yearbook. For his achievements, he was honored at an Urban League luncheon along with other honor students. The main speaker was Harry H. Pace, the president of Supreme Life Insurance Company of America. "When the luncheon ended," Mr. Johnson recalls, "I walked up to Mr. Pace and told him how much I had enjoyed his speech. He asked me what my plans were and I told him I wanted to go to college but didn't have enough money. He offered me an opportunity to work part-time at Supreme while going to college part-time. That sounded like a pretty good idea, so I accepted the offer."

Young Johnson began work in the Supreme Life office on September 1, 1936 as an all-around assistant on *The Supreme Liberty Guardian*, the insurance company's house magazine. He took copy to the printer, read proofs, saw that the photographs were in order, etc. Meanwhile, he was enrolled at the University of Chicago. Later, when he was promoted to editor of *Guardian*, he left school to work fulltime. Now John H. Johnson is Supreme Life's largest stockholder and chairman of its board of directors. In 1973, the company's assets were more than $39 million.

While editing the *Guardian*—which required him to read all magazines and newspapers and make a digest of articles concerning black people—young Johnson got the idea for *Negro Digest*, his first publishing venture. "I talked to all kinds of people," he recalls, "but I couldn't sell the idea. Nobody saw any future for a black magazine.

133

They pointed out that fifteen such magazines already had been tried and had failed. All my friends were sympathetic, but nobody came up with any money to help me get started."

Refusing to be discouraged, the young man who "never had any doubts" that he would not always be poor, simply sat down and composed "what just has to be the best letter I ever wrote." The letter offered charter subscriptions (at $2 a year) to *Negro Digest* which, at the time, was nothing more than an idea in a young man's mind. In order to mail 20,000 copies of the letter, John Johnson borrowed $500—using his mother's furniture as security for the loan. The letter was a success. "We got back 3,000 replies and that gave us $6,000 to work with," Mr. Johnson says. "That letter is what launched Johnson Publishing Company."

Circulation of the new magazine grew steadily but nothing spectacular happened until Mr. Johnson got the idea of running a series of articles written by prominent whites on the topic, "If I Were A Negro." Mrs. Eleanor Roosevelt, wife of President Franklin D. Roosevelt, was among those who responded. Her article was published and, Mr. Johnson says, "Almost overnight, circulation jumped to 150,000. We had it made."

In November, 1945, Mr. Johnson launched *Ebony*, a monthly magazine that "would show Negroes, but also whites, that black people got married, had beauty contests, gave parties, ran successful businesses and did all the other normal things of life." In 1945, *Ebony*'s circulation was 25,000. Since that time, it has climbed to nearly 1.3 million, with some six million readers. In the process of mirroring all facets of black life, Mr. Johnson also has pioneered in convincing advertisers that black Americans constituted a distinct and unique consumer market.

"I couldn't get to see anybody," he remembers of his early efforts to find advertisers for *Ebony*. "The late Eugene McDonald, president of Zenith Radio, finally gave me an appointment because I convinced him that, as president of a company, I had certain protocol rights in calling on presidents of other companies." (Mr. Johnson also knew that Mr. McDonald was interested in the exploration of the Arctic. The issue of *Ebony* he brought along "just happened to have" a story about black explorer Matthew Henson.)

"I talked with Mr. McDonald a few minutes, then he called in his advertising manager—a man we had been trying to see for a year—and asked, 'Why aren't we in *Ebony*?' The manager said, 'We're considering it, sir,' and Mr. McDonald ordered, 'See that we are.' Once we got that big one, we began to get others." Presently, some three hundred of the nation's top business and industrial firms are among *Ebony* advertisers.

Mr. Johnson shakes hands with an African dignitary during Ivory Coast visit in 1961, when he was President John F. Kennedy's special ambassador to the country's independence celebration. Others in the party were the late Robert F. Kennedy (l.) and G. Mennen Williams, then U.S. assistant secretary of state. At right, the publisher hosts Arthur Godfrey, Lena Horne and Justice Thurgood Marshall at a New York City reception marking the 20th anniversary of *Ebony* magazine.

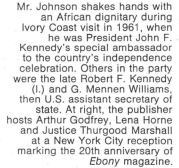

In 1950, Mr. Johnson temporarily discontinued publication of *Negro Digest* (it was revived ten years later; subsequently its name was changed to *Black World*) and launched *Tan*, an advice and confessions magazine. A year later, *Jet*, a pocket-sized weekly newsmagazine chronicling black-oriented news events was started. In 1971, *Tan* was incorporated into *Black Stars*, a magazine featuring black entertainers. By 1973, its monthly circulation was 250,000. Also by 1973, *Jet* was being sold to more than half a million readers each week. In April, 1973, Mr. Johnson published the first issue of *Ebony Jr!*, a magazine for black youngsters between the ages of six and twelve.

Johnson Publishing Company, which began in a one-room office, now maintains branch offices in New York, Washington, D.C. and Los Angeles. For several years, there was an overseas bureau in Paris. On May 16, 1972, dedication ceremonies were held for the new headquarters building in Chicago's downtown "Loop." The eleven-story steel, concrete and marble structure, built at a cost of $8 million, has been praised for its architectural and interior design, and attracts thousands of visitors each year. Its collection of works by black artists is valued at $250,000. The building is the first one built by blacks in downtown Chicago since the city's black founder, Jean Baptiste Point duSable, constructed a fur trading post in the area in 1784.

Affiliates of the Johnson Publishing Company include a book division, a book club, Ebony-Jetours (a travel service) and Ebony Fashion Fair.

In addition to his publishing ventures and his investments in Supreme Life Insurance Company ("I never really quit my job there," he says), Mr. Johnson has expanded into other areas. He is owner of Supreme Beauty Products Co. (makers of Duke and Raveen hair care products) and Fashion Fair Cosmetics. Because of his concern for the

135

Mr. Johnson receives the NAACP's 1966 Spingarn Award from author Harry Golden.

provision of housing for low and moderate-income persons, he became one of the major investors in the Lawless Gardens apartment complex on Chicago's South Side. The three 24-story apartment buildings contain 690 units, and there are 54 town houses.

Mr. Johnson is on the boards of directors of Twentieth Century-Fox Corporation, Marina City Bank of Chicago, Service Federal Savings and Loan Association of Chicago, Opportunities Industrialization Centers, and the National Conference of Christians and Jews. He is a fellow of Sigma Delta Chi, professional journalism society.

In the summer of 1972, he purchased Chicago radio station WGRT and became the first black in the city to own a broadcasting outlet.

Mr. Johnson's business success was first highlighted in 1951 when he became the first black businessman selected by the United States Junior Chamber of Commerce as one of the nation's Ten Outstanding Young Men. Other awards he has received include the Horatio Alger Award (1966), the NAACP's Spingarn Medal (1966), the National Newspaper Publishers Association's John Russwurm Award (1966) and the University of Chicago Alumni Association's Professional Achievement Award (1970). He also has received recognition from the highest levels of federal government. He was a member of the President's Commission for the Observation of the 25th Anniversary of the United Nations; was among twenty businessmen in 1955 invited by President Dwight D. Eisenhower to a stag dinner at the White House; was a member of the groups that accompanied the then Vice President Richard M. Nixon on goodwill trips to nine African countries in 1957 and to the Soviet Union and Poland in 1959. President John F. Kennedy named him a special ambassador and appointed him to a four-man delegation to represent the United States at independence ceremonies

Named as 1972's "Publisher of the Year" by the Magazine Publishers Association, Mr. Johnson receives the industry's most prestigious prize, the Henry Johnson Fisher Award, at a ceremony in New York City. From left are: Mr. Johnson, MPA President Steven Kelly, Award Committee Chairman Richard J. Babcock and MPA Chairman Harry Thompson.

of the Ivory Coast in 1961. He again was named a special ambassador by President Lyndon B. Johnson in 1963 and represented the United States at the independence ceremonies of Kenya.

Among the colleges and universities that have awarded Mr. Johnson honorary degrees are Morehouse College, Syracuse University, Malcolm X College, Central State University, Shaw University, Lincoln University, Upper Iowa College, Hamilton College, Eastern Michigan University, North Carolina College and Benedict College.

In 1972, he became the first black publisher to receive the magazine industry's most prestigious honor—the Magazine Publishers Associations' Henry Johnson Fisher Award—for outstanding contributions to publishing. In accepting the award as Publisher of the Year, Mr. Johnson talked about the kind of "responsible daring" he had employed in his business career. He said: "It is scarcely necessary to remind publishers that magazines must entertain as well as inform. But the danger here is that the publisher will blunder into the sin of dullness by mistaking his own limitations for the limitations of the public. We have to anticipate what the reader will want tomorrow by walking a step ahead of him. In fact, we have to anticipate the reader's desires and wishes by leading him, step by step, to what he really wants."

On another occasion, Mr. Johnson, who lives in Chicago with his wife, Eunice, and two teen-age children, John Harold and Linda, reflected upon his success and said: "I would be lying if I said my goals were to become a millionaire and publisher of four (now five) magazines. I guess my formula for success is picking attainable goals, then achieving them. Once you have achieved one goal, the success will give you the confidence to reach the next."

Nathaniel R. Jones

NAACP General Counsel

A Man Who Believes the American Legal System Can Be Made to Work for Blacks

"The long-term cause [of black rebellions] was the continuing practice of white racism."

Nathaniel R. Jones became general counsel of the National Association for the Advancement of Colored People in 1969—at a critical moment in the history of the organization.

During most of the middle and late 1960s, the nation's oldest and largest (1,700 chapters in all 50 states) civil rights organization was under fire from some blacks who believed it was "too accommodating to the white power structure" and thus "irrelevant to the real needs of black people."

Mr. Jones, a forty-three-year-old attorney from Youngstown, Ohio, filled a vacuum that was created by just such an argument over the organization's relationship to "the Establishment" and its tradition of fighting racial discrimination through established channels. Robert L. Carter, who had been general counsel since the position was created in 1957, had resigned after the NAACP national board fired one of his staff members for writing an article in *The New York Times Magazine* criticizing the United States Supreme Court as being segregationist. Such criticism was anathema to the NAACP, which had made significant civil rights breakthroughs (*Brown* vs. *Board of Education*,

Nathaniel Raphael Jones, general counsel, National Association for the Advancement of Colored People; born May 13, 1926 in Youngstown, Ohio; Youngstown University (B.A., 1951; LL.B., 1956). Wife: Jean V. Jones. Daughters: Pamela and Stephanie. Address: NAACP, 1790 Broadway, New York, NY 10019 (See full biographical sketch in Volume I.)

Mr. Jones (r.) was head of a three-man delegation, including his Assistant Counsel Melvin Bolden (l.) and Julius Williams, the NAACP director of military and veterans affairs, which flew to Germany in 1971 to investigate charges of racism on U.S. military installations.

In conference on racism in the military, Mr. Jones (2nd from r.) is joined by (l. to r.) Dr. John Morsell of the NAACP, Col. Harry Brooks, Maj. Gen. Frederic E. Davison, NAACP Executive Director Roy Wilkins and Julius Williams of the NAACP. Below, he reports at the Pentagon as Gen. C. E. Hutchin and Secretary of Defense Melvin Laird listen.

1954) in cases brought before the Court.

Controversy over the article resulted in the resignation of the entire staff of nine attorneys, leaving the NAACP with a rebuilding job to be done in its once potent legal department.

Mr. Jones, a man who strongly believed that the American legal system could be made to work for black people, was the right man for the job. Before assuming his NAACP post, he had served for three years as executive director of the Fair Employment Practices Committee of the City of Youngstown and had gained much experience in private law practice.

While working as a federal attorney (he was appointed an assistant U.S. attorney for the Northern District of Ohio in 1962), Mr. Jones became one of Ohio's top trial lawyers, handling the prosecution of crimes such as violations of banking, tax and counterfeiting laws, and mail, wire and government fraud cases.

In 1967, he was appointed deputy general counsel of the President's Commission on Civil Disorders, a position he held for one year. Mr. Jones said the results of the commission's findings on the race riots which scorched inner city areas across the nation during the late 1960s were not surprising. "The commission found that the long-term cause—the basic cause of the riots—was the continuing practice of white racism," he said.

As NAACP general counsel, Mr. Jones headed a three-man team that conducted a 1971 inquiry into the grievances of black U.S. servicemen in West Germany. A report, "Search for Military Justice," that he and his team prepared, contained a number of

Mr. Jones (c.) confers with Brooklyn, N.Y. parents prior to filing school integration suit on their behalf. From left, are Mrs. Mae Mitchell, Mrs. Dorothy Dolphin, James Myerson, Mr. Jones, Mrs. Bulena Pride, Donald Thomas, Mrs. Martha Harris, Mrs. Shirley Johnson and Mrs. James Tatum.

recommendations for remodeling the military justice system and sparked calls for major revisions in the handling of judicial and non-judicial punishment. The study also led to the appointment, in March, 1972, of the Civilian-Military Task Force on Military Justice. In its report to the Secretary of Defense on November 30, 1972, the task force, co-chaired by Mr. Jones, declared: "Systemic racial discrimination exists throughout the armed services and in the military justice system. No command or installation—and more important—no element of the military system—is entirely free from the systemic discrimination against [minority] military servicemen as individuals and as groups."

Following the presentation of that report, Mr. Jones was offered the position of deputy assistant secretary of defense for equal opportunity. The Youngstown native—born May 13, 1926, and one of three children of Nathaniel B. and Lillian Brown Jones—was on the way up. The national press, as well as Mr. Jones' hometown newspaper, *The Youngstown Vindicator*, urged him to take the job.

"The race problem is one of the most critical facing the armed services, and the question of the equality of military justice relating to blacks in uniform is one that Attorney Jones is especially equipped to handle. . . . On the basis of his record, he will go where the highest duty calls him," the *Vindicator* said.

Mr. Jones believed his "highest duty" was to remain with the NAACP. "I'm not available for the position," he told the Defense Department. "My duties as general counsel for the NAACP involve me in the broad spectrum of civil rights activities. . . . It is my conviction that I can better serve the interests of black servicemen by remaining in my position as general counsel of this organization."

The "broad spectrum of civil rights activities" in which Mr.

140

Jones was involved included attacks on segregation in Northern schools. For years, the North had escaped the turmoil surrounding school desegregation while the courts and the NAACP concentrated on ending *de jure* (by law) segregation in the South.

But Northern schools were, in fact, just as segregated as those in the South. Northern politicians claimed that nothing could be done about *de facto* school segregation because it resulted from segregated housing patterns. That argument suffered a damaging blow in 1972 when the NAACP, under the leadership of Nathaniel Jones and Louis Lucas of Memphis, Tennessee, won a federal court ruling that called for the merger of inner-city and suburban school systems to bring about school integration in Detroit, Michigan.

In its ruling upholding an earlier decision by U.S. District Court Judge Stephen J. Roth, the Sixth U.S. Circuit Court of Appeals said: "Big city school systems for blacks surrounded by suburban school systems for whites cannot represent equal protection of the law."

The victory supported an earlier statement about Nathaniel Jones, made by Roy Wilkins, NAACP executive director: "He has taken a quick and firm grasp of the complexities inherent in his assignment, and there is no question but that he will rapidly and effectively attain a position of major leadership in the legal areas of civil rights."

Mr. and Mrs. Jones (c.) attend a 1972 book party for Henry Lee Moon (r.), editor of *Crisis* magazine and editor of a book, *The Emerging Thought of W.E.B. DuBois.*

141

Quincy Jones
Composer, Musician

Quincy Jones, musician; born March 14, 1933 in Chicago, Ill.; attended Berklee School of Music, Boston, Mass., studied classical music in Paris under Nadia Boulanger; wife: Ulla Jones; children: Martina-Lisa and Quincy III. Address: 1416 N. La Brea, Hollywood, CA 90028 (See full biographical sketch in Volume I)

A Musical Genius Who Has Soared To the Highest Spot in His Field

". . . influenced by every original voice in or outside of jazz."

Quincy D. (for Delight) Jones II has been described by jazz critic Leonard Feather as "a composer who is on the brink of superstardom." Feather's description is hardly an exaggeration, for no musician—past or present—has been quite as successful and prolific in as wide a variety of musical endeavors as Mr. Jones. Despite his relative youth, Quincy Jones has established solid credentials as a jazz trumpeter, arranger, bandleader, recording director, conductor "for every singer from Frank Sinatra and Ray Charles to Sarah Vaughan and Peggy Lee" and composer of musical scores for more than forty major motion pictures.

Endowed with a seemingly magic musical touch that turns everything to gold, Mr. Jones has been as successful as a recording artist of top-selling jazz and pop hit LPs as he has in writing the music for movies and television shows. He not only wrote the musical theme for TV's "Ironside" but has given a good account of himself as an actor-singer-writer-conductor on "The New Bill Cosby Show" and has

At recording session, Mr. Jones displays the finesse which makes him one of the most sought-after conductors in the music industry.

scored numerous motion pictures. During a highly successful concert tour featuring his band and singer Roberta Flack, Mr. Jones won rave notices for his musical accomplishments as well as for his showmanship.

Quincy Jones was born March 14, 1933 in Chicago Illinois, but he grew up in Seattle, Washington, where his family moved when he was ten years old. About that time he made his first move into the musical spotlight by forming a vocal quartet and performing in church. He began playing the trumpet at fourteen, working with a small group formed by a blind singer-pianist named Ray Charles. Quincy did not get formal trumpet lessons until he was eighteen years old and won a scholarship to study with Clark Terry at Schillinger House in Boston (later known as the Berklee School of Music), taking ten subjects a day and playing strip joints at night to pay his room rent. He quit his studies two years later to join Lionel Hampton's band and subsequently Dizzie Gillespie's band, which he had helped to organize. After that, he began a highly successful career as a free-lance arranger, a career that kept him busy in the United States as well as in Europe. He spent a year and a half in Paris composing, arranging and conducting for Barclay Records. In addition, he studied under the great French musicologist, Nadia Boulanger, whose former students include Leonard Bernstein and Aaron Copland. His contact with Mme. Boulanger was fruitful in many ways, especially in that it helped put an end to his secret ambition of

Sharing a laugh with singer Ray Charles, Mr. Jones enjoys a coffee break between rehearsals. Mr. Charles had a great influence on Mr. Jones' career.

After guiding his orchestra through a complex number (above), Mr. Jones joins singer Roberta Flack (r.) in another swinging tune.

becoming a composer of classical music. More secure in his own musical idiom, Mr. Jones returned to the United States and in 1959 was hired as musical director for the Harold Arlen blues opera *Free and Easy.* Although the show folded prematurely through no fault of Mr. Jones', enthusiasm in the all-star jazz orchestra he had assembled for the show was so high that the ensemble stayed together and toured Europe in a series of highly successful concerts during 1966.

Even though he was to make his biggest mark writing musical scores of United States motion pictures—an area of film-making that, before Mr. Jones arrived on the scene, constituted a "closed shop" as far as blacks were concerned—he received his first break in film music with his score for the Swedish film, *The Boy and the Tree*, made in 1961. The first U.S. film to receive the unique Jones treatment was *The Pawnbroker* (1965). Critics everywhere hailed the musical score as one of the reasons for the movie's great success. After that, movie score offers came pouring in.

Basically a musician within the classic jazz framework, Mr. Jones' reputation, in spite of his versatility, rests mainly on brief compositions that combine the swinging big band feel of the great orchestras of the thirties with the musical developments of subsequent years. Mr. Jones prefers not to have his music categorized because, as he puts it, "It is probably influenced by every original voice in and outside of jazz, maybe anyone from blues singer Ray Charles to Ravel. I don't know or care."

Between his many musical commitments, Mr. Jones has found time to assert his blackness by helping form the Institute of Black American

144

Laughing at the fun of it all (top), Mr. Jones uses spare time to compose new arrangement (above), practice difficult piano chords (above, r.), and later (top, r.) join friends (l. to r.) Flip Wilson, Roberta Flack, and Cannonball Adderley at a Los Angeles theatre.

Music, of which he is president. He also gave his time and talent to staging shows and conducting workshops for the Reverend Jesse Jackson's PUSH Expo '72 in Chicago.

The recipient of every conceivable musical award and honor in recognition of his apparently inexhaustible creative output, Quincy Jones has given no indication that he is about to take things easy in the years to come. Writes *Down Beat* magazine's Harvey Siders, "His (Jones') Grammy awards, Oscar nominations, Gold Records and *Down Beat* awards are accumulating with such consistency that until he learns to slow down, all articles about this affable, open man should be written in pencil."

145

Barbara Jordan

Congresswoman

She Was Determined To Be 'Something Unusual'

"I always wanted to be something unusual. I never wanted to be run-of-the-mill."

By the time Barbara Jordan was elected to Congress in 1972, she had made the words "first black" obsolete in Texas politics.

In 1966, she became the first black since 1883 to be elected to the Texas Senate and the first woman ever to hold the post. During her six-year tenure, Miss Jordan was elected senate president *pro tempore* and became the first black woman in American history to serve as the presiding officer of a legislative chamber.

Then, on June 10, 1972, when both Texas Governor Preston Smith and Lieutenant Governor Ben Barnes left the state for a day, Miss Jordan became the first black to serve as governor of Texas. Some observers said that the one-day gubernatorial term was merely a publicity stunt and a waste of time. But for the wry Miss Jordan, it was

Before her election to Congress, Texas State Senator Barbara Jordan is sworn in by Judge A. L. Jefferson as Texas governor for a day (June 10, 1972) when both the governor and lieutenant governor were out of the state. She was the first black woman to serve in the capacity. After having a flower pinned on by her secretary, Nita Silberstein, she signs autographs for Capitol visitors and friends.

an honor that increased her political appetite. "Someday," she told a group of reporters who covered the event, "I may want to retain the governor's seat for a longer period of time."

The comment was typical of the thirty-six-year-old lawyer-politician, the youngest of three daughters of the Reverend and Mrs. Benjamin M. Jordan of Houston, Texas. "I always wanted to be something unusual," says Miss Jordan, who was born in Houston on February 21, 1936, and who was reared in Houston's predominantly black, low-income Fifth Ward. "I never wanted to be run-of-the-mill."

Her desire to excel and to be different was accented heavily by a

147

Congresswoman Jordan, known as a "no nonsense" legislator when she was in the Texas Senate, has been assigned to Judiciary Committee in the U.S. House of Representatives.

strong "no-nonsense" self-control and an equally powerful leadership ability. Thus, there have been numerous stories about the congresswoman's "egocentrism," "rudeness" and "aloofness." As Miss Jordan's mother, Mrs. Arlyne Jordan, once explained, most of the criticism stemmed from her daughter's unique style. "Barbara has always been like that. She always had a takeover attitude. Even when she was a little girl, she was able to get her older sisters to do things for her."

While a tenth grade student at Houston's Phillis Wheatley High School, Miss Jordan decided to become a lawyer. Her decision was influenced by the successful career of Edith Sampson, a noted black lawyer from Chicago who later became a Cook County (Ill.) circuit court judge.

Miss Jordan finished high school in the upper 5 per cent of her class and went to Texas Southern University where, in 1956, she graduated *magna cum laude* with a B.A. degree in history and political science. She graduated from Boston University School of Law in 1959 and returned to Houston to begin a law practice that was interrupted frequently by politics. The first such interruption came in 1960. In a

148

Prior to her campaign for a congressional seat, Miss Jordan gets a big hug from President Lyndon B. Johnson, who was one of the staunchest supporters of her political career.

move that yielded important personal and political backing in later years, Miss Jordan started the first black one-person-per-block Democratic precinct organization in Houston. The objective was to win black and other minority votes for Democratic presidential nominee John F. Kennedy and his Texas running mate, Lyndon B. Johnson.

In 1962 and 1964, she "went into business" for herself, running two unsuccessful campaigns for a seat in the Texas House of Representatives. Two years later, she defeated white liberal J.C. Whitfield, a former state representative, in a bid for a state senate seat. Commenting on her victory, she said, "I didn't play up the fact of being a Negro or a woman. . . . It feels good to know that people recognize a qualified candidate when they see one."

Many of those same people recognized her as a qualified candidate in 1972 when she began campaigning in Texas' newly created 18th Congressional District for a seat in the U.S. House of Representatives. One of her most important backers was the late President Johnson, who said of her: "She proved that black is beautiful before we knew what it meant. She is the epitome of the new politics in Texas, not the politics that seeks to destroy and mess up everything in the way. She is involved in a governmental system of all the people, all the races, all economic groups."

Miss Jordan's politically lucrative ties with President Johnson, and the role she played in the creation of the 18th Congressional District, prompted her major opponent, three-term Texas State Representative Curtis Graves, a black, to level charges of "Uncle Tom-ism" and "selling out" against her. Representative Graves accused Senator Jordan of working with white state legislators to create a new congressional district at the cost of eliminating a state senate seat for Houston blacks.

Senator Jordan vigorously denied the charges and campaigned on the record she had compiled in the legislature. In six years of service, she had sponsored most of the state's environmental legislation, authored the first Texas minimum wage law, forced the state to place anti-discrimination clauses in all of its business contracts, and pushed the first package of urban legislation through a rural-minded state government dominated by white males.

"Apparently, the voters believed me and bought my record instead of Graves' charges," she said after her congressional victory. "I received more than 80 percent of the vote. That speaks for itself." Her opponent, who was running for the same congressional seat for which he had accused Miss Jordan of "selling out," received a scant 11 percent of the vote.

As the lady said, that speaks for itself.

Percy Lavon Julian
Research Chemist

Brilliant Scientist Is Noted for Research with Life-Saving Drugs

Percy Lavon Julian, president of Julian Associates and director of Julian Research Institute in Franklin Park, Ill.; DePauw University (A.B., 1920; honorary D.Sc., 1947), Harvard University (A.M., 1923), University of Vienna (Ph.D., 1931) and numerous honorary degrees. Wife: Anna Johnson Julian. Children: Percy and Faith. Address: 9352 Grand, Franklin Park, IL 60131 (See full biographical sketch in Volume I.)

"Youths today are seeking self-identification to signify their struggle to find who they are. Properly explored and executed, this resolve could be the harbinger of the greatest emancipation vouchsafed to us in three-and-a-half long centuries."

Untold thousands of persons around the world are alive and well today because of the genius and tireless efforts of Dr. Percy Lavon Julian, a research chemist whose many life-saving and health-restoring discoveries have established him as one of the most distinguished scientists of his time. Apart from his pioneering contributions to science, he has distinguished himself as a crusader for equal opportunities for blacks and as a civic leader and philanthropist.

Dr. Julian is credited with 162 scientific publications and 105 patents. Included among his many discoveries are the successful synthesis of physostigmine, a drug used in the treatment of glaucoma; the synthesis of the female sex hormone progesterone, and the synthesis of a compound "S" from soybean sterols which makes possible the low-cost production and thus wide availability of cortisone, a so-called "miracle drug" that has a wide variety of applications in the combatting of disease. Among his non-medical discoveries is a chemical foam used to extinguish fire. It is said to have saved many lives after airplane crash-landings and is used by a number of city fire departments.

Dr. Julian was born April 11, 1899 in Montgomery, Alabama. He was one of six children of James Sumner Julian, a railway mail clerk, and Elizabeth Lena Julian. He went to elementary school in Montgomery and later attended the State Normal School for Negroes, a private institution from which he graduated in 1916. Encouraged by his family, especially his father, who wanted him to become a physician, young Percy enrolled at DePauw University in Greencastle, Indiana. His going away to college was an important family event. Consequently, not only his parents went to the train station to see him off, but also his ninety-nine-year-old grandmother who, as a young slave woman, had picked a record 350 pounds of cotton in one day, and his grandfather, who had paid with two fingers of his right hand for violating a code forbidding slaves to learn to read and write.

Dr. Julian is shown with J. V. Steinle of the Johnson Wax laboratory in Racine, Wis.

Although he had always been a top student in his class at the State Normal School, Percy discovered that he was "not ready" to do college-level work. As a result, he was obliged to take two years of remedial courses until he had made up the deficiency. While at DePauw, he slept in the attic of a white fraternity house where he waited on tables to pay for his room and board. Despite these humble circumstances, he graduated in 1920 as valedictorian of his class, and was a member of Phi Beta Kappa and Sigma Xi honorary societies.

Against his father's wishes and the advice of his professor, both of whom saw no future for a black man in the field of chemistry, Mr. Julian was adamant in his determination to prepare himself as a chemist. Unable to secure the lucrative fellowship at DePauw to which his extraordinary academic record entitled him, he accepted a post as instructor in chemistry at Fisk University. After two years, his first big break came in the form of an Austin Fellowship for graduate studies in chemistry at Harvard University.

He received his master of arts degree from Harvard in 1923. Again he was unsuccessful when he applied for a teaching assistantship at Harvard in order to finance graduate studies in chemistry. But somehow, with the aid of minor fellowships, he was able to continue there for another three years, after which he accepted a chemistry professorship at West Virginia State College. In 1928, he resigned in order to become an associate professor and head of the chemistry department at Howard University. In 1929, with the aid of a General Education Board fellowship, he went to Europe for doctoral studies

151

Respected in his field, Dr. Julian is shown with P. Dwight Joyce, chairman and president of the Glidden Paint Company (above). Below, he receives an honorary degree from K. Roald Bergethon, president of Lafayette College.

under the world-famous Austrian chemist, Professor Ernst Spath, at the University of Vienna. In 1931, armed with his newly-earned doctorate, Dr. Julian returned to the United States to resume his work at Howard—this time with the rank of full professor. He resigned a year later to accept a position as a research fellow at DePauw, his alma mater. In 1935, he married Dr. Anna Johnson, a sociologist.

After four years at DePauw, Dr. Julian had become widely acclaimed as a brilliant chemical investigator. This, however, did not help him in securing a faculty appointment at the school, or, for that matter, at any other predominantly white university. Disillusioned with the academic community, Dr. Julian, in 1936, decided to try his luck in the field of industrial chemistry. After accepting a research position with the Institute of Paper Chemistry in Appleton, Wisconsin, he and his employers discovered that an old Appleton statute prohibited "the housing of a Negro overnight." Unwilling to commute in order to oblige the discriminatory ordinance, Dr. Julian resigned and accepted the post of director of research of the Soya Products Division and the Vegetable Oil and Food Division of the Glidden Company of Chicago, one of the biggest paint manufacturers in the nation. Never before had a black man held a position of such responsibility in modern chemical industry. Glidden never had reason to regret its decision to hire him, for as a direct result of his discoveries of new processes, the firm's profits from soybean products rose from $35,000 to $135,000 in one year. Also, of the 105 patents Dr. Julian received, 66 were assigned to Glidden.

While making news in his profession, Dr. Julian quite unintentionally made a different kind of news as a private citizen. In 1950, shortly before moving into a newly purchased, fifteen-room home in an elegant, formerly all-white neighborhood of Oak Park, a suburb of Chicago, arsonists attempted to burn down the home. Not in the least intimidated by the incident, the Julians moved in, determined to exercise their right to live in any house they could afford to purchase. They were challenged again less than a year later in June, 1951, when a bomb tossed from a speeding car exploded beneath the bedroom window of the two Julian children, Faith and Percy Jr. who were, respectively, seven and eleven years old at the time. Fortunately, nobody was harmed. Each attack on the Julian home resulted in expressions of indignation and regret in the Oak Park community. In 1954, the Julians were harassed once more when they received anonymous letters threatening the lives of their children, including a newly acquired foster son, Rhoderic, ten, if they did not leave Oak Park. Again, Dr. Julian resolved to stay. "This is our home," he said at the time, "and we're going to stay here. We're American citizens and we're entitled to do this. I'm on the lookout and will not stand for anyone taking my

Widely active in civic affairs, Dr. Julian is shown at a Japanese-American citizenship meeting in Chicago.

Success in the worlds of industry and science has characterized Dr. Julian's illustrious career.

property. We'll die before they do it." Today, the racial incidents are all but forgotten and the Julians are among the most respected and honored—and certainly the most famous—citizens of Oak Park.

In 1954, Dr. Julian founded his own Julian Laboratories, Inc. in Chicago, and the Julian Laboratorios de Mexico in Mexico City. Eventually he added a company in Guatemala, Empress Agro-Quimica Guatemala, to his thriving chemical enterprises. While he is still actively engaged in chemical research (in 1973, at seventy-four years of age, he still worked ten to twelve hours a day), Dr. Julian in more recent years has narrowed down his responsibilities. In 1961, he sold Julian Laboratories to the pharmaceutical firm of Smith, Kline and French for $2,338,000, staying on as its president. The same year, he also sold his plant in Guatemala to the Upjohn Company, another major pharmaceutical firm. In 1964, he founded the Julian Research Institute, which he serves as director, and Julian Associates, Inc., of which he is president. His laboratories are in Franklin Park, Illinois, a Chicago suburb.

In addition to his earned degrees, Dr. Julian is the recipient of fifteen honorary doctorates, including D.Sc. degrees from De Pauw, Howard and Fisk universities, and Morehouse College. Among his many awards are the Spingarn Medal of the NAACP, which he received in 1947, the Silver Plaque Award of the National Conference of Christians and Jews (1963) and the Chemical Pioneer Award of the American Institute of Chemists (1968).

Much of Dr. Julian's very little spare time is devoted to serving young people as a member of the Board of Regents of the State of Illinois and as a trustee of DePauw University, Fisk University, Howard University, South Union College (Wadley, Ala.), Roosevelt University and the Chicago Theological Seminary.

While applauding the new spirit of black identity among today's black youths, Dr. Julian deplores a concomitant tendency among some black students to isolate themselves from all except those who are black. "They [many black students] are asking for all-black dormitories, societies and associations in colleges . . . [and many] are attempting to force their ideas upon young students who are afraid to speak up and challenge them," he says. "Youths today are seeking self-identification to signify their struggle to find who they are. Properly explored and executed, this resolve could be the harbinger of the greatest emancipation vouchsafed to us in three-and-a-half long centuries."

Robert O. Lowery
New York City Fire Commissioner

Robert O. Lowery, fire commissioner, New York, N.Y.; born April 20, 1916 in Buffalo, N.Y.; attended the College of the City of New York, studied at New York University School of Public Administration and at Michigan State University National Institute on Police and Community Relations; widower; Daughters: Mrs. Leslie Ann Strickland and Mrs. Gertrude Erwin. Address: 110 Church St., New York, NY 10007 (See full biographical sketch in Volume I.)

Commissioner Lowery confers with Mayor John Lindsay about matters relating to his administration of the city's fire department which has the largest payroll of any fire fighting unit in the U.S.

He Is Boss of the Biggest Fire Department in the Nation

Commissioner Lowery (c.) presides over a conference with members of his staff. They discuss committee reports and prepare to take action on matters concerning New York fire fighters.

". . . resistance still exists to the entry of blacks into this field . . . but considerable progress is being made."

Robert O. Lowery is the boss of the largest fire fighting organization in the world, the 15,000-member fire department in New York City. Not only is the department the largest in size, it also has the largest budget (currently $330 million annually) and is the busiest. In 1971, there were some 280,000 alarms sounded in the city, an average of 768 each day. During the same year, there were 125,573 fires, an average of 344 each day. And as in so many other calamities that afflict urban life, the chief victims of fires are people in the poorer areas of the city—in this case, the areas where many blacks and Puerto Ricans live. About 53 percent of all the fires and most of the 292 fatalities occurred in such areas during 1971.

The fifty-six-year-old Commissioner Lowery, who was born in Buffalo, New York and raised in Harlem, is acutely aware of the destruction that fires wreak in urban black communities. "Fire problems, which are closely related to social problems," he explains, "are a major sign of a deteriorating community. There are many fires in ghetto areas because of overcrowdedness and the presence of older, more rundown buildings which are built so close together that when a fire occurs it can endanger a whole block because it spreads and burns faster." As a primary example of social conditions causing fire hazards, he cited the perennial problem of heating old buildings in the winter. The tenants aren't provided with enough heat. Thus they set up makeshift methods of warming their often overcrowded apartments, thereby increasing the danger of fire.

Supporting his position that "the major objective of an urban fire department is to prevent fire, to protect life and property from fire and to minimize the adverse aftereffects of fire," the commissioner, who is the first black man ever to head a major U. S. fire department, has instituted a program to educate people about fires. He also has launched a

155

Visiting one of the fire houses in New York, Commissioner Lowery chats with members of the fire company, using personal diplomacy to maintain his men's confidence in department leadership.

program to encourage better relations between the department and the public and to recruit more blacks, who are currently only 4 percent (600 men) of the firemen under his command.

There have been problems in getting the programs off the ground, due mainly to meager finances, but due also, especially in the area of recruitment, to resistance from within the department itself. "To a great extent," Commissioner Lowery says, "the fire department has been a father-son operation, and the close-knit almost family-like atmosphere that exists in most fire houses has made many men strong advocates of the status quo."

Commissioner Lowery insists that, in return for his attempts to bring better fire protection to their communities, blacks must assume some of the responsibilities. I know the conditions that exist in many areas," he says, "but when all is said and done, it still boils down to the fact that people cause fires with carelessness. Most fires occur in the home—in kitchens and in bedrooms. People must understand that their cooperation is needed in fire prevention." The usually even-tempered commissioner, who has been a fireman since 1941,

156

Visiting the scene of a fire, Commissioner Lowery gets a first-hand look at his fire fighters in action.

almost "loses his cool" when discussing the subject of false alarms—most of which occur in the poorer, more fire-prone districts of the city. In New York City in 1971, 38 percent, or 105,129 out of 286,170 fire alarms were false. Commissioner Lowery calls these figures "deplorable and disgraceful," adding that "the condition adversely affects the fire protection of every resident in a city constantly looking for funds—but it can cost lives." He cites cases where deaths have occurred because firemen were answering a false alarm when a real fire broke out.

Running the department has not been an easy assignment for the quiet-spoken commissioner. When he took command in January, 1966 (he was New York City Mayor John V. Lindsay's first cabinet appointment), the department was going through a number of changes. Firemen were meeting with increasing hostility in some areas of the city, the firemen's union was beginning to flex its muscles, and the city was experiencing a serious fiscal crisis. As the first black commissioner in a department that traditionally had been headed by Irish-Americans, Mr. Lowery met stiff pockets of resistance, some of which, though weakened, still exist. His executive assistant, Vincent Collymore, says, "The fire department is a microcosm of the American society and reflects its general attitudes. There were, and continue to be, incidents that happen which we feel are directed toward Commissioner Lowery. For instance, rumors were spread that he was adjusting exams to give promotional advantages to blacks. We haven't been able to identify the sources of this kind of smear talk, but we look on it with a judicious eye because such charges have never been leveled at a previous commissioner."

The comissioner, who initially joined the department simply "because I needed a job," is aware of these attitudes but shrugs them off. "I don't want to gloss over the fact that resistance still exists to the entry of blacks into this field," he says, "and departments in every city will reflect the attitudes of the public generally. But considerable progress is being made, thanks in part to the good work of organizations composed of black professional firefighters, such as the Vulcan Society in my own city."

Commissioner Lowery's record is unblemished, and a *New York Times* survey on corruption among New York City civil servants quoted an unidentified source as saying: "The fire department is the most honest agency in the city. It is well-known that you can't bribe a fire department inspector." Good leadership is at least partially responsible for that record. Commissioner Lowery provides that leadership.

Jackie "Moms" Mabley

Comedienne

Jackie "Moms" Mabley, comedienne; born in Brevard, N.C.; high school graduate, Washington, D.C.; has played since 1923 to packed clubs and theaters across the U.S., first comedy record album in 1960 sold over a million copies, TV star since 1967; has three daughters. Address: 445 Park Ave., New York, NY 10022 (See full biographical sketch in Volume I.)

Black America's 'First Lady of Laughter'

". . . show people live the way the rest of the world ought to live: always doing things for somebody else, helping one another."

"If there ever was a time when people needed to laugh, then now is the time." That is the philosophy of one of the most unusual women in show business—Jackie "Moms" Mabley, black America's "First Lady of Laughter."

Born more than seventy years ago (she says her age is "my business . . . just say I was born in 19 nothing!") in the North Carolina mountain town of Brevard, her father, Jim Aiken, a landowner and businessman, named her Loretta Mary. Perhaps because she grew up in a large, religious family, Moms' childhood interest in entertainment began with her participation in various church activities. Realizing at an early age that people are instantly attracted to clowns, she started portraying funny characters in religious pageants, leaving the longer, more boring roles to her friends. Apparently it worked, for at the age of twelve she was the star of numerous school plays, and at thirteen she was the community's favorite young comedienne. By fourteen, she had seen a touring vaudeville troupe and was firmly convinced that her future lay in entertainment. Thus, with the blessings of her mother, Mrs. Mary Aiken, and the encouragement of her great-grandmother, Mrs. Harriette Hunt, Loretta moved to Washington, D.C., where she lived with relatives until she finished high school. Her next stop was Buffalo, New York, where she roomed in a boarding house with friends in show business. Because of her penchant for mothering entertainers and others in need of sympathy, she was nicknamed "Moms." Commenting on this, she says, "You know, show

158

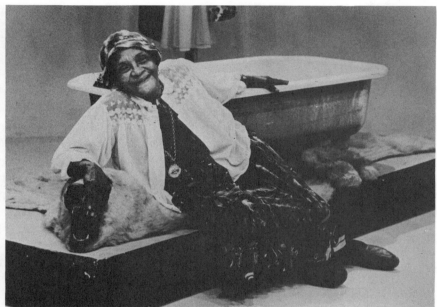

people live the way the rest of the world ought to live: always doing things for somebody else, helping one another."

A few months later, she met the comedy team of Buck and Bubbles, who steered her to her first role in a show called *The Rich Aunt From Utah*. She originally played different parts, dancing and telling jokes as the show toured the East and Midwest for two years. But with the help of comedienne Bonnie Bell Drew, Moms worked out her

159

Attending funeral services for Louis Armstrong, Moms displays the more serious side of her personality. Her nephew accompanies her.

own comedy monologue and went on to play with Tim Moore, Dusty Fletcher and Pigmeat Markham. By 1923, she was appearing in New York City, where she frequently shared the stage with such notables as Louis Armstrong, Duke Ellington, Count Basie and Cab Calloway. She also became a close friend of singer Sophie Tucker and Eleanor Roosevelt, wife of the future president of the United States.

Moms started playing to packed houses across the country—in college auditoriums, concert halls and big-city theaters such as Harlem's Apollo and Chicago's Regal, and in several Playboy Clubs. Since her formula consists of a rambling, witty discourse peppered with unexpected earthiness and hipness, her brand of humor soon became a favorite. By 1960, she began her recording career by selling more than a million copies of her first joke album, earning a gold record in the process. By 1972, ten albums had followed, including one on which she sang "Abraham, Martin and John"—a song that made her a top choice of disc jockeys in all the major cities. Her popularity also landed her a role in the film *Boarding House Blues*, in which, ironically, she managed a rooming-house for out-of-work entertainers.

Moms told her first joke before a television camera in 1967 when Harry Belafonte invited her to appear on his all-black comedy show. Her humor, which ranged from publicly removing her false teeth to cracks about her fondness for young men, led to appearances on the Mike Douglas, Bill Cosby, Merv Griffin, Smothers Brothers and Flip Wilson shows. About her teeth, she quips, "Let me tell you, I take 'em out to be comfortable—anywhere I want to be comfortable. If they bother me, out they come. I once took 'em out in the White House."

Today, after more than fifty years in show business, Moms Mabley's views and quips are as modern as the headlines. She plies her listeners with witticisms about child-raising, current politics and the never-ending battle of the sexes. Her stage technique is disarming. With a comfortable chair as her only stage prop, she usually performs in a bizarre array of clothing: a wrinkled print dress with a sagging hemline, knee-length wool stockings rolled at the top, and over-size house slippers. When the laughter fades, she is likely to remove her false teeth, inspect them and say in a buzz-saw voice: "I believe in being in season, and old men ain't in season. Ain't nothin' an old man can do for me but bring me a message from a *young* man." And while the audience is still in stitches, she lays on another: "My first husband was very jealous, though I don't know why. There was nothing I *wouldn't* do for him and nothing he *would* do for me, so we spent most of the time doing nothing."

160

Sincerely religious, Moms is a member of the late Adam Clayton Powell's Abyssinian Baptist Church in Harlem. She has three daughters and six grandchildren. On the matter of child-raising, she says, "Don't teach 'em to watch traffic lights when crossing the streets. Damn the lights! Watch the *cars*. The lights ain't never killed nobody."

Since she has never learned to drive and does not drink, Moms spends most of her free time either playing chess, checkers and canasta, or watering her house plants with champagne. Still, the "Clown Princess of Comedy" remains, in her words, "Just Moms, that's all. That's M-O-M spelled forward and spelled backwards, too. Sideways, it's M-O-M, and upside down, it's W-O-W . . . that's WOW!"

Although her reputation was built on machine-gun wit, much of Moms' humor lies in her "tacky" appearance. She has been an entertainer for more than fifty years.

Henry W. McGee Jr.

Post Office District Manager

He Sacrificed His Vacation Time
In Order to Get a College Education

*"I may be the only person in post office history who took his annual
leave an hour or two at a time in order to take some university course I
couldn't take otherwise."*

Henry W. McGee, who began as a sixty-five cents an hour substitute
mail carrier for the Chicago Post Office in 1929 and worked his way up
through the ranks, is today the district manager of the Chicago
Metropolitan Area Postal Service. He is in charge of some 40,000
employees who staff the Chicago area's four major mail-handling
facilities and 250 post offices. Before being promoted in 1972, Mr.
McGee was postmaster of Chicago, whose main post office, with
28,000 employees, is "the world's largest mail-processing facility
under one roof."

When he became postmaster of Chicago in 1966 (President
Lyndon B. Johnson appointed him upon the recommendation of the
late U.S. Senator Paul Douglas of Illinois), Mr. McGee inherited all the
problems that were plaguing the huge Chicago operation as well as

*Henry W. McGee, district
manager of the Chicago (III.)
Metropolitan Area Postal
Service; born Feb. 7, 1910 in
Hillsboro, Tex.; Illinois
Institute of Technology (A.B.,
1949), University of Chicago
(M.A., 1961). Wife: Attye Belle
McGee. Children: Henry W. Jr.,
Penny, Sylvia. Address: 120 S.
Riverside Plaza, Chicago,
IL 60688 (See full biographical
sketch in Volume I.)*

the postal service in general. These included the problem of recruiting capable personnel to handle the ever-increasing volume of mail as well as that of lingering discrimination in hiring and promotion policies. While greatly improving his post office's efficiency, and thus its mail-handling capacity, Mr. McGee made equal employment opportunity a reality. During his five years in office, he increased the number of black supervisors from approximately two hundred to more than seven hundred. Many of these supervisors were subsequently promoted to high-level administrative positions. However, although he made no secret of his deep concern for the just treatment of black employees, Postmaster McGee kept the promise he had made during his swearing-in ceremony: "There will be no reverse discrimination. Advances will be based on merit. Each employee will be treated with dignity and respect." Making good on that promise earned Mr. McGee the respect of all employees, black and white.

The eleventh of twelve children of William and Mary McGee, Henry was born February 7, 1910 in Hillsboro, Texas. When he was four years old, his mother died. By the time he was thirteen years old, the family had settled in Kansas City, Missouri, where Henry received his secondary education. While in high school, he distinguished himself as an actor in drama class and as an orator in the annual junior-senior oratorical contest.

In 1927, young McGee moved to Chicago to live with his older brother, the Reverend Ford W. McGee, who was to become a bishop in the Church of God in Christ. Henry enrolled at Crane Junior College as a pre-medical student. After completion of the two-year course, he transferred to Lewis Institute. The Depression and marriage to a former classmate, Miss Attyle Belle Truesdale, in 1931 called a temporary halt to his studies. He recalls that while working as a substitute clerk-carrier, "We were lucky to get two hours of work a day—sometimes." To supplement his meager income, he also worked part-time as an insurance salesman. "If I made $10 a week," he remembers, "I was in good shape." It was not until 1935 that he received his permanent appointment as a full-time clerk and thus was assured an income to support his family. During the forties and fifties, he and his wife attended alternately in college, juggling their spare hours between the post office and child-rearing. "I may be the only person in post office history who took his annual leave an hour or two at a time in order to take some university course I couldn't take otherwise," Mr. McGee says.

In 1944, when her oldest child, Henry Jr., was twelve and her second child Sylvia, was nine, Mrs. McGee enrolled at Roosevelt University. She received a bachelor of arts degree in 1946, the same

Mr. McGee takes inspection tour (top) through Chicago's vast Main Post Office. Above, he watches a postal employee sorting mail.

Mr. McGee presents "Key of Opportunity" to two post office scholarship winners (above). Above right, he honors winner of Mailman of the Year award and (at right) interviews Mr. George R. Downes, director of the British post office, on weekly radio show *Mail Call* on Chicago's WGN Radio.

year the youngest McGee child, Penny, was born. Meanwhile, Mr. McGee enrolled at the Illinois Institute of Technology. When he had to work at night, he went to school during the day—and vice versa—he recalls. In 1949, he received a bachelor's degree in public administration—the same year that Henry Jr. finished high school. While Mr. McGee took a break from the classroom because of the family budget, Mrs. McGee took a leave of absence from her teaching post and enrolled at the University of Chicago to study for a master's degree in education. She received that degree in 1959. Her graduation was the signal for Mr. McGee to return to school, and he promptly enrolled in a master's program at the University of Chicago. His persistence in pursuing an education was rewarded in 1961 when he received a master's degree in political science.

Mr. McGee feels that preparing himself educationally, even at a time when opportunities for blacks in the post office were very much circumscribed, had a great deal to do with his advancement—

first to supervisor, then to Chicago Post Office personnel director, post master and finally district manager. A former president of the Chicago NAACP and presently president of the Joint Negro Appeal and a member of the board of directors of the Community Fund of Chicago, Mr. McGee is a firm believer in working within the system to advance opportunities for blacks. Pointing to his own career, he says: "I had faith in the ultimate fairness and justice of the American democratic system. Somehow, I felt that white America would some day recognize the gross injustice accorded black America and would open doors of opportunity to blacks who prepared themselves."

Residents of Chicago's Hyde Park area, the home of the University of Chicago, Mr. and Mrs. McGee look with pride on their college-trained children, all of whom have professional careers. Although he now has five grandchildren, Mr. McGee confides that he would love to return to school—if he could only spare the time.

"Citation for Public Service" from the University of Chicago is presented to Mr. McGee by Mrs. Fay Horton Sawyer (above). At right, he is joined by fellow postal officials Mr. Alonzo J. Jernigan (l.) and Leon J. Hillman on the occasion of the trio's 43rd anniversary in postal service.

Thurgood Marshall
Supreme Court Justice

Thurgood Marshall, associate justice, U.S. Supreme Court; born July 2, 1908 in Baltimore, Md.; Lincoln University (A.B., 1930), Howard University Law School (LL.B., 1933). Wife: Cecilia Suya. Children: Thurgood Jr. and John. Address: U.S. Supreme Court, Washington, DC 20543 (See full biographical sketch in Volume I.)

Once He Was 'Mr. Civil Rights'; Today He Is Mr. Justice Marshall

"Negroes must earn their way to higher achievement. They can't get it by throwing rocks, preaching anarchy or making demands that go beyond reason."

The man who almost single-handedly forced white America to concede that rights guaranteed by the United States Constitution apply also to the nation's blacks is Thurgood Marshall, a civil rights giant whose landmark courtroom victories were the legal battering ram against racial barriers during the 1940s, 1950s and 1960s. As the first—and so far only—black man to hold the position of associate justice of the United States Supreme Court, Mr. Marshall looks back on an extraordinarily brilliant career in constitutional law.

Prior to being elevated to the nation's highest court by President Lyndon B. Johnson in 1967, Justice Marshall served two years as U.S.

Mr. Marshall, who was director and counsel of the NAACP Legal Defense and Educational Fund (1940–61), meets (top photo) with NAACP lawyers to plan legal challenges of racist laws in Mississippi. Above, as U.S. solicitor general (1965–67), he stands outside his office.

As the first black U.S. Supreme Court Justice, Judge Marshall (r., standing) poses with justices (l. to r., standing) Abe Fortas, Potter Stewart, Byron R. White and (seated, l. to r.) John M. Harlan, Hugo L. Black, Chief Justice Earl Warren, William O. Douglas and William J. Brennan Jr.

solicitor general, the lawyer who argues U.S. government cases before the Supreme Court, and before that, as a U.S. district judge for the Second Judicial Circuit (New York).

Justice Marshall achieved his greatest distinction from 1940 to 1961 while serving as director and counsel of the NAACP Legal Defense and Educational Fund. In that position, he argued thirty-two cases before the Supreme Court, winning twenty-nine of them. Of these, the most famous was *Brown* vs. *Topeka Board of Education*, the historic school desegregation case. That pivotal 1954 decision broke the "separate but equal" doctrine of the American judicial system. Writes black historian Lerone Bennett Jr. of Mr. Marshall: "By succeeding brilliantly in the courts, he demonstrated the limitations of the courts. By becoming the indispensable hope of the ghetto, he proved, in the end, that no one man could do it alone. Yet, for all that, Marshall came close. Although he was a lawyer, his leadership ranged

167

Thurgood Marshall as a child in Baltimore, Md. in the early 1900s.

far beyond the confines of the courts. He dramatized litigation, made it understandable, and gave Negroes a new vision of battle. Because of him the Fourteenth Amendment became as real and meaningful to Lenox Avenue as the cop on the beat.''

Justice Marshall was born July 2, 1908 in Baltimore, Maryland. The son of a country club head waiter and a teacher, he was christened ''Throughgood'' but explains, ''By the time I reached the second grade, I got tired of spelling all that out and had it shortened to 'Thurgood.' '' Following his graduation with honors from Douglass High School in Baltimore, he attended Lincoln University in Pennsylvania and received his bachelor's degree *cum laude* in 1930. Barred from Maryland University Law School because of his race, he enrolled at Howard University Law School. Mr. Marshall graduated *magna cum laude*, then set up private practice in Baltimore. From 1933 to 1937, he became a champion of the poor—people who could not afford legal fees. Paradoxically, he built up one of the largest law practices in Baltimore but still had a struggle to pay his rent.

In 1936, Mr. Marshall became part-time assistant to his former law professor, the famed NAACP special counsel Charles Houston, this time as the veteran lawyer's part-time assistant. The Houston-Marshall team plotted the basic NAACP strategy for a massive legal attack on racial inequities. It was Mr. Marshall who prepared the brief in the 1938 Supreme Court case that resulted in granting blacks the right to enter the University of Missouri Law School. That same year, Mr. Houston retired to private practice and Mr. Marshall succeeded him as special counsel at NAACP headquarters in New York. In 1939, the NAACP legal staff became a separate organization as the NAACP Legal Defense Fund and Mr. Marshall was made its director.

As director of the new organization, Mr. Marshall played a key role in the most important shift in black policy since Reconstruction— from an insistence on equal facilities to an open attack on segregation. Beginning with the *Sweatt* vs. *Painter* case, an attack on the segregated law school of the University of Texas, Mr. Marshall succeeded in getting the Supreme Court to rule on the validity of segregation by convincing the Court that equality involved more than physical facilities. He also . won such important key cases as *Smith* vs. *Allwright* (1944), ending segregated primaries, and *Morgan* vs. *Virginia* (1946) invalidating state laws segregating interstate passengers.

Justice Marshall explains his predilection for constitutional law by citing it as the ''ultimate solution'' to many of the black man's racial problems. ''The average guy doesn't suffer so much from prejudiced congressmen in Washington as he does from the local elected official. Once you get the laws on the books, it will be the political action that

168

After winning the 1964 landmark U.S. Supreme Court decision outlawing school segregation, Mr. Marshall celebrates his victory with his secretary, Alice Stovall, and Edward Dudley.

In a 1965 photo taken shortly after his appointment as solicitor general, Mr. Marshall poses for pictures with his wife, Cecilia, and sons, Thurgood Jr. and John.

Summoned to the White House in 1967 for a historic meeting with the late President Lyndon B. Johnson, Judge Marshall (then a U.S. Circuit Court judge) is told of his appointment to the Supreme Court.

will have the most lasting effect. Men will be elected to office who will enforce the Constitution rather than ignore it."

169

Winston E. Moore

Penologist

"Blacks who do nothing but go whoopin' and hollerin' in the streets only bring about more repressive measures. We've got to be willing to stick our necks out by filling positions of responsibility."

Winston E. Moore, executive director of the Cook County (Ill.) Department of Corrections; born Sept. 5, 1929 in New Orleans, La.; West Virginia State College (B.S.), University of Louisville (M.S., psychology); wife: Mable Moore. Address: 2600 S. California Ave., Chicago, IL 60608 (See full biographical sketch in Volume I.)

He Reformed 'the World's Worst Jail' by Insisting on Humane Treatment of Inmates

Director Moore chats with Presiding Criminal Court Judge Joseph Powers at main entrance of Chicago's Cook County Jail.

One of the nation's most outstanding persons in the field of corrections is Winston E. Moore, a New Orleans-born psychologist who is executive director of the Cook County (Illinois) Department of Corrections (comprised of Chicago's Cook County Jail and House of Correction), Mr. Moore is in charge of some 1,000 jail staffers, 3,300 inmates and an annual budget of nearly $12 million. He was promoted to executive director in 1970 after accomplishing what many had thought of as an impossible feat—the reforming of the formerly scandal-ridden Cook County Jail. When he accepted the post of County Jail Superintendent (warden) on March 14, 1968, he inherited what one news account described as "a veritable jungle of sexual perversion, dope traffic, extortion and bestial violence—the worst institution of its kind in the annals of modern penology." Some newspapers simply referred to it as "the world's worst jail." Because of these "scandalous conditions," Mr. Moore's predecessor had been fired. Today, because of the humane and progressive policies instituted by Winston Moore, Cook County Jail serves correction officials throughout the nation and abroad as an example of effective and enlightened jail management.

Normally a congenial, easy-going man, Mr. Moore had put in exactly five minutes on his new job as warden at the county jail when circumstances forced him to give the public a sample of his tougher side. While holding his first press conference, he learned that thirty-five female inmates had gone on a rampage after one of them had dumped soap powder into their dinner of spareribs, presumably in protest over the poor quality of the food. Leading a squad of guards, Warden Moore charged into the women's tier and, without resorting to disabling spray or rough tactics, restored order in less than twenty minutes. To show the rebellious ladies once and for all who was wearing the pants, he had them locked up in their cells without their usual evening meal.

The first battle of his new career had been won. By acting decisively, he had averted the spreading of the outburst to other parts of the jail and thus the possibility of a major catastrophe.

His next move was aimed at putting an end to the notorious "barn boss" system instituted by his predecessor. Under that system, exceptionally tough and brutal inmates (not infrequently convicted murderers) had been given authority to keep other prisoners in line. Excesses fostered by the "barn boss" system had provided the daily press with numerous horror accounts. "There will be no 'barn bosses' by Monday morning," announced the warden on Friday evening, just twenty-four hours after taking office. Then, in an unprecedented and unexpected move, he cracked down on some thirty "barn bosses" by rounding them up and confining them to isolated cells. After that, he personally led a cell by cell shakedown for weapons and other contraband—a search that yielded an arsenal of knives. Miffed by the shakedown, the inmates touched off another disturbance in which several guards were pushed around, but the disorder was quickly quelled.

By Monday, as Warden Moore had promised, the infamous inmate rule at the jail had become a thing of the past. "I want every inmate to know that *we* are the new 'barn bosses,' " the warden said at the time.

The new warden soon discovered that his main problem was less the inmates than the inept guards he had inherited from the previous jail administration. He was particularly annoyed over the excessive absenteeism among the old-timers, charging at one point that the jail had been put in jeopardy because only eleven guards of the twenty-three scheduled to work had shown up. The others, he said, "didn't even have the courtesy to call in sick."

To nobody's surprise, hardly any of the old-timers took kindly to their ebullient new boss and his new-fangled ideas about jail efficiency and humane treatment for all inmates, regardless of the nature of their

Mr. Moore inspects jail's arsenal with one of his aides (top), then chats with Capt. Henry Montgomery (above), a veteran jail guard officer.

Testifying in 1968 before U.S. Senate Investigations subcommittee in Washington, D.C., Mr. Moore warns that federal money handed to Chicago juvenile gangs may have created a "Black Mafia."

171

During talent show at jail, Mr. Moore kids with young inmates (above) in audience. Above right, he and rights activist-comedian Dick Gregory, serving a short term for "civil disobedience," share a joke in jail yard where (right) folk singer Joan Baez teams with inmate band in musical act.

After "clean-up" of Cook County Jail, Mr. Moore is congratulated by Cook County Sheriff Joseph Woods who appointed him to superintendent's post. Mr. Moore remained in his post, even after Republican Woods was voted out of office and replaced by a Democrat.

172

crimes. Warden Moore threatened to fire all of the old guards unless they shaped up. He actually had to fire only fifteen of them; the rest, nearly one hundred, saw the writing on the wall and quit.

While Warden Moore's reforms did not endear him to those guards who were either unable or unwilling to cooperate, they won him a great deal of respect from the inmates themselves. Said one of them, frequently jailed comic and black activist Dick Gregory, who did a forty-two day stretch (and hunger strike) at Cook County Jail: "He (Warden Moore) is straight. He's the best warden of any jail I've been in." Said another, less prominent inmate: "Most of the cats in here dig Warden Moore because he understands us and treats us fair. If you carry yourself like a man, he treats you with respect." And another, who was awaiting trial on a murder charge: "I know a jail is a jail, and all a fellow wants is to get out. But the warden has made it almost a nice place."

Born September 5, 1929, Winston Moore, the only son of a mail carrier, enlisted in the army at sixteen and served three years (1946–49) in the Pacific. Honorably discharged as a staff sergeant, he worked for a year as a longshoreman in New Orleans, then enrolled in college under the GI Bill, earning a B.S. degree from West Virginia State College and an M.S. degree in psychology from the University of Louisville (Kentucky). After graduate studies at Louisville, he worked two years as a psychologist for the Louisville Juvenile Court, then moved to Chicago where he met and married his wife, Mabel, a teacher in the Chicago public schools.

At home, Mr. Moore helps his wife, Mabel, a Chicago school teacher, with a project.

Unable to find employment in his profession, Mr. Moore took a post office night job sorting mail while continuing his studies at the Illinois Institute of Technology (in Chicago) where he came within a thesis' reach of a Ph.D. in psychology. His big break came in March, 1961, when he was hired as a psychologist by the Illinois Youth Commission's Reception and Diagnostic Center (for juvenile delinquents). By November, he had risen to the position of clinic director. In 1966, he took a job as staff psychologist with the Youth Opportunity Center of the Illinois State Employment Service, and two years later accepted the Cook County Jail appointment that led to his present post.

Mr. Moore firmly believes that, in order to become liberated, black people must try to run as many institutions as possible, and that only those blacks who are willing to stick their necks out by filling positions of responsibility are contributing to black progress. Conversely, he is convinced that blacks "who do nothing but go whoopin' and hollerin' in the streets" only bring about more repressive measures. "Being in the field of corrections," he says, "I happen to know something about crowd control. I know that, if necessary, any crowd can be controlled. Any riot can be stopped."

173

Constance Baker Motley

U.S. District Judge

Constance Baker Motley, U.S. district judge, Southern District of New York; born Sept. 14, 1921 in New Haven, Conn.; New York University (A.B., 1943), Columbia University Law School (LL.B., 1946). Husband: Joel Wilson Motley Jr. Son: Joel Wilson III. Address: United States Courthouse, New York, NY 10007 (See full biographical sketch in Volume 1.)

From Civil Rights Lawyer To Federal Judge

"It's a long road with no heroics. You win by preparation and experience, that's all."

U.S. District Judge Constance Baker Motley's long record of glowing achievements in jurisprudence and civil rights has firmly established her as an extraordinary example of black womanhood.

Judge Motley was born September 14, 1921 in New Haven, Connecticut. She is one of eight children of Willoughby and Rachel Baker. Her father, after coming to the U.S. from the West Indies, worked as a chef for Skull and Bones, the Yale fraternity. Although New Haven's black residents were few, Constance Baker developed an early interest in black history, no doubt because it was incorporated into her biracial Sunday school class at an Episcopal church.

The Bakers could not afford to send their daughter to college, but nearly two years after graduating from high school, the opportunity came. Clarence Blakeslee, a wealthy Connecticut contractor who had supported a number of black projects, was so impressed with her intelligence and her delivery as she spoke at a public meeting that he offered to finance her college education. In 1941 she entered Fisk

174

Constance Motley, assisting local attorneys in cases throughout the South won landmark decisions in the NAACP legal onslaught against segregation. A 1961 Georgia ruling opened the doors of the University of Georgia to black students for the first time.

University, majoring in economics.

After a short while, however, she moved to New York and completed undergraduate work at New York University in two and a half years, earning an A.B. degree in economics from NYU's Washington Square College in 1943. She enrolled at Columbia University Law School and met Thurgood Marshall, chief counsel for the National Association for the Advancement of Colored People's Legal Defense Fund and, later, a justice of the U.S. Supreme Court. Mr. Marshall arranged for the astute young law student to work for the LDF as a legal clerk, and when she received her law degree from Columbia in June, 1946, she became a full-time employee on the legal staff. During the same year, she was married to real estate broker Joel Motley Jr. They have one son, Joel III.

While working for the Legal Defense Fund, Attorney Motley participated in all of the major school desegregation cases brought to the courts during the period. She was chief counsel for James Meredith in his long fight to enter the University of Mississippi, and for students admitted to several other Southern state universities, notably the universities of Alabama, Florida and Georgia. On the elementary school level, she was chief counsel for black children in such cities as Atlanta, Georgia; Pensacola, Jacksonville, Daytona Beach and Sarasota, Florida; Hillsboro, Ohio; New Rochelle and Hempstead, New York, and Englewood, New Jersey.

Attorney Motley also tried numerous cases and argued appeals involving segregation protest demonstrations, discrimination in housing, recreation, transportation and public accommodations. From October, 1961 to December, 1964, she won nine of the ten civil rights cases she argued before the U.S. Supreme Court. These law suits involved the right to counsel in criminal cases, defense of students arrested in sit-in demonstrations throughout the South prior to enactment of the Civil Rights Act of 1964, school desegregation plans, discrimination in public recreational facilities, and desegregation of public transportation facilities and services. She became known as a force to be respected and reckoned with in any hall of justice.

175

For over a generation a spot on the NAACP Legal Defense Fund staff has been
the aim of young lawyers dedicated to using their skills and abilities in the cause of
black and other minority people denied of due process. Here, Attorney Motley
and Legal Defense Fund lawyers plan strategy for upcoming case.

When a vacancy occurred in the New York State Senate in
February, 1964, Mrs. Motley ran for the office. She was initially rejected
for nomination by Democratic elements on the theory that she was a
middle-class woman who could not get the black working-class vote.
Despite sharp opposition from political bosses, she ran anyway. She
won after a short, quiet campaign that gained in intensity near the end.
The victory made her the first woman senator in the state's history. She
was re-elected in November, 1964, and served until February, 1965
when, in a special election, the New York City Council chose her to fill a
vacancy as president of the Borough of Manhattan. She was re-elected
in the city-wide elections of November 1965 to a full four-year
term with tri-party endorsement: Democratic, Republican and Liberal.

Judge Motley has received more than seventy awards from
organizations and eight honorary degrees from universities—testimony
to a brilliant law career. She was appointed to her present lifetime
position as a United States District Judge for the Southern District of
New York on September 9, 1966 by President Lyndon B. Johnson. By
1972, she was earning $40,000 a year.

Her advice to young blacks planning careers in law is: "It's a long
road with no heroics. You win by preparation and experience, that's all.
Preparation and experience."

176

The civil rights struggle of the sixties took Northern-born and bred Constance Motley into the heart of the Southland, where her wit and humor eased many a tense moment.

Left, with Rev. Fred Shuttlesworth, Roy Wilkins, Rev. Ralph Abernathy and Dr. Martin Luther King Jr. Above with Dr. Lozette Hale and Mrs. M. L. King, Jr.

Appointed U.S. District Judge by President Lyndon Johnson, Mrs. Motley receives congratulations from Thurgood Marshall and (r.) from her mother, Mrs. Rachel Baker.

Gordon Parks Sr.
Photo-journalist, author, and movie director

In His Difficult Fight for Success, He Chose to Use Pictures and Words

Gordon Alexander Buchanan Parks, photo-journalist, author, composer and movie director; born Nov. 30, 1912 in Ft. Scott, Kan.; Maryland Institute (Doctor of Fine Arts); Farm Security Administration cameraman under Rosenwald Fellowship (1942–43), Life magazine photographer for many years; Children: Gordon Jr., Roger, David and Toni (Mrs. Jean-Luc Brovillaud). Address: Warner Bros.-Seven Arts, Hollywood, CA 90028 (See full biographical sketch in Volume I.)

One of America's most talented men, Mr. Parks has distinguished himself as a photographer, writer, composer and film director. His work has brought him numerous awards, honorary degrees, etc. His books include *The Learning Tree* and *A Choice of Weapons*; his musical scores include a piano concerto and three piano sonatas, and he has directed the movies *The Learning Tree, Shaft* and *Shaft's Big Score.*

"I dreamt big—dreamt that I could become the first black film producer, director . . ."

Gordon Parks Sr. knew the tough, seamy side of America before he became a distinguished photo-journalist, author and movie director. For blacks, the road he traveled is familiar. Yet, Mr. Parks is one who made it—no doubt because, from the arsenal of available weapons, he chose to use pictures and words.

"I think that these have been more effective," he says, "than the more violent weapons such as the gun, the knife, the club or other weapons that you might use. And this choice was made not by me but by my mother many years ago in Kansas. She admonished me early in life that I should never let my color stand in the way of success. I've simply lived by her philosophy and am not the least bit sorry."

Gordon Alexander Buchanan Parks was born November 30, 1912, on a farm in Fort Scott, Kansas, the youngest of fifteen children of a cattle-herding family. His mother died when he was sixteen and young

Mr. Parks sits with the New York Orchestral Society during taping of his *First Concerto for Piano and Orchestra.*

On location during filming of his autobiography, *The Learning Tree*, Mr. Parks pauses during break in scene rehearsals.

Early in his career, Mr. Parks was a photographer for Standard Oil Company. He is shown with photographers Arnold Eagle and Charlotte Brooks.

Gordon was sent to live in St. Paul, Minnesota, with his married sister and her husband. His father's parting words were, "Boy, remember your Mama's teachin'. You'll be all right."

Once he reached Minnesota, things went smoothly—until he quarrelled with his brother-in-law. "I was thrown out into the cold," Mr. Parks recalls. "It was thirty degrees below zero, one of the worst winters I've ever known. My brother-in-law didn't like the idea of my coming into his home and disrupting it, I suppose." Completely on his own and with nothing but his clothes, Gordon Parks had to become a man overnight.

"Those are the years I fought. I fought the cold as well as the discrimination, the indignities that were heaped upon black boys at that time. In the end, this is the reason I wanted to find some way to communicate with people. I didn't know what lay ahead of me, but I believed in myself. My deepest instincts told me I would not perish."

Mr. Parks kept himself alive, holding down a string of odd jobs. He worked in a pool room in Minneapolis, in a flophouse in Chicago, Illinois, and in a jail in St. Paul, Minnesota. He became a "hunt-and-peck" piano player, a cowpuncher, a dock-hand; he tried his luck as a professional basketball player, a porter, and a dining car waiter. In the meantime, he daydreamed and composed a few lyrics on weekends. One day he broke the monotony by going to the movies.

"I went to see a newsreel about the bombing of the *Panay*, an American gunboat in China," he recalls, "and there was this terrific footage by a man named Norman Alley. And when the lights went up there was Alley himself on the stage, talking about how he'd stayed at his camera position while the bombs were falling. That made a tremendous impression on me."

Although he was working as a dining car waiter at the time, Parks

179

A highly respected movie director, Mr. Parks guides actor Richard Roundtree (l.) through a scene in *Shaft*.

bought a book about photography and read it on the run between Chicago and Seattle. He also had the luck to meet the late photo-journalist Robert Capa and he told him of his dream of becoming a photographer for *Life* magazine. "If you really mean that," said the famous cameraman, "then stop all the talk and start making that dream come true."

When Mr. Parks reached Seattle he used part of his pay to purchase his first camera, a $7.50 Voigtlander Brilliant he chose from a dusty pawnshop shelf. "I bought that particular brand," he recalls, "simply because it had a fancy name and not because it was such a good camera." Mr. Parks made his first pictures on a rainy day in Seattle in 1937. He ambled down to Puget Sound, began shooting pictures of sea gulls and ended up falling into the water. He held onto his camera until firemen fished him out with a rescue hook.

He dried himself off and took the film back to Minnesota. Arriving in St. Paul, he showed his film to the Eastman Kodak people there. They developed the film, praised his ability and three months later gave him an exhibition in Minneapolis. In 1938, while working as a waiter at the Minnesota Club, he was given another chance to prove his ability as a lensman by Mrs. Frank Murphy, a wealthy, understanding Irish socialite who frequently sponsored fashion shows in St. Paul. She put two of Mr. Parks' pictures in the window of her store—a display that caught the attention of Mrs. Joe Louis, who invited him to work in Chicago, where he was given a darkroom at the South Side Community Art Center in return for his photographic services.

By 1940, Mr. Parks' photography was good enough to earn him a
Julius Rosenwald fellowship, he had put on a number of
photo exhibits in Chicago and had received wide critical acclaim for his
one-man shows at the South Side Center. The Rosenwald grant was
the first awarded for photography and sent Mr. Parks to Washington to
work as a cameraman with the Farm Security Administration under the
guidance of Roy Stryker, who prodded him, sweated him and made
him *see* and *feel* a picture before he allowed the anxious young
photographer to use a camera. It was there that he began to develop
a strong documentary approach in portraying the intimate lives

After attending the 1971
premiere of *Shaft* (l.), Mr.
Parks appears at a
benefit reception (below)
with (l. to r.) boxing
trainer Drew ''Bundini''
Brown, Richard
Roundtree, and Howard
Sheffy, president of the
Guardians, a black
police organization.

181

of black people.

After a year with the FSA, Mr. Parks was chosen for service with the Office of War Information. He filmed the war effort on the domestic front, New England industries, and a dramatic series of pictures of North Sea convoys. The OWI later assigned him as a correspondent with the 332nd Fighter Group. Although he recorded its activities in the States and was prepared to accompany it overseas, congressional leaders withdrew his visa because "they thought a black unit shouldn't get so much publicity." Mr. Parks resigned and in 1945 started working with Roy Stryker again at the Standard Oil Company. He made pictures of Standard Oil holdings in the Arctic Circle and in South America. The shots brought him to the attention of *Life* magazine editors, who engaged him as a staff photographer in 1949. Working for *Life*, Mr. Parks developed versatility and his striking, individual camera style.

Some of Mr. Parks' important assignments with *Life* were stories on a Harlem gang leader, segregation in the South, crime in the United States, and the plight of an underprivileged Brazilian boy named Flavio, about whom he also wrote and directed a documentary film. As a *Life* photographer, he traveled to every corner of the world, gliding easily from raw realism to graceful fashion portraits—an art that earned him the A.S.M.P. "Magazine Photographer of the Year" award in 1961. He also received the Newhouse Award in photography from Syracuse University as well as honors in the Art Directors show competition.

As a "weekend composer," Mr. Parks wrote several musical

Mr. Parks poses with film stars Ron O'Neal of *Super Fly* and Cicely Tyson of *Sounder*.

182

Lauded by the NAACP for his "unique creativity . . . outstanding achievements," Mr. Parks receives the organization's 57th Spingarn Medal (1972) from Dr. Clifton R. Wharton, president of Michigan State University.

compositions, including *First Concerto for Piano and Orchestra* which was performed in 1953, and three piano sonatas performed at Philadelphia in 1955. In addition, he has written two books on photography, *Flash Photography* and *Camera Portraits*; a 1963 novel, *The Learning Tree*, and his autobiography, *A Choice of Weapons*, which was published in 1966. His book *Photos and Poems* appeared in 1968. A year before, in 53 countries, he was voted the photo-journalist who had done most to promote understanding among the nations of the world. Still expanding his potential, Mr. Parks brought *The Learning Tree* to the screen in 1968.

"I was very anxious," he reflects, "to do something about the many dreams I had as a boy. I dreamt big—dreamt that I could become the first black film producer, director and whatever. That had to be a big dream because no black man had been allowed to assume that position before. I knew I had to go to Hollywood with a portfolio that would be impossible to turn down. That's why I had to write my book, adapt it to the screen, write the screenplay, direct it, cast it, produce it and write the music—because I wanted it to be a pure memoir of my parents."

Following mild success with *The Learning Tree*, Mr. Parks went on to direct the number one box-office hit, *Shaft*, the black blockbuster starring Richard Roundtree, whom Mr. Parks hand-picked, groomed and coached for stardom in 1971. A year later, Mr. Parks repeated his success by filming the sequel, *Shaft's Big Score*.

Mr. Parks has three grown children: Gordon Jr., a photographer and film director in his own right, David and Toni.

183

Henry G. Parks Jr.

President, H. G. Parks, Inc.

Henry G. Parks Jr., business executive; president of Henry G. Parks, Inc. (Parks Sausage Company) in Baltimore, Md.; born Sept. 20, 1916 in Atlanta, Ga.; Ohio State University (B.S.). Divorced. Daughters: Grace (Mrs. L. D. Johnson) and Cheryl. Address: 501 W. Hamburg St., Baltimore, MD 21230 (See full biographical sketch on Henry G. Parks Sr. in Volume I.)

"I got used to being thrown out of places and then going back. I guess I grew through adversity."

Mr. Parks Came Up With a Successful Recipe

Before Henry G. Parks Jr. graduated from Ohio State University as an honor student, he was advised by his placement counselor to do three things and he would "easily become a success in any major corporation you choose." Mr. Parks was told to change his name, go to South America to acquire a Spanish accent, and then come back to the United States. These suggestions might have been a success formula for the young black student of marketing in the late 1930s. But Parks never gave it a try. Instead, he replied that he would not run from anything, least of all himself.

Since then, Mr. Parks has tried to prove that blacks in America "don't have anything to run *from*, just a lot to run *toward*. I think I have proved that black businessmen not only can be successful, but that they can be successful on the same terms as anybody else."

Mr. Parks' model of success is his $10 million public corporation, H. G. Parks, Inc., which he founded in Baltimore, Maryland in September 1951. The sausage company, of which he is president and chairman of the board, has been developed into a regional concern that now supplies several million pounds of breakfast meat annually to twelve thousand stores on the East Coast from Washington, D.C., to Boston. Its customers include supermarkets in white, middle-class suburbia

184

Visiting assembly line area of
his plant, Mr. Parks talks
with employees.

(75%) as well as independent stores in black communities. His
business, which first sold stock to the public three years ago, is said to
be a nearly perfect example of black management.

The tall, distinguished-looking businessman cleared the hurdle of
being recognized in the white man's marketplace. He is now
approaching the second hurdle—that of giving leadership to those
who now give recognition to his accomplishments. This self-imposed
goal, he believes, will allow him "to see American businessmen in
general do what Parks Sausage is doing."

His business, he proudly claims, is at the forefront of consumer
goods. Although sausage is subject only to state inspection, he has
invited federal inspection of his plants from the start. For years, his meat
has been coded to indicate when it should be withdrawn from store
shelves. Mr. Parks also points to his employer-employee relations as a
good example for American businessmen to follow. He went to the
unions before they came to him.

Obviously some industrial and commercial businesses agree with
Mr. Parks' business tactics. He has been named to the boards
of two major corporations—First Pennsylvania Corporation and the
Magnavox Company. He is also a vice-president and a director of
Tuesday Publications, Inc., a Chicago-based publishing company that
produces the monthly *Tuesday* newspaper supplement.

185

Henry Parks is a self-made man who is a fighter by nature. Born September 20, 1916 in Atlanta, Georgia, to poor parents who both worked as domestics, his boyhood was spent in Dayton, Ohio, where he attended public schools. At Ohio State University he did graduate work in marketing and served as president of the Interracial Society, the Inter-Fraternal Council, and the Alpha Phi Alpha fraternity.

After graduating from Ohio State, Mr. Parks went to work with Dr. Mary McLeod Bethune at the Resident War Production Training Center in Wilberforce, Ohio, and from there moved on to try his fortunes in New York City. There he owned and operated a variety of enterprises, including a theatrical booking agency. After an abortive attempt at forming a soft drinks company with Joe Louis (the boxing champion) and his wife, to be called Joe Louis Punch, he moved to Baltimore where he engaged in various businesses—drug store operation, real estate, and cement block production—before he launched the Parks Sausage Company in 1951. He got together with several other young men and decided that there was a growing demand for a "southern style, well-seasoned sausage."

In nearly every phase of the young company's operations, problems were encountered: financing, production, distribution, sales and the securing of raw materials. Plant operations were set up in Baltimore, where the general offices and plant are now located, in a rented building. Six persons performed all operations of the company.

But Mr. Parks and his associates held to his "reverse marketing" strategy. The black consumer is the center of this strategy. From the start, his focal point was the black community which, he believes, relies heavily on brand names as insurance of quality because, he notes, "the ghettos have traditionally been the dumping ground for bad products."

With this in mind, Mr. Parks got his start selling to six stores in black Baltimore. He took his product, made from an old Virginia recipe that has been adapted to mass production techniques while still maintaining homemade values, and sponsored breakfasts for black ministers. His saleswomen promoted the product in beauty shops; salesmen campaigned in the barber shops and shoe-shine stands. A barker dressed as "Parky the Pig" paraded the streets passing out free sausage.

Soon, his product was in demand in the black community. And eventually, in the final phase of his strategic plan, black shoppers carried this demand into the broader marketplace.

About a year later, Mr. Parks got his break. He signed up his first chain in Washington, D.C. By using basically the same tactics in market after market, he won over every major chain on the East Coast.

186

Mr. Parks is now vice president of the Chamber of Commerce of Metropolitan Baltimore and is a member of numerous civic and business groups. Mr. Parks has succeeded to the point where his company's 1971 sales reached $10.4 million. The secret of his success must certainly contain determination and energy as ingredients. As he once said: "I got used to being thrown out of places and then going back. I guess I grew through adversity."

Mr. Parks' marriage ended in divorce some years ago, and he lives quietly in Baltimore, and enjoys playing golf and watching football, as a spectator. His elder daughter, Grace Gainelle Johnson lives nearby with her husband, L. D. Johnson, and two grandchildren; his younger daughter, Cheryl, is a stewardess for Eastern Airlines.

THE WHITE HOUSE
WASHINGTON

April 7, 1953

Dear Mr. Parks,

The carton of pork sausage which you left at the gate of the White House for the President and me was delivered to us a few days ago. It was indeed very kind of you to present us with such a generous supply, and we have found, as you predicted, that it is delicious. Thank you so much for this friendly gesture.

The President joins me in sending you our warm regards and best wishes.

Mamie Doud Eisenhower

Mr. Henry G. Parks, Jr.
2509 Pennsylvania Avenue
Baltimore 17, Maryland

Shortly after Mr. Parks founded his business, his Washington, D.C. manager, Clay Wilson, delivered (top) a sample of Parks Sausage to White House guard Captain W. J. McCarthy for President and Mrs. Dwight D. Eisenhower. Publicity about Mrs. Eisenhower's letter of thanks (above) helped the sausage become popular.

Mr. Parks personally samples a batch of sausage before it is shipped from Baltimore to his thousands of customers.

187

Lois Mailou Jones Pierre-Noël

Artist and Teacher

An Artist Acclaimed Wherever Her Sunlit Paintings Are Seen

Lois Mailou Jones Pierre-Noël, professor of design and watercolor painting, College of Fine Arts, Howard University; born Nov. 3, 1905 in Boston, Mass.; attended six art schools in the U.S. and Paris, France; Howard University (A.B., magna cum laude, 1945); husband: Vergniaud Pierre-Noël. Address: Box 893 Howard University, Washington, DC 20001 (See full biographical sketch in Volume I.)

"I feel that it is the duty of every black artist to participate in the current movement which aims to establish recognition of works by black artists. . . ."

Lois Mailou Jones (Mrs. Vergniaud Pierre-Noël), professor of design and water color painting at Howard University's College of Fine Arts, has excelled as a creative artist both in the United States and abroad. Long before the works of black painters were taken seriously or admitted at art exhibits, Boston-born Mrs. Pierre-Noël had been widely recognized as an artist of considerable talent. A recipient of numerous awards, including the Achievement in Art award presented to her by Haiti's former president, Paul E. Magloire, Mrs. Pierre-Noël is represented in sixteen permanent collections in the United States and in several foreign countries. She has some twenty one-woman shows to her credit and has entered her work in more than thirty group exhibitions. In 1962, she was elected a Fellow of London's prestigious Royal Society of Arts.

While Mrs. Pierre-Noël's paintings are largely characterized by their vivid colors and their strength in structure and design, a survey of her works underlines the versatility of their creator. Included are impressionistic Parisian street scenes and sunny landscapes from southern France—painted during the artist's frequent visits to that country over the years. Then there are paintings done in Haiti— decorative, often cubist impressions of Haitian life and scenery, and somber, mystic compositions filled with voodoo symbols inspired by her contacts with that Caribbean nation since her marriage in 1953 to Vergniaud Pierre-Noël, a Haitian and also a distinguished artist. In addition, her work includes American seascapes, portraits, African and Afro-American compositions, and abstract designs.

Mrs. Pierre-Noël's life and her career have been as varied as her art. Born November 3, 1905, she established solid academic credentials before beginning to paint seriously. A graduate of the Boston Museum School of Fine Arts, which she attended on a four-year scholarship, she also has certificates from the Boston Normal Art School and the Designers Art School and has attended Columbia, Harvard and Howard universities. She received an A.B. degree from Howard and studied at the Academie Julian in Paris and at several art schools in Rome.

After receiving her teaching certificate upon graduation from

188

Mrs. Pierre-Noël is shown at work in her studio (top). Above is her watercolor, *Magic of Nigeria.* At right is another of her works, *Ubi Girl from the Tai Region.*

The artist and teacher conducts a figure-drawing class as a part of her assignments at Howard University, where she is professor of design and watercolor painting.

the Boston Museum School, she applied for a vacant teaching position at her *alma mater* but was turned down and told to "go South and help your people." After a brief career as a free-lance designer in Boston and in New York, she took the advice and in 1928 accepted a position as head of the art department of Palmer Memorial Institute in Sedalia, North Carolina. Two years later, she joined the Fine Arts Department of Howard University and has remained there ever since.

Although Mrs. Pierre-Noël's paintings were exhibited and acclaimed by the world famous Société des Artistes Français in Paris as early as 1938, it was not until 1953 that one of her paintings was exhibited in the United States—at the Corcoran Gallery of Art in Washington, D.C., and then only after it had been entered by one of her white friends. The reason for this subterfuge was the Corcoran Gallery's rule prohibiting the displaying of black artists' work. Mrs. Pierre-Noël's oil painting was awarded first prize by the unwitting judges in the annual exhibition, but she waited for several years before she decided to claim her award from the surprised gallery officials. It was because of such experiences that she adopted France as her spiritual homeland. "It gave me my first feeling of absolute freedom," she explains.

In 1954, the Haitian government commissioned Mrs. Pierre-Noël to do a series of paintings of the island. She once spent six weeks there conducting a survey of contemporary Haitian painters, sculptors and ceramicists for Howard University. Detesting to be typed, she emphasizes that her preoccupation with Haiti is just one of her many interests in "black art," which she defines as "works done by black artists in an effort to bring about an awareness that black artists exist. It establishes for them 'black identity.' "

Although profoundly proud of her black heritage, she rejects the

Mrs. Pierre-Noël is popular with her students. She has been employed as a teacher in Howard University's Fine Arts Department since 1930.

190

The artist attracts a crowd on a Paris sidewalk (top). She is shown below with her artist husband, Vergniaud, a native of Haiti. Below (right) she is seen with Mrs. Robert F. Kennedy at a one-man exhibition of her works at Howard.

idea that all works by black artists must be based on "the black experience." She explains: "I feel that it is the duty of every black artist to participate in the current movement which aims to establish recognition of works by black artists. [But] I will continue to exhibit in 'black art shows' and other shows the works which express my sincere creative feelings. Whether these works portray the 'black experience' or 'heritage' or are purely abstract is immaterial so long as they meet the highest standards of the modern art world. The major focus must be to achieve for black artists their just and rightful place as *artists*."

191

Sidney Poitier
Actor

Sidney Poitier, actor; born Feb. 20, 1927 in Miami, Fla., grew up in the Bahamas; attended public school in Nassau, studied with private tutors; served in U.S. Army during World War II; won Academy Award (1963) as best actor for Lilies of the Field. Was married to Juanita Hardy in 1950. Children: Beverly Pamela and Sherri. Address: Columbia Pictures, 1438 Gower St., Los Angeles, CA 90004 (See full biographical sketch in Volume I.)

In An Era of Black Superstars, An 'Old-Timer' Remains at the Top

"I used to go to pictures and when I saw a Negro on the screen I always left the theater embarrassed and uneasy. . . ."

In an era when black superstars emerge with almost each new black film, Sidney Poitier, an "old-timer," remains the biggest of them all: an unquestioned box-office giant who has earned the privilege of choosing only those roles in which he finds meaning, of bringing to the screen only those images which he feels do not demean black people in any way. "Years ago, before I became an actor," Mr. Poitier has said, "I used to go to pictures and when I saw a Negro on the screen I always left the theater embarrassed and uneasy. There he was, devoid of any dignity . . . good maids who laughed too loud, good butlers afraid of ghosts. In the old days, it was a matter of taking whatever parts were offered, just to eat."

Sidney Poitier was born February 20, 1927 in Miami, Florida. He was the only one of seven sons and two daughters of Reginald and Evelyn Poitier born in the United States. His father, a tomato farmer in Nassau, Bahamas, often sailed to Florida with his wife to

Mr. Poitier's acting technique came to the attention of movie fans in *Blackboard Jungle*, one of his earliest films.

sell his produce. Sidney was born during one of the trips. He grew up in the Bahamas and did not start school until he was eleven years old. Two years later, his father's business folded and Sidney was forced to drop out of school to help support his family.

At fifteen, he returned to the city of his birth and tried his hand at many jobs. Unhappy with racism in Miami, he rode freight trains to New York City. Before he was sixteen, the young Poitier had worked in New York as a drug store clerk, parking lot attendant, ditch digger, trucker and longshoreman. He joined the United States Army at eighteen and served four years, working as a physiotherapist in an army mental hospital. Upon his discharge, he resolved to stay on in New York and do ''something constructive'' with his life.

One day, after spending the night on a Harlem rooftop, he spotted an advertisement. The American Negro Theater was looking for actors. After flunking two auditions , mainly because of his singsong West Indies accent, he landed a job as a backstage worker. In exchange for acting and speech lessons, Poitier became the theater's janitor. Slowly learning acting techniques and advancing gradually to bit parts in weekly productions, he finally caught the eye of James Light, a show business producer, who saw his latent talent. There was power in his voice, an electric stage presence, a soul of many emotional shades. Mr. Light knew that the young actor was destined for greatness.

Through Mr. Light, Sidney Poitier won parts which attracted

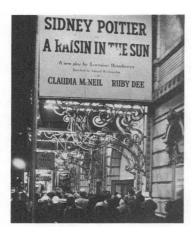

After successfully starring in *A Raisin in the Sun* (above), Mr. Poitier shares a laugh with his wife, Juanita (c.), and playwright Lorraine Hansberry.

As a dock worker in *A Man Is Ten Feet Tall*, Mr. Poitier locks loading hooks with actor Jack Warden (above). A more recent film, *In the Heat of the Night*, starred Mr. Poitier in the role of a black detective pitted against Southern bigots (right).

critical attention. On Broadway he began to cause small ripples in *Lysistrata, Freight* and *Anna Lucasta*. But it was the role of Miller in the film *The Blackboard Jungle* (1956) which made him famous. The film itself opened to bad reviews but Mr. Poitier's portrait of a young black delinquent was praised as "sensitive," "vivid," and "beautiful."

Earlier, he had appeared in *No Way Out*, (1950) which was followed by *Cry the Beloved Country* (1952); *Red Ball Express* (1952); *Go, Man, Go* (1954) and *Goodbye, My Lady* (1956). His other pre-1970 films included *Edge of the City* (1957); *Band of Angels* (1957); *Something of Value* (1957); *Porgy and Bess* (1959); *All the Young Men*

194

Mr. Poitier's portrayal of a maverick who befriends nuns (above) in *Lilies of the Field* was excellent enough to win the 1963 Academy Award as best actor. At right, he and actress Ann Bancroft pose with the coveted "Oscar."

A civil rights supporter, Mr. Poitier speaks (above) at a benefit rally in New York City, joins his friend Harry Belafonte (above, right) after presenting a $70,000 check to Mississippi civil rights leaders, and discusses fund-raising plans (right) with Mrs. Harry Belafonte (l.) and Dore Schary.

(1960); *Paris Blues* (1961); *Pressure Point* (1962); *The Long Ships* (1964); *The Greatest Story Ever Told* (1965); *Patch of Blue* (1966); *The Slender Thread* (1966); *The Bedford Incident* (1966); *In the Heat of the Night* (1967); *For Love of Ivy* (1968); *Guess Who's Coming to Dinner* (1968); *The Lost Man* (1969).

In Germany, Mr. Poitier won the Best Actor award of the Berlin Film Festival and an Academy Award nomination for Stanley Kramer's *The Defiant Ones* in which he played an escaped convict. The New York Drama Circle award was given to him for his role in *A Raisin in the Sun* (1961), a film version adapted from the Broadway play in which he had starred in 1959.

196

An astute businessman, Mr. Poitier discusses a joint production venture (above) with actor Paul Newman and singer-actress Barbra Streisand. He co-stars with friend Harry Belafonte (above, right) in *Buck and the Preacher*, directed by Mr. Poitier. During an appearance on the "Soul!" television show (right), he and Mr. Belafonte discuss the film.

In 1964, Sidney Poitier broke the color barrier which had kept the Oscar from those black actors starring in principal roles. To thunderous applause, he accepted the coveted award as Best Actor for his performance as a drifter in *Lilies of the Field*.

From that historic night, Sidney Poitier was an unchallenged "superstar," who could name his price.

Emerging in the 1970s as a film director, Mr. Poitier and his life-long friend, Harry Belafonte, produced *Buck and the Preacher*, a film dealing with the role of black men and women in the conquest of the American West.

Riding the tide of critical acclaim for *Buck and the Preacher*, Sidney Poitier admits that there are no more frontiers for him as an actor: "I have no desire to do Othello," he says. "I want to work someday exclusively as a director to control the image of blacks on the screen."

197

Ersa H. Poston

President, New York State Civil Service Commission

500,000 Employees Are Under Her Supervision

"In our family, education was an obsession. Accomplishment was something that was driven into me every moment of my life."

Personal achievement has seldom been a problem for Ersa H. Poston, who, as president of the New York State Civil Service Commission, holds the highest appointive office ever given a black person in the state. When the children on her block were still learning proper table manners, young Ersa was being groomed by her paternal grandmother in the habits and attitudes that guarantee success. "In our family, education was an obsession," she recalls. "Accomplishment was something that was driven into me every moment of my life."

Mrs. Poston, whose staff of seven hundred persons serves some one-half million New York civil servants, was born in 1921 in Paducah, Kentucky. When she was only four, her mother, a Cherokee, contracted fatal tuberculosis and young Ersa was taken care of by her paternal grandparents who ran a small hotel and a cafe in the town. It was naturally assumed that she would enter some profession. By her freshman year in high school she had decided on medicine, but despite her superior grades in other subjects it was discovered that she had no aptitude for science. A social work career was another possibility—and Ersa eventually adopted it as her life's occupation. "I think I first

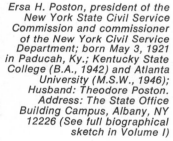

Ersa H. Poston, president of the New York State Civil Service Commission and commissioner of the New York Civil Service Department; born May 3, 1921 in Paducah, Ky.; Kentucky State College (B.A., 1942) and Atlanta University (M.S.W., 1946); Husband: Theodore Poston. Address: The State Office Building Campus, Albany, NY 12226 (See full biographical sketch in Volume I)

became interested in social work during the Depression when so many people around us were going hungry," she recalls. "My grandfather was a railroad switchman and continued to work during those dark days, so we were never in need. Grandma turned the house into a kind of soup kitchen, and there was always something to eat for both whites and Negroes."

Ersa enrolled in Kentucky State College and graduated in 1942. After working for two years, she resumed her education, earning a master's degree in social work from Atlanta University. She moved north to take a job with the Hartford (Conn.) Tuberculosis and Health Association, but when the opportunity arose she moved on to

On opposite page, Mrs. Poston takes her oath of office from N.Y. Secretary of State John Lomeco as Governor Nelson Rockefeller looks on. Above (top), after being named chairman of President Nixon's Advisory Council on Intergovernmental Policy, she meets with other members of the Council. Above, she and CBS-TV news correspondent Joan Murray attend a Links, Inc. luncheon in New York City. At right (above), she receives an award from the Public Personnel Association.

New York and a position with a YWCA neighborhood project. Four years later she joined the City Youth Board and later took a job with the State Division of Youth.

Meantime, in 1957, she married Theodore Poston, a fellow Kentuckian who, as "Ted" Poston, was a well-known journalist with the *New York Post*. Mrs. Poston was gaining new experience in her field, and when the State of New York asked her to assume the directorship of its new Office of Economic Opportunity, she recalls, "I said, 'Yes, just give me the chance.'" Three years later, in 1967, she was appointed by Governor Nelson A. Rockefeller to her present position, which she describes light-heartedly as "a gigantic assignment."

The commission is responsible for guaranteeing that merit alone is the determining factor in the hiring and advancement of all state personnel. It also functions as a training institution, a complaints bureau and an employee-relations service. Aside from her administrative duties, Mrs. Poston presides over a three-member quasi-judicial board which arbitrates disputes over questions of discipline, examinations, disqualifications, salary and title arguments, extension of service beyond mandatory age, and the administration of a state Employee Suggestion Program. In addition, by working through the Governor's Council, she has the power to obtain or to prevent legislative action.

One of the commission's more interesting programs is a career development plan which over the last several years has trained and employed thousands of persons with modest education for careers in state government. "Many are people others have given up on," says Mrs. Poston. "Yet our retention figure is 70 percent. Ages range from eighteen to the sixties. We have mothers and children in the same classes. There's nothing particularly mystical about it. We've just gone into the ghettos and found candidates. We have to have social commitments if we are going to meet our manpower needs. After six weeks of orientation, with remedial work for some, they start in an agency as employee-trainees. The program is designed to start workers on a career ladder and then help move them up."

Other areas of concern to Mrs. Poston and her commission are a regionalization program to bring civil service facilities closer to the people, and the broadening of opportunities for women in higher echelons. "We want to recruit more women in certain top occupational categories—in technical and managerial jobs," she says. "Now, many of our women employees are in clerical and secretarial positions. The situation is better than it used to be but there needs to be more improvement. Capable women need opportuniies to move to more responsible positions."

When Governor Rockefeller announced Mrs. Poston's appointment, he called her "an able administrator and a creative planner of programs to expand opportunities and horizons." He might have added that she is a committed and conscientious person with a deep sense of responsibility to an assignment. Upon his election in 1968, the then President-elect Richard M. Nixon offered Mrs. Poston a "high" civil service post. She declined, explaining that there was much to be done in her present position with the State of New York. She did eventually accept a position as chairman of the federal Advisory Council on Intergovernment Personnel Policy. The job did not conflict with her assignment in New York.

200

Mrs. Poston receives the Doctor of Laws degree in 1971 at Union College in Schenectady, N.Y. (top), and receives the 1970 Woman of the Year award (above) from the Business and Professional Women's Club of Albany, N.Y. At right (above) she has dinner with her husband, Ted.

Mrs. Poston is the only female in Governor Rockefeller's cabinet and is the highest-ranking female in the state government.

Among her friends and colleagues she is famed as a hostess and for the elegance of her wardrobe. A gourmet cook, she frequently entertains dozens at dinner. Her specialties are Mexican and Spanish dishes and homemade bread. She is also a dedicated reader of mystery novels. "They are my go-to-sleep material," she says. "I can't handle heavy professional journals at bedtime. I usually get too disturbed." Her working hours are frequently erratic but she regularly commutes between her office in Albany and the Brooklyn townhouse she shares with her husband. They have no children of their own but there are several godchildren.

"Ersa gets active in some small group, like a sorority," says Mr. Poston, "and before you know it they're 'doing something for community youth.' We go to a movie preview in a Brooklyn theater, and five little Irish girls, the usherettes, who knew her when she was working for the YWCA in Manhattan, descend on us in the middle of the picture and the rest of the time there is conversation. We seem to spend half our life surrounded by Ersa's little followers."

Says Mrs. Poston herself in providing a summary of her work: "We're always planning *for* people instead of *with* people. We've got to involve in leadership the people for whom the program is intended. It's going to be a tough assignment—but exciting."

201

Alvin Poussaint, M.D.
Psychiatrist

His Probing Analyses Help Blacks to Know Themselves

"... the white man cannot give Negroes black consciousness. They have to give it to each other."

On May 15, 1934 Alvin Poussaint was born in New York's East Harlem, the son of a printer. His parents were descended from the Poussaint family who lived in French-dominated Haiti during the nineteenth century and eventually emigrated from the South to New York City. One of eight children, Alvin was stricken by rheumatic fever at the age of nine, and was hospitalized for six months. During that time, he became an avid reader. His desire to read was fostered by a sister-in-law "who was very interested in encouraging me in school and listening to me talk and giving me books to read," he says. "Consequently, I became sort of academically focused."

Stimulated by such concern, he completed junior high school with an evident aptitude for mathematics and science. He successfully competed for a place in prestigious Peter Stuyvesant High School, one

Alvin Poussaint, M.D., associate professor of psychiatry, Harvard University Medical School; born May 15, 1934 in New York, N.Y.; Columbia University (B.A., 1956), Cornell University (M.D., 1960), University of California at Los Angeles (M.S., 1964). Address: Harvard Medical School, 25 Shattuck St., Boston, MA 02115 (See full biographical sketch in Volume I.)

of New York City's most respected schools. He was swept up by a wave of excitement, and intellectual competition.

Each day, however, as he left school, and returned to the ghetto on 101st Street he realized the differences between his contrasting worlds. It was not long before his community was consumed by the drug traffic of the 1950s. He saw many of his "running buddies" crushed by the effects of drugs. His first major decision was the rejection of the drug culture. "Every so often one of [my friends] would die. If he didn't die from an overdose, he would end up in jail for stealing, and it didn't seem worth whatever he was getting from it to participate in it, although there was a lot of pressure in the community on the kids to become drug addicts."

He graduated from Peter Stuyvesant with his heart set on going to Yale University, but the elder Poussaint felt it would be more "practical" if his son stayed near home. Consequently, he enrolled at New York's Columbia University, which he initially disliked. The Columbia University environment was not open socially to blacks, who were excluded from events by the "unspoken rules" of segregation.

Abhorring the ignorance and irrationality of racism, the young Columbia student decided not to let it cloud his direction. In the fall of 1956, he found himself at New York Hospital on East 68th Street. Young Poussaint sat through classes for endless hours—the only black American in a class of eighty-six students. He was often warned of

Dr. Poussaint is shown in his office at Harvard (above). At right, he talks with colleagues at the Neuropsychiatric Institute at UCLA, where he formerly served as chief resident.

203

racial problems ahead. Certain professors it was said, "would never have a black intern in their surgery program." "I think some of the professors genuinely doubted whether blacks could do certain things," he says, "which was a kind of white supremacy syndrome."

Dr. Poussaint was developing an interest in the emotional problems which result from white racial chauvinism. All his life, he had faced racial slurs rooted in white fantasies, not in reality. The racist faculty members; the "closed" events at Columbia—were a microcosm of the larger social disease. Dr. Poussaint committed himself to understanding the sickness of American racism through psychiatry.

When the Neuropsychiatric Institute of the University of California at Los Angeles accepted his application for internship, Dr. Poussaint was excited. He felt that his career was ready to take off. His four years at UCLA were not free from racial prejudices. His superiors, Dr. Poussaint recalls, even went so far as to ask white nurses if they objected to receiving orders from a black intern. However, Dr. Poussaint steadily impressed his abilities on the minds of the doctors, staff and fellow students at the school; in his last year at UCLA he was selected chief resident and became the head of the intern training program.

Dr. Poussaint involved himself in the civil rights drama of the early sixties. His personal struggle as a student was mirrored in the larger one beyond the academic walls. From Jackson, Mississippi, a former classmate, Bob Moses, the Student Nonviolent Coordinating Committee leader, called on Alvin Poussaint to fight with him and others on Southern soil. Jackson at the time was a civil rights "war zone."

It gave Dr. Poussaint the perfect opportunity to see racism in its most acute forms. He saw black powerlessness in the face of white power. He saw liberal whites assuming—falsely—that they were to lead a black movement. He saw the price that had to be paid for a few moments of assertive black manhood and realized the psycho-sexual dimensions of the racial problems between blacks and whites. And wondered, "What are we to do with our rage?"

Stokely Carmichael's plea for Black Power, Dr. Poussaint felt, focused on the major problem of black powerlessness: "The psychological castration of the society of black people accounts for the abnormal amount of aggression of Negroes. Negroes need much more of a voice in the direction of their communities—in their schools, in their welfare services and police."

In mid-1966, Dr. Poussaint became an assistant professor of psychiatry at Tufts University Medical School. At Tufts he studied the nature of the black man's "double consciousness," and analyzed six different personality types from the oppressed black

204

Dr. Poussaint appears with the
Rev. Jesse L. Jackson of
Operation PUSH during visit to
the organization's headquarters
in Chicago.

Dr. Poussaint, a bachelor, has
frequently been seen with
actress Diana Sands, with
whom he is shown at a
New York restaurant.

community. His studies in the black personality and the American
racial climate resulted in a series of probing articles, including
"A Negro Psychiatrist Explains the Negro Psyche" (1967), "Blacks
and the Sexual Revolution' (1971), and "Why Blacks Kill Blacks (1970).

Dr. Poussaint became the associate dean of students at Harvard
Medical School in 1969 and continued his work in investigating the
black American's inward turmoil—"an American, a Negro; two souls,
two thoughts; two unreconciled strivings; two warring ideals in one dark
body, whose dogged strength alone keeps it from being torn asunder."

"We must face the fact that America will have black segregated
communities for a long time to come," Dr. Poussaint said.
"Unfortunately the white man cannot give Negroes black
consciousness. They have to give it to each other."

205

Leontyne Price

Opera Singer

Leontyne Price, concert and opera singer; born Feb. 10, 1927 in Laurel, Miss.; Central State College (B.A., 1949), studied at Juilliard School of Music (1949–52). Address: 1133 Broadway, New York, NY 10010 (See full biographical sketch in Volume I.)

Miss Price is shown in 1957 in the opera, *Dialogues of the Carmelites*, in which she had a starring role.

Mississippi-Born Soprano Continues Reign as a Star of the Opera World

"I had to get used to . . . being a token black. That carried with it . . . the absolute necessity for being at my best always."

There were at least three good reasons why the new Samuel Barber opera might be a traumatizing experience for Leontyne Price. The opera, *Antony and Cleopatra,* was having its first performance ever and the part Miss Price would sing was still undefined. As the opening work of the Metropolitan Opera at its plush new quarters in New York City's Lincoln Center, it would attract the attention of the world and as close scrutiny by the critics as one could imagine. As for the singer herself, it was a personal challenge, one marking the first occasion she had

206

Among the numerous operas in which Miss Price has appeared are those in which she is seen at left and above. One of her first appearances was (in December, 1955) in *The Magic Flute* (right) with the NBC Opera Theatre, while her Metropolitan Opera roles include *Girl of the Golden West* (center) and *Il Trovatore*, (left).

opened with the Met since her role in *Girl of the Golden West* launched the 1961–62 season five years earlier.

Miss Price has frequently relived that experience. "Maybe that was a kind of turning point," she says. "For the next season or two I kept on doing opera and other things, but sometimes it seemed I just didn't know where I was."

The opera and its celebrated soprano were smash successes, but the challenges it presented to the self-appraising artist convinced her that her life and her career needed evaluating. Thus if opera-goers were deprived of Miss Price's talent during 1971–73, it was due to a "sabbatical" which she took to devote more time to concert tours. "A career can always stand freshness," she explains, "and I'm trying to ward off being a stagnant opera singer. For the last two seasons I have concentrated on recitals, and the challenge of bringing to life nineteen or twenty characters in one recital is greater than only one over many hours. Recitals were really what I started out to do. And I love them. When I got caught up in opera, Lady Luck was very good to me."

This ability to assess oneself objectively is a tell-tale mark of the consummate artist. And the toughness it requires is consistent with Miss Price's life which, in spite of a talent that

207

in fifteen years has made her a celebrated operatic figure, has been a series of challenges, with the percentages all against her.

Mary Leontyne Price was born to James and Kate Price, a carpenter and a midwife, in Laurel, Mississippi, on February 10, 1927. Her first musical experience was at St. Paul's Methodist Church, where she played the piano and sang in the choir. It was during this time that her ambitions seem to have been kindled. In a poem written when she was only eleven, she promised: "I'll work harder and harder to do my best. On my laurels I'll never rest."

Poetry, apparently, was not one of her fortes, but by the time she had completed her high school training, she was an accomplished musician and set out to be a music teacher. She majored in music at Central State College, Wilberforce, Ohio, where she graduated *cum laude* in 1949 before going on to study at New York's Juilliard School of Music. The slow development of her musical gifts convinced the young Leontyne that teaching was not for her. But she did have her doubts about a life on the stage. At the time, she recorded: "I'm worried about the future because I want to be a success."

One source of this worry was an obvious one: money. For a Mississippi girl of somewhat humble parentage, a career as a

Miss Price and Franco Corelli sing (left) in *Il Trovatore* at the Metropolitan Opera. At right, before a Chicago Lyric Opera performance of *Turandot*, she and soprano Birgitt Nillson pose backstage for photographers.

Miss Price is shown with Sir Rudolf Bing upon his retirement as general manager of the Metropolitan Opera Company.

concert singer was unpromising. For any young artist, whatever the circumstances, there is a period in which substantial support must be supplied. Nor was it likely in the 1940s that the racism so rife in the classical music world would allow her the chance to adequately shape a career. The first of her problems was peremptorily solved. Mrs. Elizabeth Chisholm, a well-to-do white woman with whose daughters Leontyne had played as a child, offered help, as she had done frequently in the past, and the faculty at Juilliard encouraged her to continue. Thus, with growing faith in her abilities, she continued at the school, studying with Florence Page Kimball, a former concert singer.

It was about this time that she started to think about opera. She debuted as Mistress Ford in a college production of Verdi's *Falstaff*, acquiring a passion for opera that has never left her. "I really love opera," she says today. "I love it when it is at its best, with costumes, scenery, lighting, orchestra, dancing—it's the greatest of the art forms."

In 1952, composer Virgil Thompson selected her for the part of St. Cecelia in a revival of his *Four Saints in Three Acts,* which played on Broadway. Her handling of the assignment so impressed Ira Gershwin that he asked her to sing Bess in *Porgy and Bess,* which played for two years on Broadway and eight additional months on tour in Europe.

Porgy did more than launch Miss Price's career. She fell in love with a member of the cast, baritone William Warfield, an important singer in his own right. Their five-year marriage ended in divorce. While in Europe with *Porgy,* Miss Price came under the influence of several contemporary composers, including Igor Stravinsky, Henri Sauget, Lou Harrison, William Killmayer and John La Fontaine, all of whose works she performed on the continent. And she caught the ear of Samuel Barber, whose *Hermit Songs* she performed later at the International Conference of Contemporary Music in Rome. She was the only American artist invited.

Miss Price's career in grand opera began in the mid-1950s with the role of Floria in Puccini's *Tosca,* performed on NBC television. and with her 1957 appearance, as Madame Lidoine in Poulenc's *Dialogues of the Carmelites*, her dream of becoming an opera star began materializing.

Other of her standout roles of that period: Aida in the oft-revived opera by Verdi; Leonora in the same composer's *Il Trovatore;* Donna Elvira in Mozart's *Don Giovanni,* and the lead in Carl Orff's *The Wise Maiden*—all with the San Francisco

Miss Price appears in recorded concert with the student choir of Rust College in Mississippi.

Opera. With Chicago's Lyric Opera she sang in Massenet's *Thais,* the role of Liu in Puccini's *Turandot* and principal parts in both *Aida* and *Madame Butterfly.* Abroad, she appeared at La Scala in Milan and with conductor Herbert von Karajan and the Vienna State Opera.

Miss Price's debut with the Metropolitan Opera was in early 1961. She sang Leonora in *Il Trovatore*, receiving a forty-two-minute ovation at the conclusion of the performance. The following autumn, she opened the Met's season in Puccini's *Girl of the Golden West.* She was only the fifth black person to sing with the Metropolitan since Marian Anderson's debut in 1955.

Since her debut in *Falstaff* in 1952, Leontyne Price has appeared in twenty-five operas, by composers ranging from Gershwin to Poulenc, Monteverdi to Samuel Barber. She has made some thirty record albums for three major record labels, has performed 124 times (up to 1973) at the Metropolitan, and has made extensive concert appearances in the United States and around the world. Of the many comments on her abilities, one review stands out: "Phenomenal—the voice of the century!"

Miss Price lives in a modest town house in lower Greenwich Village in New York City, but spends months at a time back home in Laurel, Mississippi, with her ailing mother, who is now in her

210

Miss Price and comedian Nipsey Russell appear at a fund-raising drive for sickle cell anemia research. At right, with singer Lena Horne, she was included among stars in a "Harlem Homecoming" in 1972.

eighties. She has credited her parents with much of her success. "My mother's flamboyant vivacity and wonderful sense of excitement—that's what gets me out onto the stage," she once said. "And my father's character and pacing of life—that is what sustains me."

Miss Price, who was a recipient of the NAACP Spingarn Award (1965), says racism has been largely responsible for her determination. "I had to get used to the idea of being a token black," she says. "That carried with it, I felt, the absolute necessity for being at my best always or at least trying to be at my best. It was like an athlete who has so many times at bat. You feel that you have to connect every time." On another occasion she declared: "I feel [about my art] that it is the strongest way, the most complete way, that I can speak. I can best express myself through a gift that God saw fit to give me."

And like many an artist, even the gifted and successful, Leontyne Price admits that life is often lonely. "But I never remember it when the applause is going on," she says. "Somehow the success, the grandeur of the opera house, the love of the public wipe out the loneliness. Singing is the most important thing."

211

Charley Pride

Country-Western Singer

Charley Pride, country music singer; born March 18, 1939 in Sledge, Miss.; high school graduate. Wife: Rozene Pride. Children: Kraig, Dion and Angela. Address: Jack D. Johnson Talent, Inc., Box 40484, Nashville, TN 37204 (See full biographical sketch in Volume I)

The Something Special He Has Given Country Music Is Called 'Soul'

On a 1971 Christmas tour of U.S. military bases, Mr. Pride trades jokes with comedian Bob Hope.

"Certainly I'm unique in country music. But each of us is unique. I just happen to have a permanent tan."

The Grand Ole Opry had been an exclusive mecca for white performers until Charley Pride came along in 1967 with his guitar and golden baritone voice and took over the stage of the great old music hall in his own very special way.

Ironically, Charley Pride, born March 18, 1939 in Sledge, Mississippi, has excelled in a musical genre which does not attract a mass following of black people. As a young child working beside his parents, seven brothers and three sisters in the cotton fields, Charley Pride acquired his love for country music from listening to early radio broadcasts of the Grand Ole Opry. Born in the midst of "blues" country, he explains his attraction to blue-grass music this way:

212

A smelter for the Anaconda Mining Company before breaking into entertainment, Mr. Pride converses with Jim Routzen (above), his foreman on the old job.

Mr. Pride, who once played professional baseball, still often works out during Spring training with the Milwaukee Brewers.

"I ended up in country music because I'm an individual. When I was a kid back in Mississippi, my ear heard a sound my heart liked. I didn't like the music some say I am supposed to like just because of a pigment in my skin. Certainly I'm unique in country music. But each of us is unique. I just happen to have a permanent tan."

Country music, however, was not Mr. Pride's first love. When he was quite young, he admired the greatness of Jackie Robinson and sought to emulate his idol in baseball. At sixteen, he packed his bags and left Mississippi, to seek employment in the now-defunct Negro American Baseball League. He was a pitcher-outfielder with the Memphis Red Sox for several years. (Later he played for the Birmingham Black Barons.) He made it to the majors in 1961 and played for the Los Angeles Angels. Between baseball seasons, he worked for Anaconda Mining's tin-smelting complex in Great Falls, Montana, and as a nightclub singer in the evenings. Yet baseball did not seem to be his real calling. "I was up and down, up and down all the time," he said of his baseball career. "I was always getting hurt and just when I'd get close to the top, it seemed the door would close . . . cracked elbows or cracked ankles."

In the 1960s, the doors began to swing open—and country music was never the same again. One evening in 1963, the late Red Foley happened to catch Charley Pride's act. Mr. Foley, a member of country music's hall of fame, was impressed with Mr. Pride's obvious talent and invited him to come to Nashville for an audition. "I don't care whether you're black, green or purple," he said in admiration. "You ought to go to Nashville."

Red Foley's words hung about in Charley Pride's head for a long time, but his heart was still set on becoming a great baseball personality. However, when Casey Stengel of the New York Mets rejected him, he put away his glove, spikes and his childhood dreams of baseball greatness. Again, he packed his bags. On his way home to Mississippi, he remembered Mr. Foley's invitation and stopped in Nashville, where he charmed the producers at RCA Records and became the first black pioneer in country music.

At first, there were numerous skeptics, but Charley Pride, characterized by an easy disposition and a ready smile, proved that he was black gold. With his recording "Just Between Me and You," he launched himself into super-stardom, becoming a Number One country music attraction.

Mr. Pride may have been nursed on the blues of Muddy Waters, but he has no hang-ups about being a black man who sings country style. "At an early age, I was told by my older brother and sister that I wasn't supposed to be singing that kind of music. They asked, 'Why do

213

you sing it?' and I said, 'Because I like it.' But then they said, 'It's *their* kind of music.' In my way of thinking, all of it is our music. For some reason, it's supposed to be 'your' music because you're pink, or 'your' music because you're black. When you think of country music, what used to be called hillbilly, you think of one color of skin. Well, it just happened that I came along when society was at a certain point and was accepted. When I first started out, it wasn't well thought of for a black man to admit he liked country music.''

At his first major concert in January, 1967 the white audience did not know he was black until he appeared on stage. ''Now you folks don't be alarmed by this tan of mine,'' he told his startled audience. ''Just sit back and relax 'cause I'm here to sing some good country music.''

With those words ''Country'' Charley Pride, as he is called by his thousands of admirers, became the Jackie Robinson of country music. And, like his baseball idol, he slugged out the ironies of his situation to win the applause of many. Honors came his way, distinguishing him as a gifted and exceptional talent. He was voted Entertainer of the Year in Country Music and the Male Vocalist of the Year in 1971, an honor bestowed upon him by the once lily-white Country Music Association.

Mr. Pride's many hits include ''Does My Ring Hurt Your Finger,'' ''I Know One,'' ''I Can't Believe That You've Stopped Loving Me,'' ''Let Me Live''—all classics of the genre. In 1971, his country gospel hit, ''Did You Think To Pray,'' won him the coveted Grammy Award.

Charley Pride and his wife, Rozene, whom he married while serving with the United States Army for two years, live in Dallas, Texas with their three children: Kraig, Dion and Angela.

The little black boy who once *picked* cotton in the fields of Mississippi now knows that *singing* about cotton fields produced much more pleasure—and much more gold.

214

A gifted performer, Mr. Pride (far left) puts "soul" into his country-western tunes, joins the Western Gentlemen (left) for a group number, and later signs autographs (right) for his fans.

At a post-show reception (l.), Mr. Pride and his wife, Rozene, enjoy some time together.

215

Wilson C. Riles
California Superintendent of Schools

The Education of 4,500,000 Children
Is a Responsibility He's Happy to Have

"Win, lose or draw, I wouldn't have it on my conscience five years from now—knowing all I knew about the condition of the [school] system—that I didn't try."

Wilson C. (Camanza) Riles, is California's state superintendent of public instruction. An elected official, he is responsible for overseeing the education of 4.5 million school children in more than eleven hundred school districts. He has an annual budget of $2.5 billion and an administrative staff of more than 2,300. The first black man ever elected to a statewide office in California, Mr. Riles attained his position in 1970 with the support of 3.25 million voters who gave him the highest number of votes ever cast for a black man in a single election in United States history. Since his job entitles him to sit on the University of California Board of Regents, he also is the first black voting

Wilson C. Riles, superintendent of public instruction, State of California; born June 27, 1917 in Alexandria, La.; Arizona State College (B.A., 1940; M.A., 1947). Wife: Mary Louise Riles. Children: Michael, Narvia, Wilson Jr. and Phillip. Address: 721 Capitol Mall, Sacramento, CA 95814 (See full biographical sketch in Volume I)

member of the university's ruling body. In addition, his post automatically makes him a trustee of California State College and secretary and executive officer of the State Board of Education.

Born June 27, 1917 near Alexandria, Louisiana, Wilson Riles was orphaned at the age of eleven after the death of both his mother and his father, a crew chief in a turpentine camp. He was adopted by a childless couple in his father's crew and was taken to Elizabeth, Louisiana. After graduating from McDonogh High School in New Orleans, he went to Flagstaff, Arizona, where he worked his way through Arizona State College (now Northern Arizona University) by carting food from the cafeteria to the infirmary for $15 a month, and by teaching Sunday school. He spent three years in the Army Air Corps before returning to Arizona State to earn a master's degree in school administration. Rising through the ranks he compiled such a distinguished record that in 1965 he was named associate superintendent of the California State Department of Education, heading a $100 million-a-year Federal Compensatory Education Program aimed at improving the education of children of low-income families. Four years later, he was promoted to the position of deputy superintendent in charge of special education. Mr. Riles was not flattered by the promotion, which nominally put him next in command to his boss, Superintendent Max Rafferty. "What he (Rafferty) really succeeded in doing," says Mr. Riles, "was [to] take me away from the program and put me in a window-dressing position."

Highly critical of his boss's conservative outlook in running the department, Mr. Riles, in 1966, began talking with a few school district superintendents—all white—around the state about the possibility of one of them seeking the top job. Many agreed that it was time for a change, but, as Mr. Riles explains it, "No one whom I thought able to do the job came forth." Finally, he made up his mind: "Win, lose or draw, I wouldn't have it on my conscience five years from now—knowing all I knew about the condition of the system—that I didn't try."

Mr. Riles had never been in politics, although he felt he knew something about the political process. One of the first things he did in preparation for the task was to go to a highly successful San Francisco public relations consultant who had already brought home some of the state's political winners. "You can win," the public relations man told him. "It'll be tough, but you can win." Somewhat encouraged, he consulted his wife of thirty years, Mary Louise, who was horrified at the very idea of his tackling such a monumental job, and told him so. "Then," remembers Mr. Riles with a smile, "my wife said something no middle-aged man wants to hear: 'At your age, you ought to be tapering off anyhow.'" That did it, as far has he was concerned. If he

217

had not really intended to run before, he certainly was going to run now. He took a year's leave of absence, rather than quit his post as

After winning election as state superintendent of schools, Mr. Riles and his wife (l.) thank supporters. At right, after taking over his new job, he attends a meeting of the state board of education (he is executive secretary of the board). With him is board chairman Henry Gunderson.

In the office, Mr. Riles is an easy-going person but is passionately involved in programs to improve the quality of education for California children.

deputy superintendent. "When you file for office," he explains, "you have to put something down under 'occupation.' I didn't want to say 'unemployed.' " He sent his boss a memo, telling him he was going to seek his job. "I think he possibly thought it was a big joke," he remembers. But Superintendent Rafferty was to find out that his deputy was dead serious.

As campaign money began to trickle in, Mr. Riles and his supporters supplied the hard work, night and day, and somehow managed to make it through the 1970 June primary. With 25.2 percent of the vote in a field of nine candidates, Mr. Riles was in second place behind Superintendent Rafferty, who gathered 48.6 percent—not enough for a majority. Then the two front-runners prepared for a showdown during the November runoff. In the end, Mr. Riles swept through the polls with a majority of five hundred thousand votes out of nearly six million cast.

Since taking office, Superintendent Riles has surprised many by going ahead with the program he outlined during his campaign. He sent all top state officials a six-point plan for easing California's crucial education problems and has succeeded in enlisting the support of many of them.

He has been instrumental in the hiring of black personnel. He made that intention clear the day he started his new job and told his department heads: "We're going to have an integrated department. I'm not going to run out with a pad and pencil and make quotas. But if there are 15 percent minorities in the state and you go out and look at your staff and you don't have 15 percent minorities, then you know you're not overdoing it." At the same time, he said: "Good people don't grow on trees—black, brown or anything else. You're going to have to go out and find them."

To run his educational empire, Superintendent Riles, a father of three sons and a daughter, arrives in his office in Sacramento's State Capitol at 8 A.M. each weekday morning and works until after six in the evening. Frequently, he returns to the office after dinner at home to work until around 11 at night. For his dedication, he receives an annual salary of $35,000.

Invitations for speaking engagements, conferences and other personal appearances pour in from all over the country at the rate of about 1,000 a month. But, as he explains: "Obviously, I have to say 'no' to 95 percent of them or else I wouldn't be doing anything but make speaking engagements. Frankly, I think, having been elected, it's time for me to get the job done." Most Californians have all the confidence in him that he will do just that.

219

Diana Ross

Entertainer

Diana Ross, singer and actress; born March 26, 1944 in Detroit, Mich.; high school graduate (1960); began singing with two teen-age friends, Mary Wilson and Florence Ballard, and they became world-famous as the Supremes; star of the film Lady Sings the Blues (1972). Husband: Robert Silberstein. Children: Rhonda and Tracee. Address: Motown Record Corp., 6464 Sunset Blvd., Hollywood, CA 90028 (See full biographical sketch in Volume I)

Her Belief: 'If You Think You'll Succeed, You Will Be Successful'

"You can't just sit back and expect people to do things for you. You've got to get up and do it yourself."

In the world of entertainment, success means pressure to remain a success, but Diana Ross doesn't mind. "Pressure made the diamond," she says, and the fact that she has sung her way from sock hops to superstardom proves it. As a peerless stage performer, solo disc artist and Oscar-toned actress, Miss Ross reigns supreme.

Diana Ross was born March 26, 1944 in Detroit, Michigan. Her parents, Fred and Ernestine Ross, raised Diana and her five sisters and brothers in a ghetto housing project where poverty squeezed them three to a bed and forced Mr. Ross to work at two jobs.

"It wasn't so bad," Diana recalls. "I didn't think about it as a ghetto. If I wanted a nickel or a penny, daddy gave me one. I had fun."

An inveterate tomboy throughout her early childhood, Diana romped and climbed until the lure of sewing and fashion design classes claimed her attention at Cass Technical High School. As a blossoming young lady, she made her own pleated skirts and supplemented her father's income by working as a dishwasher in a downtown cafeteria.

Meanwhile, Diana's religious upbringing prompted her to join the Olivet Baptist Church and become a member of its choir. She liked singing well enough to imitate radio tunes, trill for family visitors and

During her tenure as star of the Supremes, Miss Ross makes a television appearance with the Temptations.

Against a drawing of the Supremes, Miss Ross poses for one of the glamor photos that helped make her famous.

harmonize with two of her girlfriends between classes. When auditions for a school musical came up, Diana was rejected because the director did not like her voice. Crushed but not defeated, she corraled teenagers Mary Wilson and Florence Ballard and formed her own singing group. They thumbed rides to various sock hops and talent shows, averaged about $15 a week in earnings and finally bolstered enough courage to audition for Motown Records mogul Berry Gordy Jr. Realizing the importance of education, Mr. Gordy advised the trio to finish high school before pursuing their musical careers.

Diana graduated from Cass Tech in 1960 and, accompanied by Mary and Florence, returned to Motown for a second audition. True to his word, Mr. Gordy listened and signed them to a contract as the Primettes, a background group for the Primes (now known as the Temptations).

"I was very determined," Miss Ross recalls, "and they finally noticed me and realized that I was a wiry little skinny kid who was going to do something."

After a name change and a few flop singles, that "something" turned out to be the Supremes—whose tune, "Where Did Our Love Go?" hit the top of the charts with Diana Ross singing the lead. Subsequent hits followed, including "Baby Love," "Stop in The Name of Love," and "Come See About Me"—all featuring Diana's mellow soprano backed by the liquid harmony of Mary and Florence.

221

As star of her own television special, "Diana!" Miss Ross romped through a stirring medley of songs (above) and comedy routines (above, r.) with comedian Bill Cosby. Below, she mimics Charlie Chaplin.

"I never thought I wanted to be a singer," Miss Ross reflects. "I more or less grew into it. It was a hobby and I enjoyed it. It was something I did for pleasure. I studied modeling and dress designing because I thought that was the direction I wanted to go in, but things started happening with my singing and . . . zoom!"

Led by Diana Ross, the Supremes soon emerged as one of the world's hottest show business acts. Throughout the 1960s, they remained the top pop style-setters and the best-selling recording artists in musical history.

In January, 1970, however, Miss Ross left the group to make a bid for stardom as a single. "We parted on completely friendly terms," she says. "I left them because I was getting many good offers from movie companies, nightclubs, and for television appearances. The basic material I used in the Supremes' act was the same all the time and I reached a point where I felt I had to do a little bit more."

Groomed by Berry Gordy and backed by the vast resources of the Motown empire, Miss Ross quickly established herself as a versatile nightclub performer whose charisma drew mammoth crowds. Time after time, she dazzled audiences across the country with a sizzling array of musical selections woven around dances and elegant costume changes. By June, 1971, she had starred in her own television special, "Diana!" featuring the Jackson Five, Bill Cosby and Danny Thomas as her guest stars. Her songs included "Ain't No Mountain High Enough" (a 1971 Grammy Award nominee), "Reach Out and Touch Somebody's Hand," "My Man," "Don't Rain On My Parade,"

222

Miss Ross is interviewed during her appearance at the 1972 NAACP Image Awards ceremony in Hollywood.

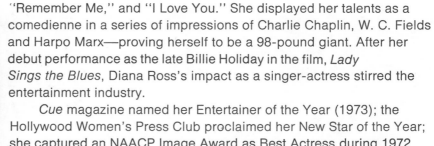

"Remember Me," and "I Love You." She displayed her talents as a comedienne in a series of impressions of Charlie Chaplin, W. C. Fields and Harpo Marx—proving herself to be a 98-pound giant. After her debut performance as the late Billie Holiday in the film, *Lady Sings the Blues*, Diana Ross's impact as a singer-actress stirred the entertainment industry.

Cue magazine named her Entertainer of the Year (1973); the Hollywood Women's Press Club proclaimed her New Star of the Year; she captured an NAACP Image Award as Best Actress during 1972 and landed the Golden Globe Award as Most Promising Actress of 1973. She added those honors to the ones she had previously received: Top Female Vocalist of the Year (*Billboard*, 1970); The World's Most Popular Singer (*The New Musical Express,* 1970); Female Entertainer of the Year (NAACP Image Award, 1971), and World's Leading Female Singer (*Disc and Music Echo,* 1971). By late 1972, Diana Ross was being touted for an Academy Award as Best Actress of the year.

Today, married to Beverly Hills public relations man Robert Silberstein, Miss Ross spends most of her time being a mother to her daughters, Rhonda Suzanne and Tracee Joy. For recreation, she plays tennis and chess.

"I've learned a lot of things since the early days," she says, "but one of the most important things is, whatever you do, make yourself happy—because how you feel is the way you go. The image you have of yourself is important. If you feel like a failure, chances are you'll fail. If you think you'll succeed, you'll be successful. You can't just sit back and expect people to do things for you. You've got to get up and do it yourself."

Audiences everywhere can say, "Amen."

After making her film debut as singer Billie Holiday in *Lady Sings the Blues* (above), Miss Ross was nominated for an Academy Award as Best Actress of 1972. At right, she chats with Motown president Berry Gordy Jr., who discovered her as a singer and coached her to success as an actress.

223

Richard Roundtree

Actor

Richard Roundtree, actor; born July 9, 1942 in New Rochelle, N.Y.; attended Southern Illinois University. Divorced, he is the father of Kelly and Nicole. Address: Metro-Goldwyn-Mayer, Inc., 10202 W. Washington Boulevard, Culver City, CA 90230 (See full biographical sketch in Volume I)

He Made the Name 'Shaft' Known Around The World

"I don't think that all the things John Shaft does on screen are admirable, but the fact of his presence is enough to redeem whatever negative aspects he may possess."

To millions of film-goers throughout the world, the name Richard Roundtree is synonymous with the name "John Shaft," for it was Richard who breathed life into his fictional counterpart in the top-grossing, trend-setting movie, *Shaft*. And it was as John Shaft that Richard Roundtree emerged from relative obscurity to become an overnight sensation as the first black private detective and super-hero in a motion picture.

Born July 9, 1942 in New Rochelle, New York, Richard grew up under the watchful eyes of his mother, Katheryn Roundtree, a housewife, and his father, John Roundtree, a garbage collector, caterer and an Elder of the Pentecostal Church. One of the smallest of his peers as a child, Richard later became captain of the track team at New Rochelle High School and played offensive end on the school's highly-ranked football squad.

"I became a football star," he recalls, "and that meant a lot. People responded to me. The whole thing of the newspapers and the publicity and feeling of self-worth was good." In the school annual when he graduated in June, 1961, Richard was listed as the "Most Popular," "Best Dressed" and "Best Looking" student of the year.

Richard went on to enroll at Southern Illinois University on a football scholarship (he was a linebacker), majoring in special education, with the intention of helping children who have learning handicaps. But he began hanging around the campus theater and was eventually cast in the play *A Raisin in the Sun.* After two years at SIU, he abandoned his hope of getting a college degree and returned home to a succession of odd jobs. He worked as a fork-lift truck operator before being hired as a suit salesman at Barney's, a men's store in New York City. A friend urged him to try modeling, so he put together a portfolio and made the rounds of modeling agencies. He finally got a chance to audition for the Ebony Fashion Fair and, in 1967, was hired as a model for the Fair, which traveled to seventy-nine cities in ninety days. He was also featured in advertisements in *Ebony* magazine, and his photo was seen on thousands of containers of Duke, the hair care products for black men. But it was as an Ebony Fashion Fair model that he first began thinking about a career as an actor.

"I got the same kind of feeling," Mr. Roundtree says, "that I knew on the football field. It was like carrying the ball and getting praise for it, but I was now relating to people as I had never done before on the gridiron. People were responding to me as an individual, which was an even heavier trip than team recognition. I figured I could further that feeling if I had dialogue." During a

As a model for Ebony Fashion Fair, Mr. Roundtree gained much of the self-confidence needed later for his career as an actor. At right, in a scene from *Shaft's Big Score*, he confronts numbers racketeer Bumpy Jonas, played by Moses Gunn.

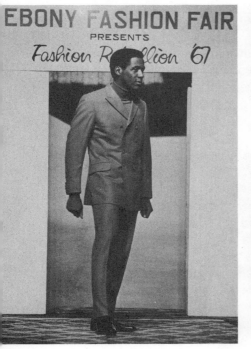

225

Mr. Roundtree rides in the annual Bud Billiken Parade in Chicago in 1972. At right, he is chased by gunmen in a helicopter in the film *Shaft's Big Score* (1972).

Fashion Fair visit to Los Angeles, he met Bill Cosby, who advised him to return to New York and enter the American Academy of Dramatic Arts. "At that point," he says, "you couldn't have told me I wasn't ready. I was going to be a superstar right then and there. But his advice turned out to be the best."

He could not afford the Academy's stiff membership fee, so he joined the Negro Ensemble Company and later appeared in three NEC productions, *Kongi's Harvest*; *Man, Better Man*, and *Mau Mau Room.* His performances led to small parts in the movies *What Do You Say to a Naked Lady?* and *Parachute To Paradise.* While his stage appearances ended with the Philadelphia production of *The Great White Hope*, his television appearances included a bit part on the soap opera "Search For Tomorrow," a brief stint on "The New Yorkers," and a segment called "Inside Bedford-Stuyvesant."

Then came *Shaft*. Competing against two hundred actors for the starring role, Richard Roundtree passed the first, second and third auditions and was then called back for a screen test, which he passed with relative ease. He was hired for the coveted role.

Working diligently to overcome the handicap of inexperience, Mr. Roundtree completed the film and became instantly popular as a cool, tough, black private eye who flexes his muscles in a squeeze play between the Mafia and Harlem mob operators. Following his successful screen debut, he went on to complete, by early 1973, two

226

of seven planned *Shaft* sequels: *Shaft's Big Score* and *Shaft in Africa*, and began putting together a "Shaft" series for network television.

"As an actor," Mr. Roundtree says, "I always thought I'd make it some day, and I visualized my first opening night for my first big picture. I figured my first film would knock everybody out. As it turned out, *I* was knocked out. It was a new experience and I was frightened to the point of numbness. The lights, cameras and people were a heavy number to pull."

Since then he has completed *Embassy* and *Charlie One-Eye*, and a TV Movie-Of-The-Week, "Firehouse." He has also made a name for himself as a singer on his first album, *The Man From Shaft.* He also has a single release called "Street Brother," and has sung on both "The Merv Griffin Show" and "The Dean Martin Show."

Reflecting on his brief but glittering career, Mr. Roundtree notes the reaction of young blacks to the screen hero he has created. "The thing I've noticed most," he says, "is that many of the young kids are like little Shafts. They really emulate that character. A lot of parents tell me that their youngsters identify strongly with Shaft, which I think is beautiful. I don't think all the things John Shaft does on screen are admirable, but the fact of his presence is enough to redeem whatever negative aspects he may possess. Let's face it. Our kids have had an overly prolonged diet of John Wayne and Doris Day."

And what does he think of the overall image of blacks on television and in movie houses?

"Basically," he says, "I think it's all positive. There's something good to be found in all of it. A lot of people put down *Sweet Sweetback*, for example. Well, whether or not they dug the black picture out there on the open market, it was something to which blacks could relate. And that's got to be positive. Of course, as more and more black films come out, we're going to get a more diversified look at black life. Now, I wouldn't suggest for one minute that *Shaft* or *Shaft's Big Score* are true depictions of black life in this country by any means. But neither are the vast majority of films depicting the life style of white America. It's entertainment, not reality. But the whites have always had, along with the exaggerations, images they could relate to in a real sense. We haven't had that. That's why at this point I feel that everything black on film deserves examination. But in another three or four years I think we'll be seeing everything from black "sexploitation" on films to love stories and historical films. It's all part of a very natural ethnic movie revolution."

From college athlete to suit salesman to model to stardom, Richard Roundtree has made his own revolution.

Mr. Roundtree attends a New York premiere with actress Gwen Mitchell who appeared with him in *Shaft.*

Carl T. Rowan

Journalist

From His Post In Washington, He Informs the World

Carl Thomas Rowan, syndicated newspaper columnist; born Aug. 11, 1925 in Ravenscroft, Tenn.; Oberlin College (A.B., 1947; honorary D. Litt., 1962), University of Minnesota (M.A., journalism, 1948). Wife: Vivien Murphy Rowan. Children: Barbara, Carl and Geoffrey. Address: 1101 17th St., N.W., Washington, DC 20036 (See full biographical sketch in Volume I)

"Abuse and danger are the price of our [black] achievements and the hazard of the dream that we hold forth to mankind."

One of the most remarkable journalistic careers is that of Carl T. Rowan whose stubborn refusal to stay in "his place" enabled him to rise from a poverty-stricken childhood in the hills of Tennessee to World War II naval officer, author of books, award-winning newsman, diplomat, sub-cabinet official and confidant of two United States presidents. Today, Mr. Rowan makes effective use, as a syndicated columnist, of the intimate knowledge of the United States government that he gained while a member of some of the innermost Washington circles. His fearless and frank comments on a wide range of issues—from the Vietnam War to black folks' hairstyles—appear regularly in some 180 newspapers throughout the nation.

Mr. Rowan, the son of Thomas and Johnnie Rowan, was born in the little Tennessee mountain town of Ravencroft on August 11, 1925. In nearby McMinnville, the young Rowan—with his brother Charles and three sisters, Jewel, Ella and Bobbie—knew a typical Southern childhood. He took his first job at one dollar a week and later advanced to hoeing bulb grass at ten cents an hour and finally graduated to the gang that stood on the bank corner waiting for someone to come along and offer any odd job, usually tough manual labor at twenty-five cents an hour.

Mr. Rowan visits with President John F. Kennedy in 1963 shortly after being named U.S. ambassador to Finland. At right, after becoming director of the U.S. Information Agency in 1964, He and his wife, Vivien, and their sons, Geoffrey (l.) and Carl Jr. pose with President Lyndon B. Johnson.

Between odd jobs, Carl stayed at Bernard High School where he was graduated in 1942 as senior class president and valedictorian. The summer following his graduation, he washed dishes and served food at the Tuberculosis Hospital in Nashville. He saved enough money to enroll at Tennessee A & I College. At college he passed nationally competitive navy examinations and in October 1943, he joined the U.S. Navy where he became one of the first fifteen blacks in U.S. naval history to be raised to officer's rank after graduation from a rigidly segregated officer's candidate school. At that time, young Rowan promised a wartime buddy—a white Southerner—to write a book on what it was like to be black in the South. That promise was fulfilled in 1953 when his book, *South of Freedom,* was published. It was listed among the best books of the year by the American Library Association.

After service as a communications officer with the Atlantic fleet, Mr. Rowan studied at Oberlin College in Ohio where he obtained his bachelor's degee in mathematics. Subsequently, at the University of Minnesota, he earned a master's degree in journalism to launch his writing career. *The Minneapolis Spokesman* and *The St. Paul Recorder* had employed him while he was still a student.

Mr. Rowan worked for the *Baltimore Afro-American* during the 1948 presidential election and eventually joined *The Minneapolis Tribune* as a copyreader. However, in the late 1950s, he switched to reporting. In many revealing exposés, his keen sense of justice and his ability to express himself clearly and fearlessly won him numerous awards, including the Minneapolis Junior Chamber of Commerce's Minneapolis Outstanding Young Man of the Year citation in 1951; the Sidney Hillman Award for the "best newspaper reporting in the nation during 1951," and the Sigma Delta Chi medallion for the "best general reporting in 1953." In 1972 Mr. Rowan was elected to membership in the Gridiron Club, an organization of Washington newsmen, and became the first black member since the club's founding in 1885.

229

As the new U.S. ambassador to Finland, Mr. Rowan visits Finnish President Urho Kekkonen (above), reviews Finnish military troops (above, r.), and attends a conference (r.) in Bonn, Germany of U.S. ambassadors to European countries.

In addition, Mr. Rowan distinguished himself as an author of books. In 1957 he wrote *Go South to Sorrow*, an analysis of racism in America, and in 1960 his biography of Jackie Robinson, entitled *Wait Till Next Year*, was published.

In February, 1961, Mr. Rowan resigned from *The Minneapolis Tribune* to accept an appointment as deputy assistant secretary for public affairs in the Kennedy Administration. In that position, he became the first black in American history to attend meetings of the National Security Council and the presidential cabinet regularly.

In 1963, President Lyndon B. Johnson appointed Mr. Rowan United States ambassador to Finland, a post he held until 1964, when he returned to the United States on his appointment as director of the United States Information Agency, succeeding the late Edward R. Murrow. In accepting the job, Mr. Rowan said: "That the president would ask me—a Negro—to take on a job of this magnitude is another mark of the increasing greatness of this country. But I expect to be *the* director of this agency, and not a Negro director."

In 1971, Mr. Rowan returned to McMinnville, Tenn., his hometown, to write an article for *Ebony* magazine. He is greeted (above) by a woman who knew him as a child.

Working in his Washington, D.C. office, Mr. Rowan prepares his column which appears in newspapers throughout the U.S.

Throughout his journalistic and political careers, Mr. Rowan has allied himself consistently with the black struggle. For black people, the road to "plenty instead of poverty, education instead of ignorance and dignity instead of submission" had to be travelled deliberately, Mr. Rowan insisted, saying that there were no short cuts to freedom. "Abuse and danger are the price of our [black] achievements and the hazard of the dream that we hold forth to mankind."

Since his return to journalism in the late 1960s as a syndicated columnist featured in major newspapers throughout the United States, Carl Rowan has continued to wage war against American racism and a variety of other explosive issues. In the early 1970s, the distinctive Rowan voice, a mixture of Midwestern and Southern accents, could be heard pounding away at issues over the radio on his program *Black Perspectives*. Those close to him, especially his wife, the former Vivien Murphy, to whom he was married on August 2, 1950, and their three children—Barbara, Carl Jr. and Geoffrey—urge Mr. Rowan to decelerate his work pace. But the man who remembers the squalor of black poverty in the Tennessee hills, replies: "Look, life is an inescapable dilemma. You compete, you work full speed, and the pressures decree that you soon leave this world; you coast, take it easy, and you find that this world soon leaves you. I don't want to get left. If I did, I could still be hoeing bulb grass."

In the finest tradition of black journalism, Carl Rowan has chosen "to plead our own cause" and to cast light on the black experience in America for the benefit of all Americans.

John H. Sengstacke

Publisher and Editor

John H. Sengstacke, publishing executive; born Nov. 25, 1912 in Savannah, Ga.; Hampton Institute (B.S., 1933), Ohio State University, postgraduate student (1933). Wife: Myrtle Picou Sengstacke. Children: John, Robert and Lewis. Address: 2400 S. Michigan Ave., Chicago, IL 60616 (See full biographical sketch in Volume I)

He Learned Early That Success Means 'Hard Work and a Little Luck'

"America's race prejudice must be destroyed" is his newspaper's creed.

John Herman Sengstacke deserves much of the credit for the extraordinary achievements of the black press in America.

In 1940, after the death of his uncle, Robert Sengstacke Abbott, who founded the *Chicago Defender* newspaper in 1905, John Sengstacke became president of the Abbott publishing empire. Guided by the spirit of his pioneering uncle, and by his own acumen, he continued the *Defender's* years-long crusades against American racism while building it into the nation's largest and most influential black newspaper chain.

Mr. Sengstacke, who was born November 25, 1912 in Savannah, Georgia, was one of six children (three sons and three daughters) of the Reverend and Mrs. Alexander Sengstacke. "From the time I was a small boy," he recalls, "my uncle (Robert S. Abbott) devoted considerable time to me. My interest in the printing trade developed naturally, since my father published a small paper in Savannah, and I began literally at the bottom as a printer's devil, eventually working up to being an assistant to my father. My uncle took charge of my education,

A founder of the National Newspaper Publishers Association, Mr. Sengstacke has served as president of the organization several times. At right, outgoing president William O. Walker, editor-publisher of the Cleveland *Call & Post*, congratulates him as he assumes NNPA leadership in 1968.

giving it the direction that led to my association with the *Chicago Defender.*"

Mr. Sengstacke began his education in the grade schools of Savannah and then went to the Knox Institute at Athens, Georgia, and subsequently to Brick (North Carolina) Junior College, from which he graduated in 1929. On the advice of his uncle, he enrolled at Hampton Institute in Virginia where Robert Abbott himself was inspired as a student. At Hampton, young Sengstacke majored in business administration and is remembered in the chronicles of Hampton as an athlete who blazed trails in track and football. He also wrote for and edited the *Hampton Script* and sang in the Hampton Quartette. His summers away from college studies were spent in Chicago where he

233

worked for the *Defender*. After his graduation from Hampton in 1933
with a bachelor of science degree, he became his uncle's permanent
assistant. To learn everything about the newspaper business, he took
courses from time to time at the Chicago School of Printing and the
Mergenthaler Linotype School, and at Ohio State University, where he
did postgraduate work in 1933.

Mr. Sengstacke worked diligently in the shadow of Robert S. Abbott
and soon learned that "success means hard work and a little luck."
When he joined the *Defender* fulltime in 1934, the paper was in its
twenty-ninth year of struggle and success. Mr. Sengstacke remembers
very well the early days when the paper was published from a small
basement in Chicago's "Bronzeville." Its slogan was planted in his
brain and became his guiding principle when he took charge of the
company: "American race prejudice must be destroyed."

The *Defender* continued to grow through the difficult years, and
produced two affiliated newspapers, the *Louisville* (Kentucky) *Defender*
(1933) and the *Michigan* (Detroit) *Chronicle* (1936). As his uncle's
assistant and as vice-president and general manager of Robert S.
Abbott Publishing Company, Mr. Sengstacke wrote numerous editorials
for the Louisville and Detroit weeklies, and his provocative articles in
the flagship paper in Chicago were widely read. By 1940, the *Chicago
Defender*, with comprehensive coverage of black American activities,
attained a value of $300,000 and was well-known throughout the United
States.

When Robert S. Abbott, often called "the lonely warrior," died in
February, 1940, the twenty-eight-year-old John H. Sengstacke
became president of the firm. The *Defender* already had a thriving
business which included modern printing facilities and a nationwide
distribution network for its national edition. As a newspaper publisher,
Mr. Sengstacke was exempt from military duty in World War II, but he
served as chairman of the advisory committee on the Negro press in the
Office of War Information, and in Chicago he headed the country's
largest war rationing board (Number Two) during the heat of the war.
From 1942 to 1945, according to Horace Cayton's *Black Metropolis*
(1945), Mr. Sengstacke's *Defender* "gave increasing space to the
exploits of Negro soldiers, to bond sales and other patriotic activities,"
but "at no time did they stop thundering away at every bit of
discrimination—from discourteous treatment of Negro soldiers in Red
Cross canteens to the diatribes of Southern congressmen."

In 1944, Mr. Sengstacke began one of his three terms as president
of the Negro (now National) Newspaper Publisher's Association, which
grew out of his call in 1940 for black publishers to come together in a
spirit of cooperation. *The New York Times* recorded that he was able to

At 1971 NNPA convention awards ceremony, Mr. Sengstacke is shown with White House Communications Director Herbert Klein (c.) and Longworth Quinn, publisher of the *Michigan Chronicle*.

Mr. Sengstacke and the late Mayor Martin Kennelly of Chicago present the *Defender's* 1954 Robert S. Abbott Memorial Award to then civil rights lawyer (now Supreme Court Justice) Thurgood Marshall.

"list among the accomplishments of the association the accrediting of Negro correspondents to the White House conferences and in war coverage, and the establishment of a Washington news bureau for newspapers represented by the association."

In 1956, the *Defender* became a daily newspaper, and Mr. Sengstacke began changing its focus. He pulled it away from its previous national outlook and began assigning his writers to saturation coverage of local news. While important national and international stories were, of course, reported, the *Daily Defender* soon became a true Chicago paper with pages of in-depth reporting on the city's huge black population. The new approach not only boosted circulation but advertising revenue as well. No longer was there a dependence on hard-to-get national advertising; local department stores, supermarkets, etc., were aimed at—and sold. And in both the *Defender* and the *Michigan Chronicle*, real estate and classified advertising developed as important sources of revenue.

Mr. Sengstacke, a member of the boards of directors of Illinois Federal Saving & Loan Assn. in Chicago and Golden State Mutual Life Insurance Co., controls three major communications enterprises: (1) Robert S. Abbott Publishing Co., Inc., which publishes the *Daily Defender*, and which is the umbrella company for four publishing companies in as many states; (2) Sengstacke Enterprises, which owns large blocks of stock in all the publishing companies, and (3) Amalgamated Publishers, Inc., which handles national advertising accounts for a number of black-owned newspapers. In addition to the *Daily Defender* and the *Michigan Chronicle*, Mr. Sengstacke's newspaper holdings include the *Pittsburgh Courier* chain (headquartered in Pittsburgh, Pennsylvania), which publishes several local editions and a national edition, and the *Tri-State Defender* of Memphis, Tennessee.

Despite the demands of the continually growing empire his uncle bequeathed to his care more than thirty years ago, John H. Sengstacke can be found almost every day moving about the *Daily Defender's* white stucco building in Chicago, reading reporters' copy, checking news coming over the wire services teleprinters, making suggestions to photographers and ordering re-writes of this article and that editorial. And remembering always what success really means: ". . . hard work and a little luck."

Kenneth N. Sherwood

Business Executive

In a 1966 photo, Mr. Sherwood stands in front of Harlem store where he began building his now rapidly expanding business conglomerate.

He Showed How To Build a Conglomerate In a Very Short Time

Kenneth N. Sherwood, business executive, is president and chief executive officer of the Kenwood Corp. and other enterprises, in New York, N.Y.; born Aug. 10, 1930 in New York City; St. John's University (B.B.A., accounting, 1951). Wife: Gloria Sherwood. Children: Michelle and Kendra. Address: 144 W. 125th St., New York, NY 10027 (See full biographical sketch in Volume I)

". . . there is no elevator to true and lasting success, because true success is usually reached step by step."

Kenneth N. Sherwood stepped into the national limelight in 1965 when he bought the old Reter Furniture Store on Harlem's noted 125th Street business strip, making his the largest black-owned store of its type in New York City.

Armed with a $20,000 personal investment and a $200,000 Small Business Association loan, he parlayed his original furniture store into an enterprise which now employs more than 125 persons and has sales of more than $6 million a year. "I want to make the finest merchandise manufactured in the country available to the people of Harlem (and my customers everywhere) at competitive prices," Mr. Sherwood pledged when he bought the company from its seventy-nine-year-old white owner.

Born in New York City on August 10, 1930, Mr. Sherwood was educated at Catholic schools and grew up in Harlem and Bedford-Stuyvesant, where his father had two full-time jobs and his

236

Mr. Sherwood and his father, Charles L. Sherwood, welcome U.S. Senator Jacob Javits of New York to the Kenwood Furniture Showrooms (above). At right (above) Mr. Sherwood hosts a 1972 visit to his Kenwood Foods Supermarket by N.Y. Congressman Ogden Reid and members of his staff.

Mr. Sherwood signs a 25-year lease with New York Telephone Co. for rental of space in one of his buildings at $200,000 a year. From left are: Kenwood's attorney, Jeff L. Greenup; Mr. Sherwood; N.Y. Telephone Co. Executive Vice President W. G. Sharwell, and Kenwood Executive Assistant A. C. Hudgins.

mother sometimes worked as a domestic. Very early in life, he decided that he wanted to compete against whites—"and succeed"—in the academic and business worlds. He realized the first of his ambitions when he graduated in 1958 as valedictorian of predominantly white Erasmus Hall High School in the Flatbush section of Brooklyn. His outstanding record won him admittance to St. John's University, where he eventually took a bachelor's degree in accounting.

Mr. Sherwood received an honorable discharge from the U.S. Army in 1953 and worked as an accountant with the Busch Corporation for nine years, then became a vice president of Reter Furniture Company.

"After college, I needed experience and started at the very bottom in business, working long hours for the 'man'," Mr. Sherwood remembers. "Education and experience I got . . . but I plodded on always, trying to learn how big business made profits; and keeping this knowledge in the back of my mind for later use. I feel that whatever success I have obtained has been due in large measure to some of the people I selected to place in key positions in my various businesses, . . . people with good reputations, and business acumen; people who look ahead in interest of what they are sharing with me."

In 1965, Ken Sherwood founded the Kenwood Company, Inc., which expanded from the furniture company and today is the parent company of ten separate and individually incorporated enterprises, each of which is headed by Mr. Sherwood, who holds the titles of chairman of the board, president and chief executive officer. The Kenwood conglomerate includes Kenwood Furniture Corporation, Kenwood Liquor Corporation, Kenwood-Shopwell Supermarkets Food

237

As New York City Mayor John Lindsay listens (c.), Mr. Sherwood speaks at opening of N. Y. Telephone Co. offices in his building. At right, he receives a 1971 "Award of Excellence" from Gov. Nelson Rockefeller of New York.

Corporation, Kenwood Doownek Realty Corporation, Kenwood Holding Corporation, Kenwood Commercial Furniture Corporation and Kenwood Programming Service Corporation.

Doownek Realty (Kenwood spelled backwards) is landlord for some of the nation's largest corporations and institutions. Metropolitan Life Insurance, New York Life Insurance, the Board of Higher Education for the City of New York, the American Red Cross, and Shearson Hammill (the first brokerage firm to open a branch in Harlem)—all are tenants of the realty company.

In addition, on April 9, 1970, Kenwood signed a lease with the New York Telephone Company, renting space to the large utility firm at a cost of $200,000 a year—a total of $5 million for the twenty-five-year period of the lease.

In the early part of 1970, Mr. Sherwood abandoned his retail furniture trade for the more lucrative commercial furniture market. "Commercial furniture is good because you're dealing with big volume. Our average sale is $25,000 with a 5 percent or 6 percent net profit," he said in January, 1973 after Kenwood Commercial Furniture Corporation signed a one-year contract to furnish and install carpet in all Consolidated Edison's offices in New York City and Westchester County. It was the first time that a black-owned company had signed such a contract with the firm and represented as much as one million dollars in business for Kenwood Commercial Corporation.

What is the secret of Mr. Sherwood's success?

"Believe in yourself is my advice to young blacks," he says. "And always seek knowledge. Learn to be a good follower if you would ever hope to be a good leader. In any field of endeavor, work hard. Be honest. Exploit your opportunities, not your fellow men. And always remember that there is no elevator to true and lasting success, because true success is usually reached step by step."

238

At a Kenwood Furniture reception, Mr. Sherwood hosts Brig. Gen. Frederic Davison and Carver Bank Vice President R. L. Hudson (left) and (right) joins Freedom National Bank President Robert B. Boyd and New York *Voice* publisher Kenneth Drew.

Hard work is something Kenneth N. Sherwood never dodged. With his companies firmly rooted in the American financial mainstream, he still works an average of twelve hours a day, a schedule which requires him to spend "far too much time" away from his wife, Gloria, and two daughters, Michelle Arlene and Kendra Jane. Nevertheless, he finds time to work in civic and community affairs. On November 29, 1972, he was appointed to the New York State Athletic Commission, filling the vacancy created by the death of baseball great Jackie Robinson. Mr. Sherwood also serves on the New York State Parks Commission and is a director of the New York City Public Development Corporation, a blue-ribbon panel that assists in planning the future of the largest city in the United States.

Mr. Sherwood and his public relations advisor, Warren G. Jackson, discuss Kenwood's successful bid (over nine white-owned firms) on an order for more than $1 million worth of carpeting for the Consolidated Edison Co.

Naomi Sims

Fashion Model

Naomi Sims, fashion model; born March 30, 1949 in Oxford, Miss.; studied at the Fashion School of Technology and New York University, both on scholarships; was the first black model to appear in a TV commercial and on the cover of a major women's magazine; voted Model of the Year by International Mannequins (1969 and 1970). Address: c/o Ford Modeling Agency, 344 E. 59th St., New York, NY 10022 (See full biographical sketch in Volume I.)

Mississippi-born Girl Becomes The Toast of High Fashion World

"I guess I always wanted to be a model . . ."

An "ebony statue," a "space age nubian princess," a "thoroughbred," —that's how the world describes Naomi Sims, who soared to the top of the fashion world as a model during 1971 and 1972.

Born March 30, 1949 to a poor family in Oxford, Mississippi, she moved to Pittsburgh, Pennsylvania to live with foster parents, Mr. and Mrs. Alfred Talbott when she was nine. Raised in the city's East End, she attended Westinghouse High School in Pittsburgh, graduating in 1967.

After graduation, she left for New York City, to live with her sister Betty, an airline stewardess, who now also has a modeling career. Armed with a scholarship to the Fashion Institute of Technology, a scholarship to New York University, where she studied psychology, and a third scholarship that enabled her to try modeling, Miss Sims was ready to seek her career.

"I guess I always wanted to be a model," she says. "But my parents didn't understand that it could be a career and pay well. They

240

Hair drawn tightly against her scalp to give her an almost
bald-look became the trade mark for Miss Sims. Here she
wears a Dominic Rompollo charcoal velvet coat lined
in ivory satin over an ivory satin halter neck, full skirt gown.

An evening kaftan covered with
shimmering pailletes shows
. off Naomi Sims' beauty.

wanted me to go to school. I knew that I wanted to be involved in
fashion in some way."

Miss Sims' success story began when she went for an interview
with photographer Gosta Peerson, whom she had found listed in the
Madison Avenue Handbook. Thinking her to be an experienced model,
Mr. Peterson photographed her right away. The photographer was the
husband of the fashion editor of the *New York Times* and Miss Sims
appeared on the cover of the newspaper's fall fashion supplement.
Naomi Sims, a virtual unknown, was now a top model commanding
$75 an hour. After two years at New York University, she quit school to
devote all her time to her new career.

A few months later, she did a national television commercial with
two white models for AT&T, and started her brilliant career.

Miss Sims was the first black model to appear in a television
commercial and the first to appear on the cover of a major women's
magazine, *Ladies Home Journal.* She was the first black to be featured
in a multi-color magazine spread in *Vogue* and the first to pose for

Tall and slim, Miss Sims often modeled bulky coats, and pants.

national ads without the company of a crowd of white models. She is often seen in the pages of *Harper's Bazaar.*

Soon after her phenomenal entry into the fashion world she appeared on the cover of *Life,* which she considers her biggest coup. In 1969 and 1970, she was voted Model of the Year by International Mannequins. Since 1971, she has been consistently on the International Best Dressed List.

Miss Sims is now also engaged in writing, starting a line of cosmetics for black women, studying chemistry, making a movie, helping underprivileged children, and working with drug rehabilitation programs. She has written a beauty book, *The Beautiful Black Woman*, to be published by Doubleday, and a cautionary tale for children "about pretty little girls with pretty white teeth who shouldn't chew gum." In a column in *Essence* magazine she gives beauty hints and refreshing things for women to make to brighten their lives.

She hopes to go back to school and study chemistry to help her in starting her new line of cosmetics, called "Naomi." "They're the result of my own ideas in make-up," she says. "The colors were developed from earth tones that I discovered while talking to a Brazilian painter. Research has revealed that the Ethiopians use earth on their faces and I believe these warm colors are complimentary to dark skins."

In her spare time, when she is not modeling, traveling, absorbed in a book or entertaining friends, Miss Sims works with the State of New York Drug Rehabilitation Program in Harlem. (She received an

In a screen test for the movie *Cleopatra Jones*, Miss Sims listens to instructions from director Jack Starrett. One of ten beauties selected for testing, Miss Sims lost the role to Tamara Dobson.

award in 1971 for that work), teaching underprivileged children in Bedford Stuyvesant (for which she received an award from the New York Board of Education in 1970), or raising funds for research into cancer and sickle cell anemia.

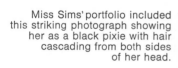

Miss Sims' portfolio included this striking photograph showing her as a black pixie with hair cascading from both sides of her head.

243

Willi Smith
Fashion Designer

In the World of High Fashion, His Name Is at the Very Top

"Sometimes I go into a place with an envelope of designs under my arm and they think I'm a messenger."

Despite his boyish looks and relatively short time in his specialty, Willi Smith is enjoying a rapidly growing reputation as one of the most talented women's fashion designers in the nation. Mr. Smith, whose clothes are sold throughout the United States at major clothing stores, attained his extraordinary success in only three years as a designer

Willi Smith, fashion designer, Digits, Inc. in New York, N.Y.; born Feb. 29, 1948 in Philadelphia, Pa.; Parsons School of Design (1972, under Philadelphia Board of Education scholarship). Address: 525 Seventh Ave., New York, NY 10018 (See full biographical sketch in Volume I.)

for Digits, Inc. in New York City. Admired by the fashion arbiters as well as by the women who wear his creations, he was nominated in 1971 for a "Winnie," the Coty American Fashion Critics Award, fashion's equivalent of the motion picture "Oscar."

Noted for designing "like it is and never like it was," Mr. Smith detests any nostalgic return to the fashions of "the gold old days," especially those days when blacks confined their wardrobe colors to black, brown and gray because they considered themselves "too dark" to wear brighter shades. Mr. Smith's love for bright colors is reflected in his creations—dresses, pants, sweaters, jackets, shorts and shirts—all done in a kaleidoscope of warm colors with such descriptive names as clear turquoise, seafoam green, coral pink and warm sand. He makes liberal use of reds, pinks and golds. "Black people were made for colors," he says. A bold innovator, Mr. Smith introduced full and pleated pants, as well as the high-rise pants.

Mr. Smith explains that he designs primarily for "contemporary women between sixteen and thirty-five, depending on their minds and bodies." He concedes that there is little, if anything, his clothes can do for the overweight woman. "My clothes are cut close to the body," he explains, "so it takes a well-shaped woman to wear them. Once I get past a size 14, I just can't cut anymore."

Unlike most Seventh Avenue designers, Mr. Smith counts heavily on young black women as his customers. "Black women," he says, "have always been fashion-minded, even when they couldn't afford to shop in the top stores. My mother and my grandmother were both very fashion-conscious and the young women of today are even more so. You can bet that when a new style comes in the young black woman will zero in on it fast. Ditto for the black male. Both bring a kind of attitude to the way they wear clothes that makes them naturals for designers." He insists that his clothes, which retail for between twenty and one hundred dollars are within the reach of the "average income" woman.

While considering himself a "black designer," he hastens to reject the idea of designing exclusively for blacks. "Like I said," he insists, "anybody with the right mind and body can and does wear my clothes." As examples, he points out that actress Melba Moore and *Cosmopolitan* editor Helen Gurley Brown are among the many women who wear Willi Smith designs.

Mr. Smith was born February 29, 1948 in Philadelphia. Because 1948 was a leap year, he celebrates his birthday only every fourth year. He traces his interest in fashions to his early teens. "At first," he recalls, "my interest wasn't pinpointed on fashion but I was always interested in art. I was lucky in that my family encouraged me." While

245

Working in his studio, Mr. Smith sketches what might become a top-seller in the Digits, Inc. line.

attending high school, he began doing drawings and illustrations of clothes by other designers, and after school and on Saturdays he worked at the Prudence and Strickland Boutique, the first black-owned business of its kind in Philadelphia. After graduation from high school in 1965, and armed with art scholarships from the Philadelphia Board of Education and New York's Parsons School of Design, Mr. Smith left for New York. He attended Parsons for two years before dropping out because "I was bored with school, anxious to work and mostly hung up on the excitement of being in New York."

He landed his first job as a fashion designer at Arnold Scassi where, he says, "I got a taste of what New York fashion is all about, but where I also found out that I wasn't interested in the high-fashion scene." He worked in several other Seventh Avenue houses, including Glenora Jr., where he received his first public recognition as an up-and-coming designer of pre-teen clothes. Two buyers, Frank Trigg and Irving Yanus, saw some of his designs and in 1969 when they decided to start Digits Inc., they hired Willi Smith as their house designer. In fact, the firm is built around his talent. The partnership has been successful; sales are soaring. Digits and Willi Smith have become nationally known names and, as a result, Mr. Smith has a financial interest in the firm.

Mr. Smith confides that his biggest inspiration is his younger sister, Doris, who models for him and helps sell his clothes. "She keeps me going, and she keeps me aware of the young consumer," he says. "Today, the person makes the garment. The young women of today don't allow the dictation of the designer and trends. They can't afford it and they just aren't interested."

While enjoying his success, the young designer is aware that the black presence on Seventh Avenue is still shaky and extremely circumscribed. "Sometimes, I go into a place in my casual clothes with an envelope of designs under my arms and they think I'm a messenger," he says. Mr. Smith, who acknowledges that some black designers are beginning to get recognition, deplores that there are only a few black fabric salesmen on the business end of the industry. He believes that blacks must get into the business area because, "A black foundation has to be laid in fashion that can perpetuate itself." He cautions young blacks who are interested in the fashion field that they must be well-trained, especially in the technical aspects, if they want to succeed. "You have to know all about fabrics, cutting, the way clothes fit. I once got a job in the library only to be close to all those books on fashion and clothes," he says.

When not designing, Mr. Smith, a bachelor, indulges in his favorite pastimes of listening "to all kinds of music," collecting art and dancing.

246

He confides that even more thrilling than dancing itself is the sight of all those girls in Willi Smith designs dancing around him.

Mr. Smith poses with model wearing one of his first (1969) successful designs for Digits, Inc. He is one of the very few blacks who have achieved success in the world of fashion design.

The Reverend Leon H. Sullivan

Clergyman and Administrator

He Makes Successes Of Youths Who Had Almost Lost Hope

The Reverend Leon Howard Sullivan, clergyman and administrator; founder and chairman of the board, Opportunities Industrialization Centers of America; born Oct. 16, 1922 in Charleston, W. Va.; West Virginia State University (B.A., 1943), Columbia University (M.A., religion, 1947) and numerous honorary degrees; ordained to Baptist ministry in 1941; pastor, Zion Baptist Church in Philadelphia, Pa. (1950–   ); winner of numerous awards for his work. Wife: Grace. Children: Howard, Julie and Hope. Address: 3600 N. Broad St., Philadelphia, PA 19140 (See full biographical sketch in Volume I.)

"I will not be content until a black man can make everything he uses, from a pair of shoes to an airplane."

Insisting that black people deserve "ham and eggs on earth instead of milk and honey in heaven," the Reverend Leon Howard Sullivan, pastor of Zion Baptist Church, the largest black church in Philadelphia, Pennsylvania, is the chief architect and proponent of a unique blend of Christianity and pragmatism based on the concept that God helps those who help themselves. "We [blacks] must close the gap of knowledgeability," says the Reverend Sullivan. "I will not be content until a black man can make everything he uses, from a pair of shoes to an airplane." Putting his energies where his mouth is, the Reverend Sullivan in 1964 founded Opportunities Industrialization Centers of America, a job-training program which now operates in more than one hundred cities throughout the United States as well as in Nigeria, Ghana, Ethiopia and Kenya, and which has trained more than 75,000 black persons in useful jobs. Also in keeping with his practical approach to religion is the fact that his church has a day-care center, a

credit union, an employment agency and a family counseling service.

Recognizing his effective leadership in black economic development, General Motors Corporation in 1971 selected him to become the first black member of its twenty-three-man board of directors—this despite the fact that he had no corporate experience and owned not a single share of GM stock. In response, he presented GM, the world's largest corporation (with assets of $829 billion), with a three-year plan aimed at improving the firm's minority involvement.

Throughout his life, the Reverend Sullivan has made a deliberate attempt to stay in touch with his roots, which reach back to a dirt alley in Charleston, West Virginia, where he was born on October 16, 1922. Because of his poverty, he did not even dare consider the possibility of going to college until a sudden spurt of growth enabled him to become a high school basketball and football star, which led to an athletic scholarship at West Virginia State College from which he graduated with a B.A. degree in 1943. At that point, he had no idea what he wanted to do, but while in college he met a number of ministers who influenced him and caused him to consider the ministry as a profession. "Black people went to church even if they didn't go anywhere else," he explains. "I felt that through the church I could reach them, teach them, inspire them and unite them around programs of real significance."

One of his first professional assignments after leaving West Virginia State was as assistant to the young pastor of New York's Abyssinian Baptist Church, the Reverend Adam Clayton Powell Jr.,

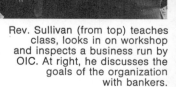

Rev. Sullivan (from top) teaches class, looks in on workshop and inspects a business run by OIC. At right, he discusses the goals of the organization with bankers.

The Rev. Sullivan receives the Lovejoy Award from Elks Grand Exalted Ruler Hobson R. Reynolds at a 1971 convention in New Orleans, La.

who was running for Congress at the time. The Reverend Sullivan became involved in his campaign and in the process learned a great deal about politics.

The Harlem of the mid-forties was a hotbed of black activism and the twenty-two year-old Charlestonian fell under the influence of A. Philip Randolph, the black labor leader and social philosopher who later became his mentor. In 1944, when Mr. Randolph threatened to march five-thousand blacks into Washington in an effort to gain defense jobs for them, Mr. Sullivan served as president of the first March on Washington movement. When President Franklin D. Roosevelt capitulated to Mr. Randolph's demands, the Reverend Sullivan realized the effectiveness of concerted social action. "I became submerged in the black issue and came to realize the importance of economics—that a man can't get out of this mess just by yelling, that he has to *do* something about it," he says.

After moving to South Orange, New Jersey to assume a five-year pastorship, the Reverend Sullivan commuted to New York, undertaking graduate studies at Columbia University (M.A. 1947) and Union Theological Seminary, specializing in community organization. After receiving his post-graduate divinity degree from Union, the Reverend Sullivan and his wife, Grace, moved on to Philadelphia and Zion Baptist. He became deeply impressed by Father Divine whom he credits with doing things "twenty years ago that we're just beginning to do now. He built businesses, schools and taught people pride, thrift and honesty." He equally respects the work of Elijah Muhammad and the Black Muslims who have consistently stressed economic programs.

Some blacks, especially some black nationalists, disagree with the Reverend Sullivan's integrationist approach to black economic development. While blacks have been the prime participants in his programs, other minorities and even whites have not been excluded. "I don't believe in all-black," he explains, "because America's not built like that and the world's not built like that. Anything we do must be developed for the benefit of everybody. Though my main interest is in black people, I am also concerned about Chicanos, Puerto Ricans and other oppressed people." Though his projects are cooperative in nature, he does not propose an overthrow of the capitalist system. "When I dealt with companies on boycotts," he explains, "it was not to destroy those companies but to make them even more viable. I believe in the enterprise system, but I work on that system to get out of it what I can for black people." Thus, the Reverend Sullivan made no secret of his reasons for accepting his appointment to the GM board. Declaring that he was not an economic expert but a Minister of God, the Reverend Sullivan, at the first GM board meeting he attended, stated

Attending his first meeting as a member of the board of directors of General Motors Corp., Rev. Sullivan is welcomed by GM chairman James Roche. At right, he talks with publisher John H. Johnson (l.) and former U.S. Labor Secretary George Schultz.

that he would be "particularly interested in training programs and in black dealerships and in black and other minority employment opportunities in General Motors plants and among General Motors vendors and producers. And I will be vitally interested in opportunities provided by General Motors for minority-owned businesses." Going a step further, the Reverend Sullivan added: "This emphasis must include my doing what I can to help the poor and the underprivileged, not only in America, but in other parts of the world, such as in the Union of South Africa. I will be intensely interested in the operations of the General Motors Corporation there, and will want to do what I can about the situation."

Despite his exalted position with GM and the many honors that have been showered on him, including a string of honorary doctorates and the Edwin T. Dahlberg Peace Award from the American Baptist Convention (1968), the Reverend Sullivan lives unpretentiously with his family, including his three children, Howard, Julie and Hope, in the integrated East Mount section of Philadelphia. One of the greatest tributes ever paid him and his work came from the late President Lyndon B. Johnson who, after visiting OIC facilities, was moved to remark: "What I have seen is not just a training program. I have seen men and women whose self-respect is beginning to burn inside them like a flame."

Rev. Sullivan and OIC executive vice chairman Dr. Maurice Dawkins (l.) present OIC's 1973 Gold Key Award to Coca-Cola chairman J. Paul Austin in recognition of his company's support.

251

Percy E. Sutton

Manhattan Borough President

Percy E. Sutton, president of the Borough of Manhattan in New York, N.Y.; born Nov. 24, 1920 in San Antonio, Tex.; Brooklyn Law School (LL.B.); intelligence officer, 99th Fighter Squadron, World War II; trial judge advocate, USAF, Korean War. Wife: Leatrice Sutton. Children: Pierre and Cheryl. Address: Municipal Bldg., New York, NY 10007 (See full biographical sketch in Volume I.)

A Political Expert Who Wields Power in Nation's Largest City

"Politics is a professional pursuit . . . an activity in which the realistic dimensions of any situation are finally, and sometimes painfully, more immediate and more important than sentimental considerations."

Mr. Sutton works in his office in the New York City Municipal Building.

Manhattan Borough President Percy E. Sutton took a load off the minds of certain people in New York City when he announced in November, 1972 that he would not run for mayor. Many whites had feared that he would try for the mayor's seat. Mr. Sutton, after all, was the highest-ranking black person in New York City government and was regarded as the city's "most articulate exponent of minority rights."

Explaining his reasons for deciding against the mayor's race, Mr. Sutton said: "I do not believe I can win in 1973 (when the election was to be held), because of the highly racially polarized nature of New York City. . . . The cost of running an effective mayoralty campaign would approach $1 million, which is hard to raise when those who would contribute know of the polarization. Blacks represent only 18 percent of my voting constituency on Manhattan Island and only 19.5 per cent of the voting constituency of the entire city of New York."

The key words in Mr. Sutton's carefully worded disclaimer were, "I do not believe I can win *in 1973*." Many political observers believed that, in making the statement, Mr. Sutton left the door open for a future try for the mayoralty.

252

After attending a meeting of the New York City Board of Estimate (top), Mr. Sutton returns to his office and gives instructions to his driver, Richard Payton. With him is his secretary, Mrs. Sylvia Schoultz.

The thinking of the political observers was understandable. Though Mr. Sutton held one of the world's most prestigious municipal jobs, the Manhattan borough presidency had lost some of the enormous built-in powers it once had. Many persons felt that Mr. Sutton—who insists that "in the nature of New York political power," his position remains "a position of great power"—burned for more *real* power, more actual control of things in his $40,000-a-year post.

The Manhattan borough presidency does offer a man with a strong personality an opportunity to make himself felt in New York City government, and Mr. Sutton has used that opportunity wisely since coming to power in September, 1966. He is one of the most popular, most visible officials despite city charter revisions that have stripped all five borough presidents (the other four New York boroughs are the Bronx, Brooklyn, Staten Island and Queens) of many administrative duties.

For example, borough presidents once had their own public works departments and were responsible for paving and sewer work in their boroughs. But by the time Mr. Sutton was elected to his first term, the office had been reduced to a ceremonial function in which the officeholder served as "mayor" of his borough. (Manhattan's polyglot constituency includes 1,600,000 blacks, whites, Puerto Ricans and Orientals, ranging from midtown millionaires to Harlem's welfare poor.) But each borough president has a vote on the City Site Selection Board—which permits them to have a voice about building projects in their boroughs—and each has two votes on the tremendously important Board of Estimate, which, together with the City Council, passes on the mayor's expense and capital budgets, thus controlling the purse strings of the greatest city of the Western Hemisphere.

By November, 1972, Mr. Sutton had served as borough president for more than six years. Was he just marking time, waiting for a good opportunity to run for mayor?

Perhaps. Born in San Antonio, Texas, on November 24, 1920, the youngest of fifteen children of Samuel J. and Lillian Sutton, Percy learned early how to be patient. His father, who was born a slave, had risen to prominence as principal of all-black Phillis Wheatley High School in San Antonio.

In his father, Percy found a life model. "While our father never actually said it in so many words . . . he was a most unhappy man," Mr. Sutton now says. "We knew all along that he was indoctrinating us to live in a yet unsegregated world; he was indoctrinating his children to challenge the segregated system and to live peacefully and effectively in an integrated society that did not yet exist."

In search of such an "integrated society," Mr. Sutton migrated to New York at the beginning of World War II, hoping to enlist in the Army

253

Mr. Sutton, accompanied by his personal assistant, Joseph Teixeira, inspects a bridge in his borough. At right, he walks through Harlem with (l. to r.) U.S. Congressman Charles Rangel (l.), Basil Paterson and David Dinkins.

Air Corps where he could use his experience as a civilian pilot. But AAC racism forced him instead to serve his country, as an intelligence officer in the famed all-black 99th Fighter Squadron and 232nd Fighter Group. He achieved the rank of captain and won combat stars in the Italian and Mediterranean theaters of operations.

During the Korean conflict, his second stay in the military, he became the United States Air Force's first black trial judge advocate. He had completed studies at Brooklyn Law School between wars.

In 1953, Mr. Sutton returned to New York City and spent the next eleven years in unsuccessful races for public office. In 1964, he finally won an assemblyman's seat in the New York State Legislature. In 1965, he drafted the first modern New York State abortion reform bill. Today, New York has one of the country's most liberal abortion laws.

In 1966, Mr. Sutton was nominated by the Democratic-controlled City Council of New York to fulfill the unexpired term of Constance Baker Motley as Manhattan borough president. Mrs. Motley, a black woman, had accepted appointment as a federal judge. Mr. Sutton was elected to the office by a vote margin that exceeded the combined vote of his two opponents. He ran for a full four-year term in 1969 and won, receiving 87 percent of the vote.

Acting as a marshal for the Afro-American Day Parade in Harlem, Mr. Sutton waves to the crowd.

Mr. Sutton's activities in Manhattan politics eventually involved him in the national political scene. It was he who nominated Representative Shirley Chisholm (D., N.Y.) as the party's presidential candidate at the 1972 Democratic National Convention in Miami Beach, Florida. Most of the national black leaders at the convention supported South Dakota Senator George McGovern, who won the party's nomination but was crushed by incumbent President Richard M. Nixon at the polls.

It was also Mr. Sutton, more than anyone else, who was responsible for the defeat of Harlem's famed congressman, the late Adam Clayton Powell Jr. To some, the move to oust Powell, which resulted in the election of Congressman Charles B. Rangel, was an indication of the borough president's "political ruthlessness."

Mr. Sutton disagreed. "Politics is a professional pursuit," he said. "It is an activity in which the realistic dimensions of any situation are finally, and sometimes painfully, more immediate and more important than sentimental considerations."

The borough president and his wife, Leatrice, have a son, Pierre, and a daughter, Cheryl.

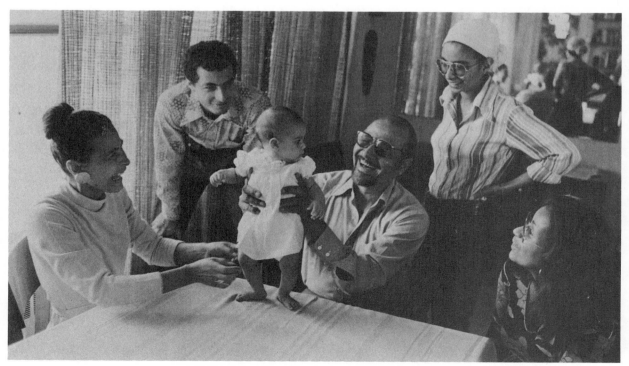

Mr. Sutton's family includes (l. to r.) his wife, Leatrice; son, Pierre; daughter, Cheryl (standing), and Pierre's wife, Charlotte, and daughter, Keisha.

255

Dempsey J. Travis

Mortgage Banker

Astute Chicagoan Negotiates
Millions in Mortgages for Blacks

Dempsey J. Travis, president, Sivart Mortgage Corp., Travis Realty Co., Freeway Mortgage and Investment Co. and Dempsey J. Travis Securities and Investment Co., Chicago, Ill.; born Feb. 25, 1920 in Chicago, he is a graduate of Roosevelt University (B.A.). Wife: Moselynne Hardwick Travis. Address: 840 E. 87th St., Chicago, IL 60619 (See full biographical sketch in Volume I.)

Mr. Travis (c.) presides at a meeting of Sivart Mortgage Corp. stockholders, including U.S. Congressman Ralph Metcalfe (to Mr. Travis' left).

"I don't get much of a chance to play the piano any more."

One of the major obstacles to black home ownership is the reluctance, or outright refusal, of white-owned banks and mortgage firms to give mortgages to blacks. The man who has done more than any other person to circumvent that obstacle is Dempsey J. Travis, president and chairman of the board of Sivart ("Travis" spelled backward) Mortgage Corporation in Chicago, Illinois. It is the largest and most influential black-owned mortgage company in the United States. (There are more than two thousand mortgage banking companies; only twelve are owned by blacks.) Sivart services about $40 million in loans—tops for any black mortgage firm.

In addition to Sivart, Mr. Travis also owns the Travis Realty Co. (which he started in 1949), the Freeway Mortgage and Investment Co. (specializing in small rehabilitation loans) and the Dempsey J. Travis Securities and Investment Co. Besides this, the dapper, quick-witted Mr. Travis is a director of Seaway National Bank, one of two Chicago banks with integrated ownership. And he is a board member of the National Association of Real Estate Brokers and founder-president of the United Mortgage Bankers of America, Inc.

256

Mr. Travis leaves the office of one of the businesses he owns. In bottom photo, he and an associate, Leo Blackburn, witness the signing of a $120,000 lease with Mr. Travis' Sivart Mortgage Corp. by a representative of Mutual Benefit Life Insurance Company of New Jersey.

UMBA was founded at the 1962 NAREB conference in Dallas, Texas, when the brokers recognized the critical shortage of mortgage money for blacks and decided to do something to relieve it.

In 1970, Sivart made arrangements with three black-owned companies and a bank to finance a $4.5 million, middle-income subdivision on Chicago's South Side. "Most black companies aren't big individually," observed Mr. Travis at the time, "but this project shows what can be done when they band together and pool their resources." Another major Sivart deal was the securing of a $10 million federal loan to build 459 moderate-cost apartments in Chicago. Since 1961, Mr. Travis has arranged about $65 million in loans on some 3,250 single-family home mortgages in the Chicago area.

Born February 25, 1920 in Chicago, the son of Louis Travis, an unskilled laborer, and Mittie Travis, Dempsey Travis attended Chicago's DuSable High School. Having played the piano since he was four years old, he formed his own combo at the age of fifteen and began playing at various dime-a-dance affairs. Only a year later, he applied and was admitted to the musicians union and thus became one of the youngest professional bandleaders in the Chicago area. By this time he was pretty much set on a music career. Even after being drafted into the United States Army in 1942, he continued his musical pursuits during off-duty hours by playing off-post "gigs" with the small combo he had formed at Camp Custer, Michigan, with some fellow GIs. After having completed Quartermaster School for Non-commissioned Officers at Camp Lee, Virginia, he was assigned as a clerk at the Aberdeen (Maryland) Proving Ground Post Exchange. Only a month later, he was made assistant manager of the Post Exchange. Another two months later, he was promoted to manager, and after another four months he was made supervisor of all Post Exchanges in the Aberdeen area. Thus, the army had stopped his musical career and launched him on a new one—management.

Following his honorable discharge from the service, Mr. Travis returned to Chicago to enroll at Roosevelt University. Still cocky as a result of his spectacular army success, he received an ego-crushing blow when he found out that he had flunked the entrance examination.

He suddenly realized how deficient his high school education had been, although he had passed all high school courses and had received good grades to prove it. In desperation, he tried to get back into the music business by rounding up his combo, but the old gang had scattered and, besides, dime-a-dance places had gone out of style. So, as his father had done before him, he got a job at the Chicago stockyards. Realizing that the job led nowhere, he quit after two weeks and took on a job filling out income tax returns. But that, too, was not

Mr. Travis confers with group of architects on plans for a new building. From left are: John Black, John J. Moutoussamy, Arthur Dubin, Mr. Travis and David Dubin. At bottom, he is shown with some of the staff of his companies.

what he wanted. Aware that his lack of education was his major handicap, he took a job with the Veterans Administration and signed up for Englewood High School night courses in accounting and social science. Since entrance examinations were not required, he had no trouble in being enrolled. Following the successful completion of his courses, he took another stab at college, this time Wilson Junior College, whose entrance requirements were lower than Roosevelt's. He was admitted, but only under one condition: he had to take a course in remedial reading. Before long, Mr. Travis made up his reading deficiency and things began to move. His self-confidence restored, he wrapped up the rest of the two-year junior college program in one year, then re-applied for admission to Roosevelt. This time, his credits from Wilson were so good that he didn't have to take an entrance examination. In one year he had his B.A. degree. Today, his Roosevelt diploma hangs on his den wall beside a framed letter from Roosevelt's dean of admissions telling him that he had been rejected.

Mr. Travis gives a diploma to Glenn Clayton, a graduate of the United Mortgage Brokers of America training program. Also shown is Benjamin Scott, UMBA's executive director.

Following graduation from Roosevelt, Mr. Travis entered Kent College of Law in Chicago. Around that time, he met and soon married Moselynne Hardwick of Cleveland, Tennessee. Before long, it occurred to him that law practice, as far as blacks were concerned, was limited largely to criminal law, which meant "dealing with unhappy situations." So he dropped out of law school and, after several uninspiring jobs, decided to go into business for himself—selling real estate. After some very lean beginnings, during which he often didn't earn enough money to afford a hot lunch, things started to pick up. They have been picking up steadily ever since.

One of Mr. Travis' big breaks came in 1961 when President John F. Kennedy put Dr. Robert C. Weaver, a black man, in charge of the Department of Housing and Urban Development. Sivart Mortgage Corporation became the first black-owned company to be approved by the Federal Housing Administration and the Veterans Administration. As a result, more and more large lending institutions were willing to back Sivart.

While prospering as a real estate broker and mortgage banker, Mr. Travis also became increasingly active in numerous civic affairs. He is a past president of the Chicago branch of the National Association for the Advancement of Colored People, a director of the Cosmopolitan Chamber of Commerce, a trustee of the Northwestern Memorial Hospital (formerly Wesley Memorial Hospital), a member of the Mayor's Commission for the Preservation of Chicago's Historic Buildings, and a member of the Board of Governors of the Chicago Assembly.

With all of his business and civic activities to attend to, Mr. Travis says—with only a mild note of regret—"I don't get much of a chance to play the piano any more."

Mr. Travis is shown at Chicago's Lake Grove Village, a housing complex his firm helped develop for the United Presbyterian-African Methodist Episcopal Conference, Inc. From left are: Dr. Russell Brown, national secretary of the A.M.E. Church, Mr. Travis, Presbyterian minister Dr. A. L. Reynolds (c.) and Charles A. Tatum, a Sivart vice president.

259

C. DeLores Tucker

Pennsylvania Secretary of State

C. DeLores Tucker, secretary of the Commonwealth of Pennsylvania; born Oct. 4, 1927 in Philadelphia, Pa.; attended Temple University and University of Pennsylvania; husband: William L. Tucker. Address: Dept. of State, Room 302, North Office Bldg., Harrisburg, PA 17120. (See full biographical sketch in Volume I.)

"Black is beautiful. Yes. But you also have to remember another 'B' and that is for 'brains.'"

The most powerful woman in state government in Pennsylvania is Mrs. C. DeLores Tucker, secretary of the Commonwealth (same as secretary of state in most other states). Hers is the third highest governmental office in the state—after that of the governor and lieutenant governor—and her work affects the lives of most of Pennsylvania's nearly twelve million people. She is the first black, and the second woman, ever named to a cabinet level post in the state's history. Mrs. Tucker, who owned a public relations firm in Philadelphia, was appointed by her close political ally, Governor Milton J. Shapp, and immediately upon her assumption of office in January, 1971, became a political force to be reckoned with.

For instance, the state constitution provides that she shall be a member of the boards of Pardons, Property and Finance, and Revenue. Members of the last decide how state money is to be deposited and invested. She's also a member of the state athletic commission, keeper

She's the Lady to See About a Lot of Things in Pennsylvania

In conference with Governor Milton J. Shapp (above), Mrs. Tucker discusses plans for staff meeting (above, right) in Pennsylvania capital, Harrisburg. She is flanked (opposite page) by Paul Waters (l.) and Rev. Percy Patrick.

Sign in parking lot always reserves a parking spot for Mrs. Tucker.

of the Great Seal of the state, custodian of the laws and resolutions passed by the general assembly, and custodian of all proclamations issued by the governor. By statutory provision, she is chairman of the State Employees Retirement Board. Nearly all the official transactions of the governor pass through her hands. She must keep a record of all death warrants, respites, pardons, remittances of fines and forfeitures, and commutation of sentences. She has complete responsibility for registering and keeping records on all the more than five hundred thousand corporations in Pennsylvania. Nineteen various occupations and professions—from barber and undertaker to doctor and engineer (some 450,000 persons in all) are licensed and regulated by her department. And finally, she conducts all swearings-in of elected and appointed officials and acts as chief protocol officer of the state.

Mrs. Tucker, a consummate politician and an energetic and no-nonsense type administrator, tackles all these responsibilities as if born for the job. Governor Shapp, who calls her "the sparkplug of my administration," says admiringly: "Before she came into office the job of secretary of the Commonwealth was a nonentity. She has thrown out most of the dead wood and made it a major department." To assist her in making changes, Mrs. Tucker has brought into the state government a host of able black technicians and professionals, one of whom, Attorney Paul Waters, notes that "the whole tenor of the state government has changed for the better for black people since she came into office." With the help of the Pennsylvania Negro Democratic Committee, of which she is vice chairman, she combed the state for qualified blacks and recommended their names to Governor Shapp for consideration. As a result, the number of blacks in cabinet and sub-cabinet positions increased from one in pre-Shapp days to twelve

261

Mrs. Tucker swears in Paul Waters (above) as first black member of Environmental Review Board. In her office (above, right) she is besieged for autographs by group of elementary school pupils from Paoli, Pa.

in 1972, and blacks are now on more than half of the state's occupational and professional boards. Previously, they were on only one. The policy change has seeped right down through the ranks. According to Mrs. Tucker, of some 2,400 people hired by the state, about 300 are black.

An astute political realist, Mrs. Tucker—who was born into a very religious family that stressed education and accomplishment to her and her sister Grace—is keenly aware that her power rests as much on support from Pennsylvania's black community as it does from the confidence of Governor Shapp. She keeps her line to the black community in good order by answering all mail that she receives and by constantly speaking to black groups across the state and the nation. Of some 125 speaking engagements she made in one year, over half were to black organizations. Speaking in the Baptist-preacher-like voice and style that she learned from her father, the Reverend Whitfield Nottage, she tells her audiences that they've got to get on the case to make progress, and her particular message to black youth is: "Black is beautiful. Yes. But you also have to add another 'B' and that is for 'brains.' Don't just stand in the corner saying 'Right On' unless you are going right on to your English, history and science classes."

As a civil rights activist, she participated in the 1965 Selma-to-Montgomery March. She also is vice president of the state NAACP. And to add to a seemingly endless list of organizational affiliations, she's the first black vice chairman of the Pennsylvania State Democratic Committee, a member of the policy council of the Democratic National Committee and was on the arrangements committee for the 1972 Democratic National Convention. She was a supporter of Senator Edmund Muskie.

Photograph of Mrs. Tucker by photographer Mrs. Lois Weissflog (c.) is presented to her by Matthew Moore, NAACP state coordinator. Presentation of photo was project of Gulf Oil Corporation.

Mrs. Tucker's ties to the black community, of course, are more than political. They are also social and emotional. She insists that blacks "who have achieved" must remember that their security is ultimately tied to the progress of the majority of black people. And she refuses to be satisfied with being the first black here and the first black there. "We must remember that back in 1875 we had one lieutenant governor, one secretary of state and one senator. Now we only have two secretaries of state and one senator. That is not my idea of great progress." She urges blacks to "organize on the local level so we can thoroughly control our wards. From that position of strength we can begin to elect mayors, county leaders and governors."

In her official capacity, Mrs. Tucker accepts declaration of candidacy form for Hubert H. Humphrey from Jerry Lawrence (c.), and former governor George Leader. At right, she and her husband William L. Tucker talk with Sen. Edmund S. Muskie.

263

Cicely Tyson

Actress

She Brought the Dignity Of the Black Woman to Movie Screens

Cicely Tyson, actress; born in New York, N.Y.; attended New York University, studied acting at the Actors Playhouse; made Broadway debut with a hit role in The Dark of the Moon *and after more than two dozen successes on stage, screen and TV, received rave reviews for her film role in* Sounder. *Address: c/o William Morris Agency, 1515 El Camino Dr., Beverly Hills, CA 90212 (See full biographical sketch in Volume I.)*

"I'm sure that God didn't intend for me to sit at a typewriter."

At the top of the Hollywood film heap, Cicely Tyson easily stands as one of the most gifted actresses around. By 1973, after a frustrating stage and screen career, she had achieved the stardom which had long eluded her. Her gripping portrayal of a sharecropper's wife in *Sounder,* one of the more provocative of black movies, was almost universally hailed by the critics. Always regarded as a top performer by blacks in the profession, but consistently underrated by whites, Miss Tyson's growth as a talented actress was stunted by the arbitrary "newcomer" label pinned on her by some in the film industry. Victimized by a shortage of good scripts and haunted by a succession of bad ones, she sacrificed false glory for minor roles and steadfastly refused to compromise. When *Sounder* promised relief, her ten-year holdout ended.

Although her age is a well-kept secret that she vows never to reveal, Miss Tyson said in 1972 that she was born "around thirty years ago" in East Harlem, New York to William and Theodosia Tyson,

264

Miss Tyson plays Rebecca in the film *Sounder*, for which she was nominated for an Academy Award in 1973.

immigrants from Nevis, smallest of the Caribbean Leeward Islands. When her father, a carpenter-painter, died in 1962, her mother made ends meet by cleaning houses while a friend looked after Cicely and her brother and sister.

Raised in poverty, Cicely knew at an early age what hardships were like. While she never went to bed without some kind of supper, she could be seen selling shopping bags on cold street corners when she was nine. Rent scales and crime drove the family from one tenement to another, until they ended up on 101st Street in Harlem, more comfortable, yet still in the midst of danger. Cicely's mother forbade her to go to the movies. Bored by her studies at the Charles E. Hughes High School and by a dull home life, Cicely turned to religion. Most of her free time was spent at the St. John's Episcopal church where she sang in the choir and played the organ and piano.

Following high school graduation, Cicely started working in New York as a secretary for the American Red Cross. She held the job until she decided to look for something more exciting. She startled her friends at the office when she strolled in one day, announced that she was quitting and marched out again to try her luck at modeling. "I'm sure," she said at the time, "that God didn't intend for me to sit at a typewriter." Her svelte figure, innocent face and perfect teeth made her an advertising man's delight and she was soon considered one of the top ten models in the United States.

After a brief but lucrative stint as a cover girl, Miss Tyson enrolled at New York University—only to drop out when a fashion editor suggested acting as a cure for her doldrums. Studying acting techniques at the Actors' Playhouse, she soon won a role in a play called *The Spectrum*, which was quickly shelved because of inadequate funds. She made her Broadway debut in *Talent '59*, staged by John Effrat, in which she

From a job as a typist (left), Miss Tyson became an international film star who was voted "Best Actress" at the 1972 Atlanta Film Festival. Above, she is greeted by Yolanda King and Mrs. Coretta S. King at the Festival.

played a character called Barbara Allen in the play, *The Dark of the Moon*. She was so distinctive in the role that she was chosen as one of the talents of the year. A few months later she appeared in the Theater Guild production of *Jolly's Progress*, in which she also understudied the star, Eartha Kitt. The following year (1962), she was a hit in Genet's *The Blacks*, a stunning play which not only featured such black artists as Moses Gunn, Roscoe Lee Browne, James Earl Jones, Raymond St. Jacques and Godfrey Cambridge, but which led Cicely to the coveted Vernon Rice Award for her electric portrayal of a prostitute named Virtue. She later won the same award for a similar role in *Moon On A Rainbow Shawl*. She topped the year off with the Broadway production of *Tiger, Tiger, Burning Bright* with Alvin Ailey, Claudia McNeil and Diana Sands. The play died, however, because of a newspaper strike that hurt publicity.

Miss Tyson ushered in 1963 by winning a regular feature role in "East Side, West Side," thus becoming the first black to appear in a key part on a television series. She played George C. Scott's secretary on the show—a refreshing departure from earlier roles but one which caused a racial stir: many television stations in the South threatened to ban the show. Her first major television appearance was on a special telecast titled "Americans: A Portrait In Verse." Among her other shows were "Naked City," "Camera Three," "The Nurses," "Slattery's People," "I Spy," "Frontiers of Faith" and "To Tell the Truth." There were also a couple of television dramas. One, "Brown Girl, Brown

At a reception for Miss Tyson in Washington, D.C., she meets Congressman Charles C. Diggs of Michigan.

Stones,'' was about West Indians coming to Brooklyn with a role for Miss Tyson in which she felt at home. The other was ''Between Yesterday and Today,'' the tale of an African family. Looking back, Miss Tyson recalls that when she applied for her first major movie role in *Twelve Angry Men*, she was told that she was too chic. She got the part when she returned in a tacky disguise. She achieved her first starring role on screen with Sammy Davis Jr. in *A Man Called Adam*.

In 1966 Miss Tyson was featured in the Broadway play, *A Hand Is On The Gate,* and in 1968 she was cast in *To Be Young, Gifted and Black* at New York's Cherry Lane Theatre. There was talk of her doing her own teleseries in 1969 but it turned out to be just talk. Nonplussed, she did ''On Being Black,'' ''The Courtship of Eddie's Father,'' and the ''Bill Cosby Show.'' During the same period, she also co-starred in the movie, *The Heart Is A Lonely Hunter*. *Pygmalion* beckoned her the following year, and she found herself starring in the George Bernard Shaw play at the Cincinnati Playhouse.

If the pace of Miss Tyson's career has been slow at times, it has been because she decided not to accept any stage or screen vehicle that would demean black womanhood. She refused lucrative offers that did not provide roles to suit her standards. When the rush for black films began, she backed away, preferring relative obscurity to work with trashy scripts. She had, after all, once acted in such invigorating productions as *Odds Against Tomorrow*, with Harry Belafonte; *The Last Angry Man*, with Paul Muni; *Who's That Lady I Saw You With?*, a comedy with Tony Curtis, and *A Matter Of Conviction*, with Burt Lancaster. In 1972, black writer Lonne Elder III wrote *Sounder* and Miss Tyson read, and liked, the role that had been offered to her. The resulting performance brought rave reviews, a host of new film offers and several film awards.

''Hopefully, this film will turn the tide,'' she says. ''People are aware of the chaos that's been going on with the black films, such as *Sweetback* and *Super Fly* and the various *Shafts*. I can't put those films down completely, because they allowed us to get our foot in the door. But now it's time we said something else. *Sounder* is a part of our history, a testimony to the strength of humankind. Our whole black heritage is one of struggle, pride and dignity. The black woman has never been shown on the screen this way before. She has always been a prostitute, a drug user or someone who has slept around. *Sounder* changes all that.''

The movie also changed Cicely Tyson's luck. The little girl who used to sell shopping bags on the streets of Harlem could be rather certain that she would not have to do that kind of work again. She has set an example of the strongest of strong black pride.

Melvin Van Peebles
Writer, Actor, Composer, Film Director

Achieving Success as A One-Man Industry

"You think you're a studio, therefore you are a studio."

Melvin Van Peebles, writer, actor, composer, film director; born Aug. 21, 1932 in Chicago, Ill.; Ohio Wesleyan University (B.A., 1953); wrote, directed, co-edited and co-scored the films, The Story of a Three-Day Pass and Sweet Sweetback's Baadasssss Song. Address: 132 rue d'Assas Paris 6, France. (See full biographical sketch in Volume I.)

Melvin Van Peebles sits comfortably in the midst of a cultural storm—and for good reason. Praised for masterminding the most daring cinematic coup in the annals of motion picture history and criticized for getting away with it, he is arguably the man most responsible for launching the black film revolution in America.

As a black man, he refused to toe the lines drawn for him by white society. As a non-conformist, he rebelled against the straitjacket success formulas prescribed by conservative studio bosses. And as a renegade film-maker, he set a screen trend that shattered box-office records, paved the way for the artistic liberation of industry blacks and established him as "the one to watch next time."

Mr. Van Peebles was born on August 21, 1932, in Chicago, Illinois, and grew up in Phoenix, a quiet Chicago suburb, where he lived "a happily bourgeois childhood." Actually, he was considered a smart-alecky brat who had a way of being very stubborn. "It was self-awareness," he says, "but people thought I was being ornery. I was just standing up for my rights."

Brash but intelligent, Melvin graduated from Thornton Township High School in Harvey, Illinois in 1949 and enrolled at West Virginia State College. After a year, he transferred to Ohio Wesleyan University, where he graduated in 1953 with a "B" average and a Bachelor of Arts degree in English Literature—an accomplishment that he rarely discusses.

Mr. Van Peebles is shown during a visit to Chicago for a promotion of his film, *Sweet Sweetback's Baadasssss Song.*

A record album which resulted from the movie is exhibited by the director.

Acting on a whim, he joined the U.S. Air Force and became a navigator-bombardier. After three years of duty, during which his "attitude" drew him several court-martial threats, he was discharged and promptly began "living as I pleased." He moved to Mexico and tried his hand at painting—a venture that satisfied him but provided little money for support of his wife and two children, Mario and Megan. He drifted to San Francisco during the early fifties and got a job as a grip-man on a cable car and wrote the text for a picture book called *The Big Heart*, a story about cable cars. When it was published in 1957 he was fired from his job because his boss "thought a grip-man should not be an author." He accused the company of racial discrimination.

"My record showed that I had never been late or absent," he says. "They said I was psychologically ready to have a big accident. I went to the Fair Employment Practices Commission. They asked, 'Did anybody call you a nigger?' I said 'No.' They asked, 'Well, how can you call it discrimination?' That experience taught me that people can juggle things any way they need to."

Undaunted, Mr. Van Peebles began working at the post office and went to movies at night. On one occasion, he saw a particularly disgusting film and left the theater with a plan in mind: he would make his own movies—"not from love, but from nausea about what I had seen." He had absolutely no knowledge of film-making. But later he edited his first feature movie (about 13 minutes long) in a closet and scored it himself; he could not afford to pay a musician. He knew nothing about chord structure, so he composed music on a kazoo. He bankrolled the film by holding three jobs at once and renting a room in his home. His buddies considered him crazy.

Hooked on his newest endeavor, Mr. Van Peebles joined the San Francisco Film Club. He threw house parties and shot footage of the guests as they arrived. Hollywood, however, was not interested in hiring anyone black except elevator operators, parking attendants—and Sidney Poitier. Disgruntled, Mr. Van Peebles packed his family off to Holland in 1959. He soon dissolved his interracial marriage, studied astronomy at the University of Amsterdam on the G.I. Bill, and toured with the Dutch National Theatre. After playing the role of a homosexual boxer in "The Hostage," he shifted his residence to Paris in 1960.

To survive hard times, Mr. Van Peebles hustled odd jobs and ended up dancing and singing black spirituals in the Paris streets for a few coins. Although his average annual income was only $600, he kept himself alive in this manner—long enough to write five novels, four of them in self-taught French: *A Bear for the FBI*, about a young boy's experiences with sex and racism; *The Chinaman of the 14th District*, a collection of short stories; *The*

Mr. Van Peebles' motion picture was one of the earliest of the current wave of black-oriented movies. Its success was instantaneous.

True American, a farce about a white man and a black man in hell; *The Party in Harlem*, which was later transformed into the play *Don't Play Us Cheap*, and *La Permission*, a story of interracial love in Paris, which became the movie *The Story Of A Three-Day Pass*.

Working under a grant from the French government, Mr. Van Peebles began writing and directing short films after joining the French Director's Guild. By the time he started receiving writing awards near the end of 1967, he was ready to meet Al Johnson, the program director for the San Francisco Film Festival, who was scouting Europe for entries. Mr. Van Peebles cornered Mr. Johnson at a party in Paris and talked about *Three-Day Pass*, which he had just written, directed, co-edited and co-scored. Mr. Johnson was impressed. Mr. Van Peebles was invited to the Film Festival as the French delegate. "That was a kick," he recalls. "Nobody believed I was the French delegate." The movie surprised the critics, and Hollywood began making offers.

But Mr. Van Peebles was in no rush to become a token black director. Instead, he began to concentrate on developing his composing ability—"with the man in the street in mind." In time, he produced three albums, including *Brer Soul* and *Ain't Supposed To Die A Natural Death*, the lyrics of which dealt with the inner lives of social outcasts. He also used the time to teach himself to play the piano.

Finally, in 1970, he signed a contract with Columbia Pictures to direct *Watermelon Man*, budgeted at $1 million and starring Godfrey Cambridge as a white bigot who mysteriously turns black. Mr. Van Peebles' first big clash with movie industry bosses occurred on the set of that movie. "Eighty percent of the energy on *Watermelon Man*," he recalls, "was spent not on the set but in fighting in the corridors of power. They wanted a white guy in blackface. I wanted a black guy in whiteface. They tried to deal in compromise but I wasn't trying to do a consensus, I was trying to do a film. I fought everybody—the author, the producer and the actors, but I got what I wanted. After it was over, I was shaving one morning and I looked in the mirror and said, 'You think you're a studio, therefore you are a studio.' Studios have all the power in Hollywood."

That experience left Mr. Van Peebles determined to do his next movie without studio backing. Bargaining with the $70,000 he had earned making *Watermelon Man*, he begged, borrowed and sweet-talked the rest from friends and gullible enemies. He hired a non-union crew, an amateur cast and rented the equipment he needed. Then he slipped into the Watts section of Los Angeles and filmed it— on the pretense that he was *not* doing what he *was* doing. Union watch-dogs shrugged the project off as a kind of "documentary black skin-flick." A few months later they realized their mistake. Mr. Van

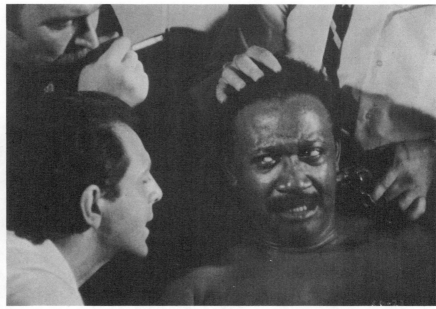

Colorful director is casual in dress. His film (right) inspired some controversy but critical reaction was generally favorable.

Peebles had filmed *Sweet Sweetback's Baadassss Song.*

Mr. Van Peebles had pulled a brilliant coup: he had written, produced, cast, directed, starred in, scored, edited and distributed the film himself—a feat that remains unparalleled. Not only that, he also wrote and sold a book about the making of the film, cut a record about it and dominated the entire publicity campaign surrounding it—all under the noses of doomsayers. The picture grossed about $12 million, broke the white film pattern and spawned today's rash of black movies.

Clinching his sudden fame, Mr. Van Peebles then turned his attention to Broadway. He produced a musical from his record album, *Ain't Supposed To Die A Natural Death*, which opened at the Ethel Barrymore Theatre on October 20, 1971, thanks to $150,000 of his own money. In 1972, he decided to stage another musical, *Don't Play Us Cheap*—financing it with earnings from *Sweetback* after first filming the production in New Mexico prior to its Broadway opening.

"After each one of these projects," he says, "there's a big council meeting inside my head. The council is convening these days. Everyone is screaming 'Me next! Me next! Me next!' "

Mr. Van Peebles is shown with comedian Bill Cosby. The director is considered one of the most creative young men in the motion picture industry.

Walter E. Washington

Mayor of Washington, D.C.

Walter E. Washington, mayor of Washington, D.C.; born April 15, 1915 in Dawson, Ga.; Howard University (A.B., 1938 and LL.B., 1948). Wife: Bennetta Bullock Washington. Daughter: Bennetta (Mrs. Jules-Rossette). Address: 14th and E Streets, N.W., Washington, D.C. 20004 (See full biographical sketch in Volume I.)

Sworn-in by Supreme Court Justice Thurgood Marshall (top. r.), Mayor Walter E. Washington is congratulated by President Nixon and Mrs. Washington. Above, he holds press conference.

His Honor, the Mayor
Of America's Capital City

*"I am unique; I have a great deal more responsibility
than I have authority."*

Walter E. Washington is the first man to hold the position of mayor
(also called commissioner) of Washington, D.C. Originally appointed
to his post in 1967 by President Lyndon B. Johnson, and
reappointed to a second four-year term by President Richard M.
Nixon, Mayor Washington took over as chief executive of the nation's
capital following the implementation of President Johnson's
reorganization plan for the District. In that arrangement three District
commissioners were replaced by one mayor, a deputy commissioner
and a nine-member city council.

Although the U.S. Congress still holds the purse strings for the
District of Columbia and can change, through legislation, what the
mayor of the council enacts, Mayor Washington has emerged as a
powerful official who enjoys the respect of large segments of the
District's citizens and of many lawmakers on Capitol Hill from
both houses of Congress and from Republicans and Democrats.

Mr. Washington was born April 15, 1915 in Dawson, Georgia.
He was the only child of William L. Washington, a factory hand, and
Willie Mae Thornton Washington. Young Walter distinguished himself as

At end of long session,
Mayor Washington (l.)
clasps hands of District
of Columbia official union
representatives after signing
new teachers' contract.

273

Interested in transportation,
Mayor Washington tries out one
of city's new midibuses.

a high school athlete, especially as a track man in the 400-yard and half-mile events.

Following graduation from Jamestown High in 1933, he worked just long enough on odd jobs to become convinced that he was cut out for more challenging occupations. He decided that a college education was the only avenue that would take him toward his ambition. While still in high school, Walter had made the acquaintance of a local lawyer for whom he had worked after classes, cleaning the law office for a dollar a day. Impressed with the bright youngster, the lawyer left him a small legacy of about $100, which enabled Walter to enter Howard University in 1934. He has been a Washingtonian ever since.

At Howard, he majored in political science and sociology. He graduated with an A. B. degree in 1938. Awarded a graduate scholarship, he enrolled at American University and began work on a doctorate in public administration. Later, he changed his mind, deciding that he wanted a law degree instead because ''the discipline of law would be very good as a supplement to public administration.''

In 1941, after scoring high on a competitive civil service exam, he landed a junior aide's job with the National Capital Housing Authority, a position which made it economically possible for him to marry his Howard University schoolmate, Bennetta Bullock. Both continued their educational pursuits—Mr. Washington during night classes at Howard University Law School, from which he received an LL.B degree in 1948. Later, Mrs. Washington, who received her Ph.D. degree in education from Catholic University in 1951, became a pioneering principal in a Washington slum school and now is the director of the Women's Job Corps. Despite their careers, the Washingtons are devoted parents. Their daughter, Bennetta (now Mrs. Jules-Rossette) is the wife of a young drama student from Martinique whom she met while studying at the Sorbonne in Paris, France.

Mr. Washington was admitted to the District of Columbia Bar in 1948 and was admitted to practice before the U.S. Supreme Court a year later. Continuing to rise within the National Capital Housing Authority hierarchy, he was appointed its executive director by President John F. Kennedy in 1961. He served with such distinction that, in 1966, New York Mayor John V. Lindsay asked him to take on the top housing post in New York City. Mr. Washington accepted the formidable task of administering New York's 141,000 public housing apartments. In effect, this made him New York's biggest landlord. In spite of his staggering work load, he made sure not to become an absentee landlord. He listened to the complaints of large numbers of tenant groups—frequently at night ''so they wouldn't lose time from work.''

After only one year in his New York post, he was summoned to

274

Washington by President Johnson who offered him the newly created office of mayor of the nation's capital. Although this meant a reduction in salary from $35,000 to $28,000, Mr. Washington accepted the challenge.

Almost from the moment he took office, Mayor Washington has waged a persistent fight against waste resulting from duplication in the city government. His many innovations have resulted in more effective crime control, better relations between the city's police and its predominantly black population, and a substantial increase of blacks in the District government's upper echelon.

Reflecting on his dependency on Congress and the resulting difficulty in effectively running the nation's capital, Mayor Washington says, "I am unique; I have a great deal more responsibility than I have authority."

Although Mayor Washington was appointed, rather than elected, to his present position, his administrative competence as well as his vote-getting potential have been duly recognized. Editorialized the *Washington Daily News*: "Someday the District of Columbia is going to have an elected mayor. When that happens, we hope Mr. Washington will be running as the incumbent. It should be a breeze."

The mayor has a concern for youth (top) as well as senior citizens (middle photo). New metro system for Washington (above) is a major project.

Mayor Washington accepts a plaque from recreation official after D.C. Youth Games win by D.C. team.

Barbara M. Watson

U. S. State Department Administrator

'Honor Through Distinction' Is A Motto by Which She Has Lived

Barbara M. Watson, administrator, Bureau of Security and Consular Affairs, U.S. Department of State; born Nov. 5, 1918 in New York, N.Y.; Barnard College (A.B., 1943), New York Law School (LL.B., 1962). Address: U.S. Department of State, Washington, DC 20520 (See full biographical sketch in Volume I.)

"Life . . . is a compromise. The important thing is not to be so stubborn that you don't give an inch. . . ."

Barbara Watson's business is minding other people's business. As administrator of the U.S. Department of State's Bureau of Security and Consular Affairs, she is the first woman to attain the rank of assistant secretary of state. The $40,000-a-year job places 3,000 federal employees under her supervision and puts her in charge of all passports and visas issued to American citizens. Another duty is to supervise the nation's 250 consular operations around the world—a task that requires her to make several overseas trips each year. She deals with problems of Americans abroad, including those imprisoned for narcotics and other offenses. Such responsibilities are a welcome challenge to Miss Watson, who believes in "honor through distinction," a family motto.

She was born Barbara Mae Watson on November 5, 1918, the

eldest of four children. Her father, the late Judge James S. Watson, came from a family involved in government and transportation and was the first elected black judge of the New York Municipal Court. Her grandfather, Israel Lopey, was a magistrate in Jamaica and her brother, James L. Watson, is a U.S. Customs Court judge in New York City. Her mother, Mrs. Violet Watson, came from a family active in retail business and real estate. Both parents migrated to New York from Jamaica, bringing with them a tradition of discipline, culture and pride which was instilled in Barbara from an early age.

"Mother was at us constantly," she recalls. "We couldn't waste time. She'd say, 'You're not on this earth just to take up space. You must justify your existence.' My father disciplined me, but it was never with a spanking. It was his *look*. Yet, there was a great deal of love. The things that meant the most to my father were law and his family—and he was very concerned about the problems of black people. He taught us that what really counts is the character of the individual, no matter what color. When he died in 1952, his words stayed with me."

Miss Watson grew up in New York City in her father's fifteen-room greystone townhouse on West 120th Street in Harlem's "Millionaire's Row"—a house with fireplaces in every room and a staff of five servants. Each Wednesday night, her parents held family conferences in their library to cultivate the children's moral and aesthetic values. Barbara's cultural interests, for example, were awakened by her father's practice of inviting prominent artists, musicians and politicians into their home. Among them were Kwame Nkrumah and Nnamdi Azikiwe, who later became presidents of Ghana and Nigeria, respectively, and

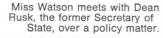

Miss Watson meets with Dean Rusk, the former Secretary of State, over a policy matter.

Miss Watson gestures during a press briefing as she discusses the sharp increase in the number of Americans being detained abroad on drug-possession charges.

writer-poet James Weldon Johnson.

Miss Watson received her B.A. degree from Barnard College in 1943 and, in the family tradition, decided to study law at St. John's University. She stayed only one week, finding the study of law too boring. "I wanted something more challenging at the time," she recalls. She worked as an interviewer for the United Seaman's Service in New York from 1943 to 1946. Following World War II, she started looking for more interesting things to do.

"It occurred to me that American business was overlooking a very important domestic market—the Negro market. Anyway, I was sick and tired of Aunt Jemimas and porters carrying luggage." In 1946, she opened a charm and model school. Her models were photographed for such magazines as *Ebony*, *Vogue* and *Harper's Bazaar* before she closed the successful enterprise a decade later to take a year's rest in Jamaica. She returned to the United States and took a position as foreign student advisor at Hampton Institute. A few months later, however, she enrolled at New York Law School. She graduated at the top of her class and was admitted to the New York bar in 1962 and was chosen as "the most outstanding law student in the City of New York" by a committee of eminent jurists. After working for two years as an attorney for the City of New York, she became executive director of the New York City Commission to the United Nations, the official liaison between the City of New York and United Nations personnel and diplomats. During lunch with the French ambassador to the United Nations in the spring of 1966, Miss Watson received a phone call

278

Miss Watson is visited in her office by her brother, James L. Watson.

from the United States State Department to "please come down." She went to Washington, completed certain documents and in July was appointed special assistant to the deputy undersecretary for administration. She was promoted to deputy administrator of the Bureau of Security and Consular Affairs in October, 1966 and became acting administrator in April, 1967. On August 12, 1968, after appointment by President Lyndon B. Johnson, she was sworn in as administrator of the bureau.

Miss Watson, who speaks French and Spanish, is a singular example of black strength, pride and intelligence in her role as a political peacemaker. "Everyone has a point," she says. "Life itself is a compromise, and if you can inject a little reason and a pinch of humor into your conferences, then you can reach some kind of agreement. The important thing is not to be so stubborn that you don't give an inch. The minute you become rigid, you lose your effectiveness; but if you bend too much, you lose your bargaining power. I try to strike that happy medium."

For Miss Barbara Watson, there is a message in that medium—one that is respected by all: "Honor through distinction." Her achievements speak for themselves.

At the end of a work day, Miss Watson heads for the apartment she maintains near her office.

279

André Watts

Concert Pianist

A Young Prodigy Reaches
Musical Maturity

André Watts, concert pianist; born June 20, 1946 in Nüremberg, Germany; studied at Peabody Institute in Baltimore, Md. and the Philadelphia (Pa.) Musical Academy; performs annually as soloist with major U.S. and European orchestras and appears on concert tours around the world; recipient of Grammy Award (1963). Address: c/o Judd Concert Artists, 127 W. 69th St., New York, NY 10023 (See full biographical sketch in Volume I.)

"[He is] a giant among giants at an age when most young men are just beginning their careers."

At the age of twenty-six—a mere baby as solo concert artists go—piano virtuoso André Watts is not only batting in the same league with such venerated keyboard veterans as Vladimir Horowitz, Artur Rubenstein and Rudolf Serkin, but does so with unparalleled commercial success. At a time when some of the most famous names in classical music fail to fill concert halls, André Watts "packs them in" like a hard rock combo for an average fee—"with much fluctuation," he says—of $3,000 per concert.

Born June 20, 1946 in Nüremberg, Germany, the son of a black GI and his Hungarian wife, Mr. Watts first came to national attention in 1962 at sixteen. At that time, illness had forced the famed Canadian pianist Glenn Gould to cancel two scheduled performances with the New York Philharmonic under conductor Leonard Bernstein. Desperately looking for a suitable replacement, Mr. Bernstein remembered the teen-ager who had performed three weeks earlier on his "Young People's Concerts" television show. Young André was engaged on the spot and given only two days to prepare.

Predictably, there was considerable skepticism, even open disappointment, when the substitution was announced. But those persons in the audience who resigned themselves to the prospect of witnessing an amateur talent show had the surprise of their lives. Within minutes, André Watts stirred the souls of even the most discriminating listeners with a flawless performance of Liszt's taxing *Concerto No. 1 in E-Flat Major*. The performance not only drew "the season's wildest ovation," it also made the front page of the traditionally reserved *New York Times*.

Music critics who at one time had cautioned that his stunning debut might have been nothing more than a single, though admittedly spectacular, flash in the pan, have long since been silenced by the young virtuoso's continued musical maturation. Today, having played with virtually every major orchestra in the United States, Asia and Europe, and with a rapidly growing number of records to his credit (he is the recipient of the 1963 Grammy Award for the "Most Promising New Classical Recording Artist"), Mr. Watts is "in solid" and his reputation as a soloist *par excellence* is no longer questioned. Paris has hailed him as "a virtuoso of the rarest sort, a pianist of exceptional class." Munich found him "magnificent by comparison with the older as well as the younger musicians." In Athens, he was recognized as "an artist who transcends all the known limits of virtuosity." Berlin stated bluntly that Van Cliburn, the one-time child prodigy from Texas, "has been replaced as the darling of the music world by André Watts." And a Teheran critic, at a loss for words, could only tell his readers that "André Watts has to be seen and heard to be believed." Perhaps the most significant tribute regarding his musical maturation was paid by a *New York Post* critic who termed his ability "a gift that defies explanation," concluding that "Watts is ageless before he has

Mr. Watts, despite his early success, is still a conscientious student and practices regularly. At right, he is shown with Leonard Bernstein, former conductor of the New York Philharmonic, who has assisted in his career.

Mr. Watts performs with New York Philharmonic and chats with admirers at concert's end. At far right, he is congratulated in Greece by Queen Anne-Marie. Queen Mother Fredericka looks on.

grown up.''

The real beginning of the André Watts saga precedes by quite a few years his memorable New York Philharmonic debut. In fact, Mr. Watts' ''overnight success'' had been a long time in the making. Despite the big break he received when he substituted for Glenn Gould, chance played only a minor part in his rise. It was his mother, Mrs. Maria Alexandra Watts, herself an amateur musician, who introduced André to the piano and to the music of the great classic composers when he was barely seven years old. At that time, they were living on U.S. Army posts in occupied Germany where André's career-soldier father, First Sergeant Herman Watts of New Orleans, Louisiana, was stationed. Plans for grooming her son for a career on the concert stage were still far from Mrs. Watts' mind although it soon became clear to her that she had a rather unusual child on her hands. ''I just wanted André to learn music for his own enjoyment,'' she recalls. ''It was just to be a part of his education, a part of his life, as it had been of mine.'' She nevertheless left nothing to chance or, for that matter, to her little musical genius. Whenever André balked at practicing, as he often did, she would rekindle his enthusiasm by telling him how hard Franz Liszt, her countryman and his idol at the time, used to practice. Each time, she recalls, André would return to the piano.

Mr. Watts arrives for a concert engagement, one of many he has performed in foreign countries.

When André was eight, his father was transferred back to the States and the family settled in Philadelphia. Despite their meager financial resources, Mrs. Watts continued her son's musical education at the Philadelphia Musical Academy. By this time the evidence was clear that André was headed for big things. Barely nine years old, he had competed with over forty young pianists and won the chance to play a Haydn concerto at one of the Children's Concerts of the Philadelphia Orchestra, a performance which led to a string of other engagements with that famed ensemble. During this period, André's parents were divorced.

Although she could have used the money, Mrs. Watts resisted the temptation of cashing in on her son's unusual gift and instead concentrated on his gradual, long-range musical development. Even after André's now historic debut with the New York Philharmonic, she and his manager, William Judd of Columbia Artist's Management, Inc., continued to use restraint, resisting numerous offers of quick money. Although André himself felt he was ready for a heavier load, they permitted him to accept only six concerts during the first year after his triumph. The following year, he was allowed to make twelve appearances and the next year fifteen. Only after he came legally of age in 1968 did they pull out all stops for a full schedule of some one hundred performances a year, all booked up three seasons in advance.

Highlights in Mr. Watts' eventful musical career include playing in Washington's Constitution Hall for President Richard M. Nixon's first inauguration; giving a concert in Teheran as part of the coronation festivities for the Shah of Iran; performances for numerous other heads of state, including the King, Queen and Queen Mother of Greece, Archbishop Makarios and Prince Juan Carlos de Bourbon and Princess Sophia. He also was presented by Zaïre (formerly Congo) President Joseph D. Mobutu with that country's highest honor, the Order of the Zaïre, following an appearance at the White House where he played after a state dinner for President and Mrs. Mobutu. Celebrating the tenth anniversary of his career early in 1973, Mr. Watts fittingly hosted one of the Young People's Concert telecasts, the same program at which he was "discovered" a decade earlier by the then host Leonard Bernstein.

Between concerts, Mr. Watts, a bachelor, lives in a large New York City apartment near Carnegie Hall. In his rare moments of leisure, he reads Chekhov, Poe and Gibran, practices yoga and listens to records. But most of his waking hours are spent at the keyboard, honing that talent that has made him a giant among giants at an age when most young men are just beginning their careers.

Clifton R. Wharton Jr.

College President

Shortly after his 1970 inauguration as president of Michigan State University, Dr. Wharton gets acquainted with students on campus.

Meeting, Beating Racism Is 'Positive Militancy,' He Says

Clifton Reginald Wharton Jr., president of Michigan State University (1970–); born Sept. 13, 1926 in Boston, Mass.; Harvard University (B.A., 1947), Johns Hopkins University School of Advanced International Studies (M.A., 1948), University of Chicago (M.A., economics, 1956; Ph.D., economics, 1958); several honorary degrees; author of numerous articles on agriculture and economics; editor, Subsistence Agriculture and Economic Growth *(1968). Wife: Dolores D. Wharton. Children: Clifton III and Bruce. Address: Michigan State University, East Lansing, MI 48823 (See full biographical sketch in Volume I.)*

Dr. Wharton takes a brisk stroll across the campus as he begins his administrative duties at the famous Big Ten university.

During his first days as president, Dr. Wharton is visited by the university's former president, Dr. John Hannah.

"I like to express my militancy by meeting the competition totally on their own ground without any special consideration. . . . Meeting white racism and competition on these terms—and beating it—is what I call positive militancy."

If success is getting what you want and happiness is wanting what you get, then Dr. Clifton Reginald Wharton Jr. is a satisfied man. His position as president of Michigan State University represents an extraordinary "first" for a black educator. His earlier achievements are no less spectacular. Not only has he been a leading figure in the development of foreign nations but he has achieved distinction in American education and research activities.

Dr. Wharton was born in Boston, Massachusetts on September 13, 1926, the son of Clifton and Harriet Wharton. His father, the Hon. Clifton R. Wharton Sr., was America's first black career diplomat and ambassador until his retirement in 1964.

285

"My father," Dr. Wharton remembers, "was a foreign service officer for forty years. He was stationed in the Canary Islands when I was a child, and later had posts all over—consul-general in Madagascar, minister to Rumania, and ambassador to Norway."

Dr. Wharton spent six years of his youth in the Canary Islands, where he learned to speak fluent Spanish. There were no American schools in the Canaries, so his mother taught him with material from a Baltimore, Maryland, correspondence school. When he reached the age of ten he went to live with his grandmother in the Roxbury section of Boston and attended the Boston Latin School (America's oldest secondary school). He enrolled at Harvard University in 1942 at the age of sixteen. While an undergraduate student, he was a founder and the first national secretary of the U.S. National Students Association. He graduated *summa cum laude* with a B.A. degree in history from Harvard in 1947.

He was the first black man to be admitted to Johns Hopkins University School of Advanced International Studies and the first to receive the M.A. degree in international studies (1948). From 1948 to 1953, he headed the reports and analysis department of the American International Association for Economic and Social Development, specializing in growth problems of Latin America. He was a research assistant and then research associate in economics at the University of Chicago from 1953 until 1957 when he joined the Agricultural Development Council, an organization created by John D. Rockefeller IV, as executive associate. He earned an M.A. degree in economics from the University of Chicago in 1956 and a Ph.D. in economics in 1958.

From 1958 to 1964 Dr. Wharton was stationed in Malaysia, directing the Agricultural Development Council programs in Vietnam, Thailand and Cambodia. During this time he also was a visiting professor at the University of Malaya (1960–64). From 1964 to 1967, he was a director of the council's American Universities Research Program and was a visiting professor at Stanford University (1964–65). He was named acting director of the council from 1966–67 and was appointed vice president in 1967. He served until his appointment as president of Michigan State University in 1970.

As a director of the Equitable Life Assurance Society, Dr. Wharton is the first black man to serve on the board of one of the ten largest United States corporations. He is also a trustee or director of several other organizations, including the Asia Society, the Overseas Development Council, the Rockefeller Foundation, the Public Broadcasting Service and the New York Museum of Modern Art.

Dr. Wharton was a member of the Advisory Panel on East Asian

Dr. and Mrs. Wharton wave to fans during intermission of game between Michigan State and Indiana while a photographer takes candid pictures. Later, the university's first family enjoy refreshment in their home.

and Pacific Affairs of the United States Department of State (1966–69) and the Southeast Asian Development Advisory Group (1966–69). In 1966 he was a member of the Presidential Task Force on Agriculture in Vietnam, and recently served on the United Nations Association of the United States panel devoted to world population and the quality of human development.

He has written extensively on economic development and is editor of the book, *Subsistence Agriculture and Economic Development.* During his first twelve months at Michigan State University, Dr. Wharton made more than forty-five major speeches, received four doctor of law degrees from various universities and was named Man Of The Year by his alma mater, Boston Latin School. In addition, he has accomplished the establishment of a Committee Against Discrimination and an Anti-Discrimination Judicial Board whose purposes are to investigate and remedy claims of prejudice on the basis of race, creed, ethnic origin or sex; started the practice of making informal visits to student residence halls to conduct "lounge dialogues" (1958-60) and resolved a student protest.

"I have never in my career," Dr. Wharton says of his new post, "knowingly accepted a position or job where race was the primary consideration. I like to express my militancy by meeting the competition totally on their own ground without any special consideration. Meeting white racism and competition on these terms—and beating it—is what I call positive militancy."

287

Frederick D. Wilkinson Jr.
Vice President, Macy's

Frederick D. Wilkinson Jr., vice president, R. H. Macy, Inc., New York, N.Y.; born Jan. 25, 1921 in Washington, D.C.; Howard University (A.B. magna cum laude, 1942), Harvard University (M.B.A., 1948). Wife: Jeane. Children: Sharon, Dayna and Frederick III. Address: R.H. Macy, Inc., 89–22 165th St., Jamaica, NY 11432 (See full biographical sketch in Volume I.)

Washington Newsboy Becomes
New York Merchandising Executive

"Of all the various types of businesses, I think retailing has the most to offer black people."

When he was an eight-year-old boy in Washington, D.C., Frederick D. Wilkinson Jr. was busy selling to the public. He sold newspapers at one time and flowers at another, but the objective was always the same—good business.

When he was a fifty-two-year-old businessman in New York City (Jamaica, Queens), Mr. Wilkinson was a vice-president of R. H. Macy, Inc., the world's largest department store, with some seventy branch outlets. One does not become a vice president of that kind of operation overnight. So Mr. Wilkinson started early.

"I decided in high school that I was going to become a businessman, even though I was not certain what kind of businessman I was going to become," he says. "I studied business administration when I went to college, and I made it a point to study every possible aspect of business. When I graduated from college, I *knew* a little about every aspect of business."

Mr. Wilkinson is shown in his office in the Macy's store in Jamaica, which serves Jamaica and Queens.

289

After graduating *magna cum laude* in 1942 from Howard University, Mr. Wilkinson entered the United States Army and served four years in such capacities as platoon leader, company commander, liaison officer, post exchange officer and trial judge advocate. His military experience included studies at the Army University Center at Oahu, Hawaii, where he received a certificate in business law and accounting. After attaining the rank of captain, he was honorably discharged in 1946.

"When I came out of the army, my interest in business had not diminished," Mr. Wilkinson says. "Therefore, I decided to enter the Harvard Graduate School of Business, where I pursued the same general course as I did in undergraduate school. I was seeking to acquire as broad a knowledge as possible, and thus I was able to more or less pick and choose the area of business which I wanted."

While at Harvard, Mr. Wilkinson was interviewed by Macy's for a position in the store chain's executive training program. He joined the program in 1948 after receiving (with distinction) a master's degree in business administration from Harvard. Twenty-five years later he is still with the giant firm.

Mr. Wilkinson was appointed a junior assistant buyer in 1949, a senior assistant buyer in 1950 and a buyer in 1952. "Becoming a buyer for Macy's was a high point in my career," he says. "It was a jumping point, a move from a junior to a senior executive." As a buyer, he purchased merchandise in the domestic market (U.S.A.) for all of the corporation's stores in New York. He also served as a corporate buyer in the foreign market; he traveled throughout Europe and the Orient, buying for the Macy stores.

Mr. Wilkinson also served as a merchandise manager of Macy's Roosevelt Field Store in New York and as administrator and manager of the Macy's store in Jamaica, Queens. In 1968, he was elected a vice-president of the corporation.

"I am the first vice president of Macy's who happens to be black," he said. "I don't regard myself as a black vice president. . . . I was not hired by Macy's because I was black; I was hired because they felt I had the qualifications to become a key executive in this company. The fact that I am black is coincidental as far as I am concerned, as far as the employees are concerned, as far as the customers are concerned, and as far as our resources are concerned. . . . I came up through the ranks."

Elaborating on his progress through the ranks, Mr. Wilkinson says: "Macy's has a system of progression which is based largely upon the principle of promotion from within, and it is structured in such a manner that one generally knows what his next step will be. I was interested in merchandising, so my progression followed the normal path of a person who is interested in merchandising, and who performs up to the required standards."

Quality performance is what Mr. Wilkinson preached to black college students while working with a National Urban League program aimed at interesting young blacks in business careers. A strong advocate of retail business careers, he says: "Of all the various types of businesses, I think retailing has the most to offer black people. Retailers are constantly looking for qualified people, and in my opinion, they are, by and large, color blind. If more qualified black people had sought positions in retail operations there would be many more in key positions. It is my hope that many more bright, qualified, young black people will seek employment in this field. In retailing, one is kept so busy doing so many exciting things that there is neither time nor the necessity to be concerned about the question of color. In this field, ability is what counts and, fortunately, the statistical tools are available to make ability quite measurable."

Mr. Wilkinson feels that his most significant achievement was "convincing my wife, Jeanne, that she should marry me."

Mr. Wilkinson, who is proud of having come up through the ranks, looks out on main floor of store he manages.

Flip Wilson

Entertainer

Flip Wilson (Clerow Wilson), comedian; born in 1933 in Jersey City, N.J.; attended high school, joined the U.S. Air Force at 16 years old; began performing in 1964 in San Francisco Cal.; star of his own NBC-TV show. Divorced. Father of four children. Address: NBC, 3000 W. Alameda, Burbank, CA 90205 (See full biograpical sketch in Volume. I)

Leading TV Comedian Spent 15 Years Preparing for Success

"If funny don't buy my shoes, I'm not gonna have no shoes. I must be honest to my work and it must take care of me...."

There is no such thing as an overnight success. Such a statement might sound somewhat trite to have been made by a top comedian whose sparkling wit has won him nationwide fame. But when the speaker in question is Flip Wilson, the sentiment is accompanied by a considerable authority. Mr. Wilson, who stars on the "Flip Wilson Show," one of the most popular comedy hours in television history, has earned the right to deliver such a sermon after more than fifteen years of practice and study of the finer aspects of what it takes to be a funny man. As Mr. Wilson has explained it: "Humor is a serious business. I set myself a fifteen-year goal to learn this business and

As star of "The Flip Wilson Show,"
Mr. Wilson (above) thrills television
audience with frantic antics, then
assumes the character of Geraldine
Jones (left, c.) for more gags with
guest stars Billy Eckstine (l.) and
Phyllis Diller.

perfect my routine. The greatest satisfaction of my life has been that
I stuck to my program. I made it on my own and I'm happy.

The odds against the attainment of such a goal were heavy. Clerow
Wilson was the tenth of twenty-four children of poverty-stricken parents
in Jersey City, New Jersey. When he was only eight, his parents were
separated and the children were shuttled in and out of foster homes and
orphanages, getting whatever schooling that could be squeezed in.
Clerow quit school when he was sixteen years old, lied about his age
and enlisted in the air force, where his talents as a quipster first found
appreciation. Fellow airmen quickly named him "Flip" (for "flipped
out"), a liberty which he rather appreciated. "I don't know where the
name Clerow came from," he once said, "but if I knew, I'd send it
back." As his renown as a comedian spread tnrough the base, Flip was
invited to perform on stage, giving hilarious lectures on such esoteric
subjects as "The Sex Habits of the Coconut Crab." Upon leaving the
service in 1954, his talent as a comic continued to develop. He was
working as a bellhop at the Manor Plaza Hotel in San Francisco when
the manager of the nightclub, obviously a man of perception, let him

293

Warming up his studio
audience with jokes (l.) Mr.
Wilson later plays a
pool shark-lover (above) in a
comedy skit with guest star
Gail Fisher.

perform onstage during breaks in the entertainment, and Flip Wilson's career as a stand-up comedian was launched. He toured the country, with only modest success, doing drunk routines and other kinds of humor, but he recognized early that comedy is a skill requiring much preparation. "No one that I've run into feels that the depths that I go into are necessary," he once observed. "But I feel that just having the natural ability is not enough. Comedy involves so much psychology and being able to speak on all kinds of subjects. You've got to read, learn, educate yourself."

For all the hilarity of his onstage demeanor, Mr. Wilson was all business when the laughter died away. He did his homework away from the stage, poring at night over the "theory" of comedy as expressed in such books as *The Laws of Humor* by Max Eastman. He soon developed his own "laws," haphazardly, as "there was no place I could go and be taught what's funny or about the technical aspects of presentation," and the fellow comics in the field were generally of little or no help. But there was always the element of professionalism. "If you pay to see someone be funny," he reasoned, "then that person is supposed to stand up and be funny; he's not supposed to stand there and practice. I'm not about to *try* to be funny. I'm going to *be* funny. . . ."

294

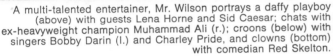

A multi-talented entertainer, Mr. Wilson portrays a daffy playboy (above) with guests Lena Horne and Sid Caesar; chats with ex-heavyweight champion Muhammad Ali (r.); croons (below) with singers Bobby Darin (l.) and Charley Pride, and clowns (bottom) with comedian Red Skelton.

He had attained something of a national reputation, at least among insiders, when the first big break came his way. Redd Foxx, another top black comic who later achieved television eminence, was appearing one night on the Johnny Carson "Tonight" show and spoke highly of Flip before a nationwide audience. The comedian was invited to appear on the show and was so hilariously successful that other invitations quickly followed. In rapid succession, he captivated audiences on the "Ed Sullivan Show," the "Today Show," the "Mike Douglas Show," the "Merv Griffin Show" and "Laugh-In." Success was at hand and it came as no surprise when the National Broadcasting Company, in 1968, announced that it had signed the now-popular entertainer to a five-year exclusive commitment contract. Two years later, Flip Wilson became the host of his own prime-time television show.

There is now seldom a week when the "Flip Wilson Show" is not among the top five programs in the television ratings. Flip Wilson jokes have become a part of the nation's folklore, and his host of characters—Killer, Geraldine and the Reverend Leroy, among others—are staple entertainment for generations of viewers. His salary has been reported as about $1 million a year. After fifteen years of touring the country, the performer, now thirty-nine, enjoys a settled life

Constantly on the go, Mr. Wilson signs autograph pads for teenage fans (above), then later poses with the Jackson Five (above, r.) after NAACP Image Awards program.

in southern California, with occasional interludes to pay visits to his four children (his ten-year marriage ended in divorce) who live in Miami. But, no one is less surprised by his success—or less affected—than Flip Wilson himself.

"I knew all this would happen," he once said. "I believed all this would happen. It's just a matter of seeing how much more of the dream is going to come true. I dreamed it all. I got the cookie in the dream."

Mr. Wilson, rather predictably, is not about to rest on his laurels. He is still the conscientious "student" of humor who knows exactly what he wants and how to go about achieving it. His success, he believes, is "a combination of many things. It's the simplicity of the grammar involved; there's nothing I say that anybody—any kid—can't understand. Plus, I think that in many instances, it's the visual jokes I do, where it is the body, the facial expressions, the gestures that make the joke. So each joke or story or line has different qualities. It's a matter of using each one. It's like a band in a total arrangement. One time it's the clarinet, another time the drum, but they're all working together. One is accented to give a particular effect.

"I've never filled out an application for a job in my life. I said to myself, 'If I'm gonna do this, then I'm gonna do it honestly. Either I'm

After a meeting (top) with Carl Stokes (l.) and Rev. Jesse Jackson, Mr. Wilson elicits smiles from two airline stewardesses (above) before taking a cool dip (r.) in hotel swimming pool.

gonna eat from being funny or I'm not gonna eat!' That makes you cut out all the bull. If funny don't buy my shoes, I'm not gonna have no shoes. I must be honest to my work and it must take care of me . . ."

Many blacks who are dedicated Flip Wilson fans, however, have expressed some doubts about the Wilson brand of humor, complaining that his material lacks effective "social" statement. He respects these opinions, but is less than over-awed. "No one knows what I have to do here [on this show] but me," he declares. "I can't let someone else tell me what to do. I'm aware of my obligations and I will do what I want to do, when it's convenient for me to do it. . . . I do it because I want to do it, not because I want to impress someone or be built up for that. I'm an artist. All I want is respect for my art."

For Mr. Wilson today, as always, it is the craft of the comedian which must determine his effectiveness. "If you really put yourself into something," he insists, "you can make it. That's it. Just an honest day's work for an honest day's dollar."

Stevie Wonder

Entertainer

Stevie Wonder, musician, singer, composer, recording star; born May 13, 1950 in Saginaw, Mich.; studied at Michigan School for the Blind and tutored privately, graduated from high school with honors (1968); made first gold record (1 million copies) at age 12. Address: Motown Record Corp., 6464 Sunset Blvd., Los Angeles, CA 90028 (See full biographical sketch in Volume I.)

He Refused to Let a Handicap Slow Him Down

"The only people who are really blind are those whose eyes are so obscured by hatred and bigotry that they can't see the light of love and justice."

"A handicap isn't a handicap unless you make it one," Stevie Wonder says of his blindness. And his remarkable career as a singer, musician and composer proves it. An electric performer who exudes raw joy, he attracts standing-room-only crowds whenever he appears in concert. Ranked as a top-drawer recording artist, many of his tunes are his own compositions. Some have sold more than a million copies each and account for the dozen gold records that Stevie had collected during the decade leading up to 1973.

He was born Steven Judkins on May 13, 1950 in Saginaw, Michigan, the third of six children. When his family later moved to Detroit, Michigan, his step-father, a bagel baker, and his mother, Mrs. Lulu Mae Hardaway, a housekeeper, enrolled him in the Michigan School for the Blind where, sightless but optimistic, he studied music and other subjects in Braille.

"When I was young," he says, "my mother taught me never to feel

Billed as a show-stopper, Mr. Wonder thrills audience with one of his many hit tunes.

After receiving a gold album from Motown Artist Relations Director Weldon A. McDougal III, Mr. Wonder thanks his fans. Below, dressed in African robe, he talks with a friend.

sorry for myself, because handicaps are really things to be used another way to benefit yourself and others in the long run. I was a normal, mischievous boy and got more than my share of punishment and whippings. I'm happy for one thing, though. I managed early to mind my mother and this kept me clean." No doubt it also had a positive effect on his learning. Guided by his sensitive touch and hearing and inspired by the recordings of black artists, Stevie soon achieved mastery of piano, harmonica and drums. "The piano didn't take too long," he says, "and I started out on a ten-cent harmonica and moved up. Then one day my mother took me to a picnic and someone sat me behind my first set of drums. They put my foot on the pedal and I played. They gave me a quarter. I liked the sound of quarters."

Those who heard him play liked the sound of his music, for as his talents grew so did his listeners—one of whom was singer Ronnie White, one of the Miracles, who arranged an audition with Berry Gordy Jr., president of the Motown Record Corporation. Mr. Gordy was so impressed with Stevie's talents that he changed the twelve-year-old's name from Judkins to Wonder and signed him to a contract on the spot. Stevie's first smash was "I Call It Pretty Music," which sold more than a million copies. It was followed by "Fingertips" and "Uptight," hit sounds that quickly established Stevie Wonder as a musical genius and earned him the respect of veteran entertainers.

No longer was he thought of as just "the little blind kid" who lived in a Detroit housing project. He was a star, a boy wonder in the highly competitive field of entertainment. Showered with requests for singing engagements, he embarked on a grueling concert tour that took him all over the United States and to England,

During cross-country tour, Mr. Wonder takes time to chat with Ebony Fashion Fair models Cheryl Maeweather and Charmeen Caldwell.

France, Japan and Okinawa. Not only was he the first Motown artist to perform overseas, but he was the first to appear in motion pictures: *Bikini Beach* and *Muscle Beach Party*. In addition, he was the first Motown act to perform on network television, including "The Ed Sullivan Show," "The Mike Douglas Show," "American Bandstand," "Where The Action Is" and "The Tom Jones Show." In the meantime, many of his outstanding singles broke the record charts; fans everywhere selected copies of "Water Boy," "Contract On Love," "High Heel Sneakers," "Nothing's Too Good For My Baby," "Blowing In The Wind," "Alfie," "A Place in The Sun," "Traveling Man," "Yesterday," "Signed, Sealed and Delivered," "My Cherie Amour," "For Once In My Life," and "Heaven Help Us All."

Although he usually writes his own lyrics or collaborates with Ron Miller, Stevie credits his mother with helping him write his best-selling "I Was Made To Love Her." "I wrote the melody and chord structure," he recalls, "but she came up with the phrases. It was the first time she worked on a song with me. It really delighted her. She used to be a gospel singer.

300

Visiting the Eye Institute of New York's Columbia Presbyterian Medical Center (above), Mr. Wonder gives pictures and albums to children with vision problems.

After a New York City performance, Stevie Wonder and friends head for a party in his honor.

Despite his hectic schedule, Stevie remained steadfast in his belief that success is no more important than education. A private tutor was hired to provide the musical prodigy with four hours of academic studies each day. His youth, his blindness and the strain of constant performances were challenges that prodded him to graduate from high school in 1968 (with honors) without a break in his career—a feat rarely achieved even by youths without handicaps.

It came as no surprise, then, when *Billboard* magazine cited Stevie as one of the nation's top single artists, or when he received both the "Show Business Inspiration" and "Distinguished Service Awards" for compelling achievements in the world of entertainment.

Through it all, however, Stevie remained the same. "I'm still basically me," he says. "I'm a happy guy who believes that no matter how big an artist becomes, he should still treat everyone on the same level. I don't want to be God and I'm not going to be a beast, either. The only people who are really blind are those whose eyes are so obscured by hatred and bigotry that they can't see the light of love and justice. As for me, I would like to see the world, the earth, the birds, the grass—but my main concern is with self-expression, with giving a part of the gift God gave to me: my music."

Success has not spoiled Stevie Wonder. His example continues to promote respect for the potential of the blind. His talents as an entertainer continue to inspire the world.

Thomas A. Wood

President, TAW International Leasing, Inc.

*Thomas A. Wood, president,
International Leasing, Inc.
New York, N.Y.; born Jan.
26, 1926 in New York City;
Columbia University (A.B.,
1949), University of Michigan
(B.S., 1951), postgraduate
studies at Massachusetts
Institute of Technology (1958),
and Wayne State University
(1953–54). Wife: Barbara Jean
Wood. Children: Kaye, Eric,
Victoria and Brian. Address:
866 United Nations Plaza, New
York, NY 10017 (See full
biographical sketch in
Volume I.)*

Mr. Wood is seen in his New York office as he negotiates a business deal. Much
of his time is spent away from the office on business trips to Africa.

Venturous Financier Sets Up Equipment Leasing Firm in Africa

*"We are providing a needed service in Africa, and assisting Africans in
. . . developing economic independence."*

Geographically speaking, the movement of Thomas A. Wood, the
founder and president of TAW International Leasing, Inc., the first
American leasing firm in Africa, really hasn't been all that spectacular.
From the street in New York City's central Harlem, where he was born
on January 26, 1926, he has moved no farther than the east side of
midtown Manhattan. However, the forty-six-year-old business executive
has travelled a considerable distance in terms of accomplishment: from
his youthful days as a member of a close-knit, hard-working family who
encouraged him to succeed, to his present position as head of his
own company, an internationally respected businessman, and a
member of the board of directors of one of America's foremost
blue-chip financial institutions, Chase Manhattan Bank of New York.

 Mr. Wood's company does most of its business in Africa and is one
of the few concerns in the world leasing heavy equipment on the

302

Mr. Wood consults with Harold A. Epps, the firm's vice president and secretary, and then dictates to his secretary, Lucille Singleton.

Executive arrives in Nairobi, Kenya during one of his regular visits to East Africa.

African continent. TAW (Mr. Wood's initials) leases construction equipment, trucks, farm machinery, and other items to private firms or governments in about ten African countries, making it possible for major projects to be started without the considerable capital which would be necessary to buy the equipment outright. Mr. Wood is enthusiastic about the role that a leasing firm can play in helping a developing nation while at the same time producing profits for its investors. "Africa is in a developing period," he says. "The whole continent is in a race with time to make life better for all its people. Most developing nations are short of funds to buy the necessary modern equipment in the quantity needed so new methods of acquisition are called for. That's where we come in."

TAW now operates in Kenya, the Ivory Coast, Liberia, Ghana, Ethiopia, Cameroon, Gabon, Zambia, Uganda and Botswana, and has regional offices in Nairobi, Kenya, for the English-speaking countries and in Abidjan, Ivory Coast, for the French-speaking countries.

Mr. Wood, whose father, a railroad porter, always encouraged him to "get into business," strongly believes and states unhesitatingly that "we are providing a needed service in Africa and are assisting Africans in their aims of developing economic independence." To reinforce his point, he notes that "of our first twenty-two leases in Ivory Coast, twenty were to Ivorians." He emphasizes that "We lease only income-producing equipment that a customer can use to earn money. For example, we will lease a passenger car for use as a taxi cab, but not for personal use." He also insists that TAW has no plans to do business in the Republic of South Africa.

Sitting in his modest, functionally furnished New York office, Mr. Wood talks confidently of TAW's future. "We plan to go into computers and even airplanes," he says, "and though right now we have to arrange for the maintenance of our equipment by the manufacturer,

Mr. Wood leaves Ethiopian Commercial Bank (above) with two of his Africa-based staff men. He and others tour Addis Ababa, (top right). At right, he reviews model of a new shopping center in the city.

we hope to eventually establish local servicing through TAW-trained personnel.'' In 1972, the company had $10.8 million in total capital available for use, of which $2.2 million was equity and the remainder short- and long-term debts. Seven million dollars of that amount came from Prudential Insurance Company, which owns 22 percent of TAW. Both TAW and Prudential have received United States Agency for International Development (AID) guarantees—the first made to a leasing company. TAW gets political risk coverage, while Prudential gets extended risk coverage for its loan and half its equity. The AID loan didn't come easily because, according to Mr. Wood, ''most of the companies which have applied for AID's Investment Guarantee Programs were generally the size of the Fortune 500 [*Fortune* magazine annually lists the 500 top companies in the U.S.], so when we applied there was a slight credibility gap.''

Mr. Wood is accustomed to starting businesses. In 1960, he and three fellow workers at International Telephone and Telegraph quit their jobs to organize Decisions Systems, Inc. and built it into a multi-million-dollar, publicly held computer firm. Mr. Wood sold his Decisions Systems stock in 1966 to found, with help from both black and white backers who had faith in his ability, TAW Development Co. and then TAW International Leasing.

Mr. Wood originally intended to start a meat processing plant in Tanzania, using a gamma radiation preserving process, but dropped the plan when the U.S. Pure Food and Drug Administration ruled that the process (now used in Israel and Russia) needed further testing.

A friend of his college days was most instrumental in guiding Mr. Wood to Africa. Earle E. Seaton, now a minister-counselor with the Tanzanian UN Mission, was a student at Howard University at the time that Mr. Wood attended Columbia University. The men met in 1949 and became close friends. Mr. Seaton went to Tanzania and bombarded his friend with letters telling him of the business opportunities there. Mr. Wood finally visited Tanzania and was convinced.

Mr. Wood has an electrical engineering degree from the University of Michigan, and has the technical knowledge, combined with a natural business talent, that makes him a truly qualified company executive in his very lucrative field.

Cocktail party gives Mr. Wood an opportunity to go over plans for company's Africa operations.

The Reverend Andrew Young Jr.

Congressman

The Reverend Andrew Young Jr., U. S. congressman, Democrat, Fifth District of Georgia (Atlanta); serves on the House Banking and Currency Committee; born March 12, 1932 in New Orleans, La.; attended Dillard University (1947-48), Howard University (B.S., 1951) and Hartford Theological Seminary (B.D., 1955); ordained minister in United Church of Christ; executive director of SCLC (1964-68) and executive vice president of SCLC (1968–70). Wife: Jean Childs Young. Children: Andrea, Lisa and Paula. Address: House Office Building, Washington, DC 20515 (See full biographical sketch in Volume I.)

Civil Rights Activist Is Georgia's First Black Congressman Since Reconstruction

"There comes a time in a democratic society when you have to do more than preach. You have to try and make the Kingdom of God become incarnate in the life of society. And that means politics."

On November 7, 1972, the Reverend Andrew "Andy" Young, a veteran civil rights activist and close associate of the late Dr. Martin Luther King Jr., became the first black since Reconstruction to be elected to the U.S. House of Representatives from Georgia.

Representing Atlanta's predominantly white Fifth Congressional District, the Reverend Young, a Democrat, scored a comfortable victory over his closest opponent, white Republican Wyche Fowler, after running a campaign aimed at winning both black and white votes. "The political and economic facts of life are that we have to stand together or we will not survive," he told a racially mixed group during his campaign. "There is no black economy and white economy. There is no real black and white education problem. In black and in white schools within this region, there is not a race problem but an education problem. You will deal with it for everybody or for nobody." The Reverend Young's

306

confidence in Atlanta's readiness "to move beyond racism" was borne out by his winning 60 percent of the vote in a district in which blacks make up only one-third of the population.

The Reverend Young's victory followed an earlier, unsuccessful attempt at winning a House seat. In 1970, he easily won the Democratic nomination, beating an old-guard white opponent, but was unable to topple the Republican incumbent, arch-conservative Fletcher Thompson, in the general election.

Born March 12, 1932, in New Orleans, Louisiana, the Reverend Young is one of two sons of a prosperous dentist, Dr. Andrew Young, and Mrs. Daisy Fuller Young, a schoolteacher. Although the Youngs were the only black family in the neighborhood in which Andy grew up, they were financially better off than their neighbors. As a result, Andy became known by his peers as "the rich kid." Because his mother had taught him to read and write before he reached school age, he was allowed to enter elementary school at third-grade level. Yet neither the fact that he lived in a white neighborhood nor his economic advantage kept him from being bussed daily to a segregated black school.

He was only fifteen years old when he was graduated from Gilbert Academy, a private high school in New Orleans. In 1947, he enrolled at New Orleans' Dillard University and a year later transferred to Howard University in Washington, D.C. as a pre-medical student. He graduated with a bachelor of science degree in 1951 at the age of nineteen. His "newly awakened social awareness" caused him to have second thoughts about seeking a medical career. Instead, he decided on the ministry and enrolled at Hartford Theological Seminary in Connecticut. He received a bachelor of divinity degree in 1955. After being ordained a minister in the Congregational Church, the Reverend Young pastored churches in Hartford; in Marion, Alabama, where he met his wife, Jean (a native of Marion), and in Thomasville and Beachton, Georgia. Mrs. Young, a schoolteacher, attended Manchester College in Indiana and did her graduate work at Queens College in New York.

Not contented with preaching, the Reverend Young yearned for a more active kind of ministry and, in 1957, accepted a position in New York City as associate director of the Department of Youth Work of the National Council of Churches. For four years, he worked with youths in such diverse areas as television programming, athletics and policy-making. Although he found his work challenging, it dealt almost exclusively with white youths and offered him no opportunity to become more involved with the progress of blacks, especially in his native South. The Reverend Young's opportunity to take part in the mounting

The Rev. Andrew Young Jr. and his wife, Jean, thank supporters (opposite page) after his 1972 election to the U.S. Congress. Below, he stands on balcony overlooking part of the Fulton County (Atlanta) district he serves.

Rev. Young is congratulated on victory by his wife (l.) and his mother, Mrs. Andrew Young Sr.

civil rights struggle in the South came in 1961 when he was sent to Georgia as director of citizenship training under a project of the American Missionary Association of the United Church Board for Homeland Ministries, financed by a Field Foundation grant. Working closely with Dr. King's Southern Christian Leadership Conference, he helped train field workers in the difficult and dangerous task of working in Deep South counties getting blacks to register to vote. Gradually, the Reverend Young became more deeply involved with SCLC and in 1964 was promoted by Dr. King to the post of SCLC executive director. In that position, he became one of the civil rights movement's chief strategists and a member of the vanguard of nationally known activists who risked their lives in an effort to secure racial equality for blacks. In the process, he took more than his share of beatings, arrests and harassment. He was in charge of the 1963 demonstration in Birmingham, Alabama, when Police Chief Eugene "Bull" Connor used police dogs on black marchers. Throughout the 1960s, the Reverend Young proved especially effective as a mediator in racial disputes— first in Birmingham, then in St. Augustine, Florida and in Selma, Alabama. He also helped mediate the 1969 hospital workers strike in Charleston, South Carolina, and, in more recent years, was a mediator between various groups in "Resurrection City" in Washington, D.C. As a key member of a major civil rights organization, the Reverend Young was instrumental in the drafting of the Civil Rights Act of 1964 and the Voting Rights Act of 1965. When Dr. King moved to Chicago to challenge Northern-style racism by marching through white neighborhoods in a demonstration for open occupancy, the Reverend Young again helped lead columns of marchers through hostile and menacing crowds. In 1968, he was among a handful of SCLC leaders who were with Dr. King when he was fatally shot from ambush while standing on the balcony of the Lorraine Motel in Memphis, Tennessee. Elevated by Dr. Ralph D. Abernathy, Dr. King's successor, to executive vice president of SCLC, the Reverend Young continued in that position until his first bid for a House seat. Following his defeat, he was appointed chairman of the Atlanta Community Relations Commission, a post from which he resigned when he entered his second, successful congressional campaign.

In addition to his civil rights activities in the United States, the Reverend Young has participated in many overseas projects such as the Overseas Work Program of the Church of the Brethren in Reid, Austria; the European Ecumenical Youth Assembly in Lausanne, Switzerland; the World Council of Churches Central Committee meeting in St. Andrews, Scotland; the American Churches for World Council of Churches Inter-American Consultation in Colombia, and an American

During 1965 voter protest march in Selma, Ala., Rev. Young (l.) stands with Dr. Martin Luther King Jr. (2nd from l.) as a federal marshal reads a court order halting the march. Below, the Youngs and their daughters watch election returns during unsuccessful 1970 campaign to unseat incumbent Georgia congressman Fletcher Thompson, a Republican.

Jewish Committee Study Tour of the Middle East in both Israel and Jordan.

The Reverend Young's achievements have not remained unrecognized. He has received a long string of awards and honors, including the Alpha Phi Alpha Man of the Year Award (1967), Howard University's Alumni Award (1968), the Young Man of the Year Award of Omega Y's Men's Club (1969) and the New Rochelle (N.Y.) NAACP Struggle for Human Rights Award (1969).

Assigned to the House Banking and Currency Committee, Representative Young divides his time between his congressional work in Washington, D.C., and his home in southwest Atlanta where he lives with his wife and three daughters, Andrea, Lisa and Paula. Explaining why he switched from church pulpit to political rostrum, he says: "There comes a time in a democratic society when you have to do more than preach. You have to try and make the Kingdom of God become incarnate in the life of society. And that means politics.

Rev. Young is sworn-in to Congress by Rep. Carl Albert of Oklahoma, speaker of the House. Observing the ceremony is Rep. Thomas P. "Tip" O'Neill of Massachussetts, majority leader of the House.

Picture Credits